THE
HOLY
ORDER
of
WATER

Hurricane Fran approaching The Bahamas and the United States in September 1996: a graphic example of water's vortex energy. (Photo: GOES-8 Geostationary Operational Environmental Satellite).

THE
HOLY
ORDER
of
WATER

HEALING
EARTH'S WATERS
AND
OURSELVES

WILLIAM E. MARKS

Published by Bell Pond Books
P.O. Box 799
Great Barrington, MA 01230
www.bellpondbooks.com

Book design by ediType

Library of Congress Cataloging-in-Publication Data
Marks, William E., 1949–
    The holy order of water : healing the earth's waters and ourselves /
William E. Marks.
        p.   cm.
    Includes bibliographical references and index.
    ISBN 0-88010-483-X
    1. Water – Health aspects. 2. Water conservation. 3. Water-supply.
I. Title.
RA591.5 .M366 2001
333.91'16 – dc21

                                                        2001003055

10 9 8 7 6 5 4 3

Printed in the United States of America

Contents

Part V   HOPE

Disclaimer

The author does not directly or indirectly dispense medical advice or prescribe the use of water as a form of treatment for sickness without medical approval. Doctors, nutritionists, and other experts hold widely varying views. It is not the intent of the author to diagnose or prescribe. The intent is only to offer health, scientific, and historical information concerning water that may help people live more fulfilling lives.

In the event this information is used without a doctor's approval, you are prescribing for yourself, which is a constitutional right, but the publisher and author assume no responsibility.

Acknowledgments

For their help in forming this book, I would like to thank my editor, Will Marsh; Mel Berger at William Morris; Chris Bamford, Richard Smoley, and Michael Dobson at Bell Pond Books; Laurie Chittenden for believing in the book; my old friends Fairleigh S. Dickinson, Jr., Alfred Eisenstaedt, Peg Littlefield, and Eric Sloane; Fran Houghton; Walter Cronkite; my father, Charles Thomas Marks, and my mother, Evelyn Pruden Marks; my brothers and sisters; my daughter Sarah; the people of Martha's Vineyard, who have a deep appreciation and love for water; and to all my water brothers and sisters of the world. And of course I give special thanks to water and all that it has provided in my life's journey.

Introduction

Water is peaceful and extends its beneficent action throughout Nature, not even disdaining those gloomy depths which the vulgar look upon with horror, for water works much as God does.
—LAO-TZU

THE MYSTERIES FLOWING FROM WATER are with us in many ways—in the life surrounding us; in thoughts generated by our water-filled minds; the smells and rhythms of our oceans; the soothing sounds of gurgling streams and fountains; the beat of our hearts; the gift of sight from our watery eyes; the ever changing clouds above; the misty fog that lightly kisses our faces; the sight of an awe-inspiring tornado; the vortex swirl of water disappearing down a drain—the list is endless.

We are living in a time when the future evolution and health of humankind and all other life forms, as well as the future of all world economies, will depend upon how we interact with this mysterious substance.

Water touches each one of us every day, for it is a mystery on which our very lives depend. Our human bodies are mostly water. Each day we must drink water so it may flow through us to do its work of nourishment and waste removal. Without this constant flow of water through our bodies, we would cease to exist.

Today, because of the questionable quality of the drinking water found in public water supply systems, it is no surprise to see health-conscious people traveling with jugs of water slung over their shoulders. Because of this growing trend, worldwide bottled water purchases have grown from 15 billion gallons in 1994 to 27.5 billion gallons in 2000, according to industry sources. Another recent development is the use of bottled water or some kind of water filtering system in many urban and suburban offices as well as homes. This is mostly due to the worldwide impact of our industrialized, chemical-dependent, and waste-laden civilization, which has caused

1

the practice of drinking naturally pure water from springs, flowing streams, and rivers to be a fading memory.

The media headlines tell us story after story of water shortages; polluted drinking, swimming and fishing waters; dammed waterways; land subsidence due to overpumping of groundwater; spreading deserts; stressed ecosystems losing water to urban and agricultural interests; destruction of our rainforests; dying oceans—and on and on. Such news helps to make us more aware of the global impact of our growing population. In 1970 there were three billion of us on the planet. Today there are six billion. By 2050 there will be more than nine billion. When the growing global water shortage is married to humanity's expanding population and the globalization of culture and economies, we face the potential of civilization failing on an epic scale.

"We are at a crucial turning point," said the National Geographic Society's Gilbert S. Grosvenor at a 1998 international Groundwater Guardian symposium. "If we do not change the way we respect and manage our freshwater supplies within the next ten years, we might as well as write off civilization as we know it."

Could these prophetic words be true?

Whatever the answer, it will soon become our living reality, so much so that some people feel the decisions we make about water may very well determine whether we are creating a future living heaven or hell here on Earth. Yet, the nonchalant attitude taken by some people toward our present worldwide water crisis is indicative of denial and/or the belief that we are victims of a fate over which we have little or no control.

Could it be that we are marking time in hope that new intelligence will arrive in time to help save us from ourselves? Nowhere is this hope more evident than in bookstores. Many store shelves and tables are now filled with books attempting to give us answers about understanding our place in life relative to our ever growing water crisis. Most of these books are dedicated to new methods, new purposes, new technologies, experimental plans, and a variety of governmental mandates. Others focus on gloom and doom without providing any constructive answers. All of the above, however, give little consideration to ancient teachings and some modern findings about the powers found within the remarkable substance of water.

Each passing day it becomes more obvious that many of the proposed solutions to our water crisis are failing. Solutions based on reactions to an immediate water crisis are proving to be nothing but Band-Aid prescriptions for postponing disaster.

The true answers for today's water crisis have roots that reach back to the creative source of our physical and spiritual realities—the same source that supports and maintains our present earthly thinking existence each passing second. With this thought planted in our watery minds, we may perhaps begin to see a way to grow solutions—solutions usually overlooked in our search for the true meaning behind today's water problems. It is a crisis that exists and lives amongst us for a reason. If we pay attention, we may learn ways in which water can be our teacher. For water is a sublime teacher with the power to create and destroy life.

In facing the truth of our worldwide water crisis, some people feel that faith will deliver us, while others believe in the fateful acceptance of whatever the crisis will deliver unto us. As I see it, the question is, do we make the choice of Achilles—better a short life full of deeds and glory than a long life without content—or do we choose a life of just sitting in our chairs and watching the show unfold on our television sets and computer screens? Yes, it can be difficult after a long day at work for you to come home and find the energy to be involved with helping to change the course of events. You may have bills to pay, mouths to feed, and worries about how you are going to survive today, tomorrow, and next week. My goodness! How can anyone in a right mind even think of asking you to take time from your life to help with the water crisis?

However, whatever your situation, there are opportunities available for you to help yourself, your family, and humanity to enjoy a better life through water, and to reduce your life's negative impact on our sensitive water world. I write these words based upon my own evolution in life.

I was raised on a self-sufficient organic farm in the "sticks" of New Jersey. I was one of nine children. We were financially poor, but psychologically rich. We grew and canned our own vegetables, raised and slaughtered our own animals (giving them a good life and thanking them for helping us survive), and forged intimate relationships with the abundance of life found within the expanses of woodlands and wetlands surrounding us.

At an early age, I and my year-older brother Lefty helped our father dig a water well by hand and set up an irrigation system for our family's vegetable garden. A day on our family farm was always full. Milk the cow in the morning and evening; mend pasture fences and maintain the barns; repair the garden tractor and other farm equipment; plow, disk, plant, hoe, weed, water, and harvest the garden; put up canned goods in the fall; care for the chickens, sheep, horse, dogs, goat, rabbits, beef steer; mow the grass—we never seemed to find the end of the list.

At age eighteen I left the farm with a small pocket of saved money to discover life on my own. I worked my way through college for five years with money from part-time jobs and the help of athletic and academic scholarships. This taught me to discover resources within myself for surviving and learning.

During my undergraduate studies at Fairleigh Dickinson University, I did extracurricular independent research in water pollution by taking my father's small aluminum fishing boat up and down rivers. Using a camera and basic water sampling gear, I gathered all sorts of industrial pollution data. This research eventually led to threats against my life as my work resulted in several industries being indicted by federal grand juries on water-pollution charges. After college, I traveled Europe and Northwest Africa to learn about historical water management practices and industrial water pollution, and to see and feel how the Sahara Desert continues to enlarge through the thoughtless actions of humankind.

Upon returning home, I briefly landed a job with the City of Newark as an environmental analyst. My job was to manage and cure the city's drinking water, floodwater, and river pollution problems. However, Newark's water pollution, drinking water infrastructure, and political problems were so entrenched that I sensed early on that there was little I could do to solve these problems by embracing a failed system.

As fate would deliver, one December day a miracle of sorts entered my life. While at a meeting with New York City officials in the Gold Room of the World Trade Center, I was struck by an epiphany-evoking vision. There on the wall, as clear as the pinstripes on the Brooks Brothers suits of the men seated across from me, was the vision of a man on horseback with a packhorse trailing behind! The horseman was slowly riding alongside a swift-flowing stream; in the background rose a high mountain covered with dark green vegetation reaching upward to a bright blue sky.

Within two weeks, I handed in my resignation to Newark's City Hall so that I could undertake a 7000-mile horseback journey from San Diego to Maine. I entitled this odyssey "Ride for Nature." Many of my family, friends, and coworkers told me I was foolish for leaving a secure job during a time when our American economy was doing so poorly. In my mind's eye, I saw that many of the people who tried to dissuade me were the foolish ones.

With meager savings and a little money from the sale of my used car and stereo equipment, I flew out to San Diego. When my brother Lefty met me at the airport, he asked, "Where is your luggage?" My response was to pull a toothbrush out of my denim shirt pocket. Within three weeks I purchased a lead horse and packhorse, along with equipage and survival gear for making tracks across America.

To earn money on the ride, I worked a variety of jobs on farms, Indian reservations, ranches, and oil fields, and spoke before many diverse groups. As I slowly trekked across our bountiful country, I asked questions and kept diaries about the nature and health of our water.

When the horseback journey concluded in Calais, Maine, my horses and I were invited to move into a pond house on the Connecticut estate of the artist and writer Eric Sloane. Living indoors took some getting used to after living outside for almost two years. The still air inside a closed room felt stagnant and suffocating. Thank goodness there was a large swing-up window overlooking the deck on the pond. Locking the five-by-six-foot window open allowed me to relocate the mattress so I could sleep with my head practically outside. In exchange for caretaking the estate, Eric and his wife, Mimi, gave me and my two horses a nice transition home while I reentered society's structured and in some ways limited existence. I must also say that Eric was an inspiration in his beliefs about the importance of farm life and respecting nature.

When Eric sold his Connecticut estate, I tearfully sold off my horses and relocated to a remote cabin with no electricity on the beautiful island of Martha's Vineyard. Soon another turning point of my life came when I consciously opted for a life of financial independence by creating wealth through work that I loved. In a span of fifteen years I founded several profitmaking environmental businesses and a nonprofit research institute. The businesses were: a state-certified water-testing laboratory and environmental consulting/engineering firm (Vineyard Environmental Protection, Inc.); an environmental research institute (Vineyard Environmental Research Institute); a publishing company (WEM Publishing, Inc.) that published *Martha's Vineyard Magazine* and *Nantucket Journal* (today known as *Nantucket*); and a local cable television talk show entitled *The Vineyard Voice*. Besides these business interests, I was also actively involved in the Vineyard community by serving as a town official to protect wetlands, surface waters, and drinking waters.

Today, at age fifty-two, I see how most of my life has been centered on water—physically, psychologically, and spiritually. This book is based on a collection of notes and thoughts that I hope will bring a better respect and understanding of water and all that it gives to life. My belief, based on experience, is that a better understanding of water will give each one of us a way of seeing ourself and help lead us to a better life.

My attempt to write about water is certainly not the first. Water stories exist from people around the globe and can be found in the earliest forms of writing chiseled in stone and clay. Therefore, I am only reflecting on, and hopefully adding a little to, the vast pool of information on water. At this time, the most important thing I feel I can do is to help awaken humanity to the urgent need to care for water as though it were a living being—for that is exactly what water is.

Part I

WONDER

Lake Baikal and Irkutsk, Russia, area, November 1994. The largest and deepest freshwater lake in the world. This NASA photo offers a look at the southern portion of the lake and the snow-covered Khama Daban Range. The lake's only outlet, the Angara River, can be seen in the lower center. The great volume of water from the Angara is captured by one of the largest hydroelectric dams in Eurasia, located near the bottom of the photograph.

ONE

The Well

WHEN I WAS A BOY, I recall one hot day during a long dry summer. On that day, the shallow well that was our farm's main water source went dry. Certainly, with all the children and animals dependent on a daily ration of water, something had to be done immediately. Our farm was so remote that no well drillers were readily available. And, even if a well driller had been available, my father would not have been able to afford him. To make matters worse, we had no farm machinery capable of drilling or driving a well point down into the water table. Our only saving grace was that the water table was relatively close to the surface, only about twenty feet down.

Being a strong man with an uncanny connection to nature, my father decided we had no choice other than to dig a new well the old-fashioned way— with shovels. Thus, my brother Lefty and I set to working long hours with our father in an attempt to solve our local water crisis.

In preparation for finding the precise location for digging a new well, my father cut a forked branch from a willow tree so he could dowse for water. My brother and I stood in awe as we watched him walk back and forth with the ends of the forked branch balanced in his hands. We noticed that the long part of the branch pointing out from the fork would take a dip downward from time to time. Eventually, my father stood in a spot between the house and the barn and stabbed the branch into the ground. "This is where we will dig," he pronounced with a sparkle in his eyes.

We began by digging a circular hole a little over three feet in diameter. After digging shovelful by shovelful to a depth of about four feet, the three of us, with much pushing and creative leverage, placed the first cylindrical concrete well casing. This casing was two feet high by three feet in diameter and, once situated, sat on the bottom of the hole. We then placed a second concrete casing on top of that one; the outside edges of the casings locked together at the seam by means of an overlapping joint.

Since my brother Lefty and I were young boys at the time, we could fit inside the casings with some room to spare for shoveling dirt. We took turns going down into the hole and filling a bucket tied to a rope. Whoever was outside the hole up above would pull the bucket up hand-over-hand and empty the dirt on the ground. Admittedly, an occasional slip while sending the bucket up or down did result in some near misses of the digger's head.

To this day, I vividly remember the rich damp odor of freshly dug earth while digging in the hole. It was a smell so sensual and seductive that I began to realize why so many gardeners and farmers think of it as a natural form of aromatherapy. This aromatherapy, coupled with my first experience of digging a deep hole into our Earth, made the entire experience an adventure of sorts.

To dig, I would stand in the bottom of the hole with the heels of my feet against the concrete well casing and dig out the center of the hole. Then I would stand inside the dug center of the hole and dig out the dirt from beneath the casing. Once enough dirt under the casing was removed, the bottom casing, along with the casings weighing it down from up above, would slip downward. As the hole got deeper, more casings were added at the top.

After digging the hole down to about fifteen feet, I began to see the sides weep water, like tears running down a face. With each bite of the shovel, there would be a sucking sound as the moist soils reluctantly released another shovelful of earth. After removing the moist dirt, I would see snakelike movements as tiny rivulets of water slowly revealed themselves as they pushed free from their dark hiding places. Even then, with the mind of a boy, I could see that before I disturbed the soil, there was a complex system of pathways through which water flowed beneath the ground. I could see how the water flowing from the sides of the hole was a small part of a much larger system of an underground network of water veins.

As I dug the hole deeper, the water weeping from the sides spilled forth with greater volume and speed, and the soil beneath my feet became wetter and softer. Also, because of the greater depth, it was getting darker and more difficult to see what I was digging. I would take my shovel, dig out a scoop from the side of the hole beneath the casing, wait a few seconds, and then watch as tiny streams of water appeared. At about seventeen feet, the water was streaming down the sides of the hole so rapidly that I began wearing boots. At this depth, my brother and I took turns climbing down a wooden ladder into the well hole to do our digging. Once one of us was inside the hole, my father would hoist up the ladder to get it out of the way so Lefty or I could get on with the digging.

Since the well needed to be deeper than the water table, my father fashioned a gasoline water pump with a long black suction hose to pump out the water. The end of the hose that sucked the water from the bottom of the hole had a rough metal screen fitted over it to prevent rocks and gravel from being sucked in and damaging the pump's internal fins. To gather the water for pumping, I would shovel out a depression in the bottom of the hole, quickly shove in a specially prepared bucket punctured with large nail holes, and then put the screened end of the suction hose inside the bucket. This setup would suck out the water to below the surface of the soil in the bottom of the hole and allow us to continue digging deeper.

I remember quite vividly the afternoon the well-digging adventure reached its climax. There was a slight chill in the air with a line of dark clouds casting long shadows across the land. It got so dark in the bottom of the well that my brother's job was to shine a flashlight into the hole so I could see what I was digging. After filling the bucket with wet sand and gravel, I'd say, "Okay, haul it away." With strong arms and hands, my father hauled on the rope and raised the heavy bucket out of the well. By then we had reached a depth of about twenty feet, and the soil on the bottom of the well was very soft and mushy. While looking upward at the disappearing bucket, I felt something moving beneath my feet—something with a life of its own, like a huge slithering snake. I became frightened. Suddenly, water began bubbling up so fast that its swift current emitted musical sounds.

Soon the air was stirring around me as it turned deathly cold and the sandy soils beneath my feet were transformed into quicksand. I let out a scream as my boots sunk quickly below the surface. I tried to free my feet but found myself rapidly sinking deeper as the mucky, smelly cold water rapidly rose around my ankles. It felt like the hands of death were gripping at my legs and pulling me under. I yelled for help as I leaned over and began hugging the pump's suction hose for dear life. Pulling with all my strength, I tried yanking my feet from the dark swirling muck. With reluctance and a sucking sound, the living muck released my right foot while keeping my boot and sock. The same result came from the tug of war to release my left foot.

With my feet free, I was able to wrap my legs around the six-inch suction hose and hold on as the icy waters quickly rose up to drown my paralyzed legs.

"Hold on, Billy, I'm sending the bucket down," yelled my father. "Grab the bucket!" both he and my brother yelled, as the roped bucket dropped next to me. "Billy, grab the bucket!" my father yelled in panic several times. So I grabbed the lip of the metal bucket with my right hand as my legs and left arm and hand clung tightly to the black suction hose. "Now grab the bucket with both hands!" my father yelled down, his eyes straining to see me as Lefty fumbled with the flashlight.

I really didn't want to let go of the hose with my legs and left arm. In a strange way, the hose had suddenly become my closest friend, like some sort of umbilical cord. "Billy! Listen to me! Grab the bucket with both hands!" yelled my father in his scary "You're in trouble if you don't listen to me" voice. Letting go of the hose with my left hand, I grabbed the bucket with both hands. "Let go of the hose with your legs!" came my father's next command. But I just couldn't get my legs to let go.

From up above, my muscular father hauled on the bucket rope with all his strength. My numbed fingers held tightly. Suddenly, the handle on one side of the bucket broke. I let out a tearful scream and let go of the bucket and grabbed back onto the black hose with both hands. By now, the deathly cold spring waters were rising up around my waist. Thinking quickly, my father pulled up the rope and tied it around the top rung of the wooden ladder. He then lowered the ladder into the well hole. When the ladder hit the bubbling quicksand below, it sank deeper and deeper until the top rung of the ladder went below the top of the well. My father then ran to a nearby apple tree and tied the rope off. Returning, he shifted the ladder close to me and yelled, "Billy, let go of the hose and move over to the ladder!" By this time, I was a shivering mess. "I'm too cold. I can't move!" I cried. In what seemed like a lifetime, my father climbed over the top of the well and came down the ladder until he was at my side. Within seconds, his strong left arm was lifting me up onto the ladder. When we reached the top of the well, my tearful eyes opened wide and greeted the golden twilight. With each deep breath I inhaled the warm air as if for the first time.

Years have passed now, and whenever I visit my brother Timothy, who bought the farm from my mother, I walk up to the old well and quietly say hello, as if to an old friend. At times, I recall laboring with my father and brother to dig the well, remember my first visit with the hidden realm of underground water, and am thankful for the experience in my lifetime. Without doubt, I also remember the joy and security the well brought to my family. The hand-dug well we installed has never gone dry, even when other wells in the area failed due to subsequent dry spells.

I lost count of the times in the remaining years of my father's life when I heard him say after drinking a glass of water, "This well water tastes good." I also think at times of the last hours of his life as he was dying of cancer. Because of weakness and internal bleeding, he found it difficult to clear the blood and phlegm from his throat. As I sat next to him in the wee hours of the morning, I would take a straw and submerge most of it into a glass of water. Then I would place my index finger over the hole on the top end, lift the water-filled straw from the glass, and place the bottom end in my father's mouth. Slowly and purposefully, I would release the pressure of my index finger at the top of the straw. As the water trickled into my father's mouth, he would move his lips and tongue to help clear his throat. As amazing as this may sound, the last words he spoke before lapsing into a coma from which he did not revive—"Mmmm, that's good water."

TWO

Cosmic Rain

Is it not of great significance that the world of the stars perme-
ates all movements of water, that water infuses all earthly life
with the events of the cosmos, that all life processes are through
water intimately connected with the course of the stars?... Thus
water becomes an image of the stream of time itself.
—THEODOR SCHWENK

RECENT DISCOVERIES about our universe tell us that water may be
present everywhere in one form or another. And, just as we say,
"Where there's smoke there is fire," we may soon be saying, "Where
there's water there is life." Searching the cosmos, scientists have now
discovered water being created in interstellar space. In interstellar
space they have also found the rudimentary constituents of life. For
instance, in 1984 scientists at the Goddard Space Center found a
bewildering array of molecules, including the beginning of organic
chemistry in the form of atoms that are found in living tissue, in interstellar space. The key words, "found in living tissue," are quite
telling. For it is these atoms that possess the spinning vortex energy
that is also found in the seemingly indestructible watery center of all
living cells.

Over the past thirty years I have learned much about water through
laboratory analysis, reading, research, other water professionals, and
travel. Information from sources such as *U.S. Water News, Science,*
Nature, American Water Works Association (AWWA), The Groundwater Foundation, Worldwatch Institute, National Aeronautics and
Space Administration (NASA), Woods Hole Oceanographic Institute
(WHOI), *National Geographic*, American Rivers, and many other
sources, is continually providing me with revelations about the subject of water. I find it exciting that with each passing year, science
is making new discoveries about the presence of water throughout
our solar system and beyond. To date, evidence of water has been

discovered on our Moon, Sun, Mars, Jupiter's moon Europa, in the so-called empty spaces between the stars (interstellar space), and in many other cosmic locations.

In December 1998, a specially designed satellite called the Submillimeter-Wave Astronomy Satellite (SWAS) was launched to detect radio waves emitted by water molecules in space. As a water researcher, I found the launching of this project to be intriguing. So, while making the final edits to this book, I picked up the telephone and tracked down the leading scientist of the SWAS project. "We're seeing water everywhere. Every region we've looked at so far contains water," reported the project's chief scientist, Gary Melnick of the Harvard-Smithsonian Astrophysical Observatory in Cambridge.

Melnick's finding is further supported by the existence of the Oort Cloud, a huge watery cloud surrounding our solar system that is made up of trillions of comets containing ice and gases. The Oort Cloud is thought to be about five billion years old, at least as old as our solar system, which means that water was present at the creation of our solar system. Some scientists believe that Oort comets may have brought quantities of water to our oceans and lakes when they struck our Earth over the past billions of years.

Cosmic clouds containing forms of water have also recently been discovered rotating around black holes that are suspected to be near the center of our universe. Forms of water have also been found to be one of the major constituents of comets. When Halley's comet last visited our solar system in 1985, scientists at Kitt Peak Observatory reported "that the comet's dominant constituent is water ice, and that much of the tenuous 360,000-mile-wide cloud surrounding it consisted of water vapor." At one point, according to Ian Stewart, the director of NASA's Halley's comet project, it was estimated that the comet was losing up to 70 tons of water a minute!

The tails of comets appear to be made up mostly of water that is carried by the solar wind as the ice in comets evaporates due to heat from the Sun. According to Paul Spudis of the Lunar and Planetary Institute at Rice University, "comets are 90 percent water in the form of ice mixed with dust." Once the solar winds dissipate the water of a comet into space, the water may refreeze into tiny ice particles or be reduced to the basic gaseous components found in plasma—the same plasma that makes up most of the universe and serves as a fuel in stars.

The Hale-Bopp comet, which passed through our solar system in

1997, also yielded secrets demonstrating that the ice in comets carry the chemical precursors for life, as reported by Dr. Dale Cruikshank, an astronomer at NASA's Ames Research Center, in a 1997 article in the journal *Science* (Vol. 275, No. 5308).

In 1986, Dr. Louis A. Frank, a University of Iowa physicist, first proposed that giant cosmic snowballs were constantly bombarding the upper atmosphere of Earth. Dr. Frank's studies, based on analysis of pictures from a NASA polar satellite, indicated that as many as twenty cometlike snowballs of about thirty feet in diameter approach the Earth every minute. According to Frank, after these comets break up, the ice water and dust fall toward our planet as a form of cosmic rain. Back then many scientists met this idea with skepticism. However, Frank continued his research as new space satellites were placed into orbit. Then, on May 28, 1997, he appeared before the American Geophysical Union convention and presented new information in support of his cosmic rain theory. As reported in the *Boston Herald* on May 29, 1997,

> Giant snowballs are bombarding the upper atmosphere, then breaking up, adding water to Earth's oceans and possibly nurturing life on the planet, a researcher reported yesterday.
>
> The snowballs are actually small comets about 40 feet in diameter that appear to be streaking toward Earth in a steady stream. However, according to data provided by NASA's Polar satellite, the snowballs are no danger to people on Earth or to spacecraft or airplanes because they break up at altitudes from 600 miles to 15,000 miles. "This relatively gentle 'cosmic rain'— which possibly contains simple organic compounds—may well have nurtured the development of life on our planet," Louis Frank of the University of Iowa said.

Cosmic water may also enter the Earth's atmosphere in other forms. In 1998, some boys in the West Texas town of Monahans saw a meteorite blaze a trail across the sky on its way to falling in a nearby yard. With fear and excitement, the boys ran home and told their parents, who promptly alerted scientists at NASA's Johnson Space Center in Houston. Not too long after picking up the meteorite, NASA scientists realized that it had a chicken or egg story to tell. As they looked at it closely, they realized that for the first time they could answer the question about which came first: our solar system or the water we find on Earth and elsewhere.

According to an article in Volume 285 of *Science* (August 27, 1999), the researchers who cracked open the Monahans meteorite were surprised to discover the actual presence of water. "The existence of a water-soluble salt in this meteorite is astonishing," wrote Robert N. Clayton of the University of Chicago.

Clayton also wrote, "Meteorites can provide insights into processes in the early solar system. However, the role played by water can often only be inferred indirectly."

The NASA team that worked on the Monahans meteorite included the noted planetary scientist Michael Zolensky. While working on this book, I telephoned Dr. Zolensky for an update. He reported that when he and other scientists opened a portion of the meteorite in their lab, "We found purple crystals of halite, or rock salt, that contained minuscule pockets of water with bubbles, which indicated that water flowed on whatever parent body spawned the meteorite." He further explained, "Chrondite meteorites, such as the one found in Monahans, contain some of the most primitive ingredients from the beginnings of our solar system. It is possible that the water found inside the Monahans meteorite could date back to 4.5 billion years or perhaps before the creation of our solar system."

"How could water exist before the creation of our solar system?" I asked. Zolensky answered, "It is possible that the water in the Monahans meteorite came from what we call interstellar water. Interstellar water can be much older than 4.5 billion years. At this time, we are keeping what is left of the Monahans meteorite in a safe place with the hope that at some future time we will be able to determine the age of water from hydrogen and oxygen isotopes. Right now, science has no way of determining the age of water."

Toward the close of our conversation, Dr. Zolensky said that he and other scientists are still researching another chrondite meteorite discovered on a frozen lake in Canada's British Columbia. This bus-sized meteorite, weighing about 220 tons, broke into pieces just before landing on Tagish Lake in January 2000. According to Peter G. Brown of the University of Western Ontario, the Tagish Lake meteorite pieces are the most pristine specimens on the planet at this time. As Brown reported in the October 2000 issue of *Science* (Vol. 290, pp. 320–25), "These data suggest that the Tagish Lake meteorite may be one of the most primitive solar system materials yet studied."

The research on the Tagish Lake meteorite and the discovery of water inside the Monahans meteorite help to provide us with clues about water being present at or before the creation of our solar system. The mythological, theological, and scientific implications of this fact have yet to be synthesized into a unifying theory.

In June 1999, NASA launched a telescope-carrying satellite called the Far Ultraviolet Spectroscopic Explorer, known as FUSE. FUSE is designed to trace chemical fossils created at the creation of the universe by focusing on the hydrogen isotope deuterium, which was created naturally only at the time of the Big Bang. If the three-year project is successful, it will tell us what conditions were like moments after the Big Bang and may also provide information about the role of water in our universe's creation.

Scientific studies have also showed that water reacts to cosmic influences. It was observed in laboratories that water used in mixing chemical solutions does not always remain the same. Further studies revealed that the water in the solutions was being influenced by shifts in the Earth's magnetic field or by explosions on the Sun. How and why water is so sensitive to such cosmic influences, even in laboratories deep underground, remains a mystery. But it is now suspected that water responds to and is interconnected in some way with all that exists in the cosmos. This means that water is a far more sensitive and responsive entity than most people ever imagined.

The connection of water on Earth with the cosmos also manifests in other ways. The most visible evidence of extraterrestrial matter coming to Earth is the meteor trails we see blazing across the night sky. It has been estimated that at least one hundred tons of cosmic dust and litter enter the Earth's atmosphere each day. So much cosmic material has come to Earth that its mass is estimated to have doubled since its beginning. This cosmic dust also plays an ongoing part in creating our weather, for the floating dust particles in the atmosphere help create raindrops. Without dust to cling to, the water vapor in our atmosphere would never fall as rain. The fact that it takes approximately one million cloud droplets to create each raindrop can leave much for the imagination during a rainstorm.

This is not to say that all our rain is created around dust from outer space, in fact far from it. Volcanic eruptions, the burning of fossil fuels and forests, and removal of vegetation all contribute to atmospheric debris. Winds blowing across unprotected soil lift fine particles of dust thousands of feet into the air in a spiral motion; eventually, these particles can travel around the entire planet. It may be that the escalating presence of dust from human activities and natural sources is a contributing factor to our violent weather and heavy rains.

The thought that every raindrop needs a dust particle for its nucleus may also serve as a doorway for our minds into the cosmic realm. We have learned that the plasma of interstellar space contains the constituents of water in gaseous form. These constituents in turn form the basis of creating water in interstellar space. Expanding on this thought in a relative fashion, we may envision our Earth as a large dust particle floating through the extensive space that makes up our universe. Just as a dust particle attracts billions of water molecules to create a drop of rain, so, too, may our Earth attract interstellar water, which in turn condenses to contribute additional water to our planet's biosphere.

The fact that water has been discovered throughout interstellar space, in my mind, gives additional credence to the sayings of our world's first empirical philosopher, Thales. Over two thousand years ago, Thales proposed that all things come from water and that all heavenly bodies, including our Earth, float in water. Water therefore may be the connecting interstellar intermediary between all matter in the universe. Just as a thrown pebble sends waves of energy rippling through every water molecule in a pond, changes in any planet or sun may also send waves of energy rippling through every water molecule throughout the universe.

THREE

Water of Life

Why, then, does water, which has no life-characteristics of its own, form the very basis of life in all life's various manifestations? Because water embraces everything, is in and all through everything; because it rises above the distinctions between plants and animals and human beings; because it is a universal element shared by all; itself undetermined, yet determining; because, like the primal mother it is, it supplies the stuff of life to everything living. —THEODOR SCHWENK

IN MY TRAVELS throughout the world, I have seen many unusual life forms. Those of us who have seen other life forms in pictures, zoos, or while traveling, may ask: Why does Earth give rise to so many life forms? Why does the geologic and archeological record tell us about other life forms that no longer exist? Are there new life forms being created today? Did the creation of new life end with the dawn of humans?

Modern science is now speculating that small microbes called extremophiles (because they survive under extreme conditions) may represent the first life form created on Earth. These microbes have been discovered in volcanic pools and in the deepest depths of our oceans in above-boiling heat where there is no oxygen or sunlight. The discovery of extremophiles follows on the heels of the discovery of hydrothermal vents and strange life forms 9000 feet deep by Dr. Robert Ballard (of *Titanic* fame) on February 16, 1977. In his book *Explorations*, Ballard wrote, "If life could flourish, nurtured by a complex chemical process based on geothermal heat, then life could exist under similar conditions on planets far removed from the nurturing light of the parent star—the sun." This thought by Dr. Ballard supports the late Carl Sagan's speculation about life existing on other planets. However, what science has yet to understand are the how and the why of life springing forth anywhere it may be found in the universe.

Before seeking to find the origin of life, perhaps it would be helpful for us to define life. However, as strange as it seems, people from all walks of life, including biologists, have varying opinions about the definition of life.

Basically, all living beings are made up of about twenty chemical elements. These elements are mostly carbon, hydrogen, oxygen, and nitrogen, and to a lesser extent chlorine, calcium, sodium, potassium, magnesium, sulfur, and iron along with small amounts of a few other elements. A curious thing about this list is that these same elements are also found in all the materials forming our Earth as well as our universe. It is in this fashion that we see life's intimate relationship with the entire universe as well as with our Earth. Life also depends on the Earth's electromagnetic field and on nutrient chemicals, as well as the flow of energy from the Sun.

But how is it that these elements can come together in such a way that life is created? In Mary Shelley's classic book *Frankenstein*, it is the power of an electrical flash that provides the necessary spark of life. Today, in an example of science following art, it is now widely believed that lightning in the ancient atmosphere played a vital part in bringing forth life on Earth.

This "lightning yielding life" theory was introduced with considerable media fanfare in the early 1950s by a graduate student at the University of Chicago named Stanley Miller, who was greatly influenced by Harold Urey, the renowned theorist on planet formation. Miller undertook a series of innovative laboratory experiments involving the frequent discharge of electricity into atmospheric conditions mimicking those of primitive Earth. What he hoped to prove was that lightning was responsible for altering the Earth's early atmosphere. If he could prove that lightning played a vital part in the creation of life on early Earth, Miller thought he might eventually be able to discover how primitive life began.

Again and again Miller sent electrical discharges flying through the watery atmosphere he created in the laboratory. After about three days, he began getting readings that he and other scientists considered astounding—the electricity had converted the atmosphere into a variety of amino acids and other relative biological ingredients that make up the very foundations of life. Once the facts of this discovery became known, Miller found himself an overnight media sensation as news sources from around the world clamored to report the story. The news stories speculated that humankind might soon discover how life first began on our planet!

The discovery of how life began has yet to materialize. Recently Miller, now at the University of California, commented, "We have learned how to make organic compounds from inorganic elements; the next step is to learn how they organize themselves into a replicating cell."

About a decade after Miller's initial experiments, his theory was reinforced by another sensational discovery. This discovery was made when our Earth was struck by the "Murchison Meteorite." At the time, it was almost as though Divine assistance was playing a part in the expansion of human consciousness. Falling to earth in 1969 in the relatively obscure town of Murchison, Australia, this carbon-rich meteor created a news clamor comparable to Miller's. Since life on Earth is based on twenty amino acids, the discovery of a range of amino acids on the surface and inside the meteorite was cause for excitement. Analysis of the inside of the meteor found amino acids and other organic chemicals similar to those obtained by Miller in his experiments. This led to conjecture that cosmic forces exerted on the meteor as it flew through space had created amino acids and other materials that were building blocks in the creation of life. Curious too was the fact that water was discovered inside the Murchison Meteorite—water that had been trapped inside the meteor for perhaps untold billions of years.

Ongoing research into the Murchison Meteorite was reported in the February 1997 issue of the journal *Science*. Dr. Sandra Pizzarello and Dr. John R. Cronin reported findings based on their recent research into the "left-handedness" of the amino acids found inside the meteorite. This recent discovery supports the theory put forth in 1991 by chemist Dr. William A. Bonner of Stanford University, who speculates that the creation of these possible life-forming amino acids may have been influenced by the circular light generated by a neutron star. This light would flow in a corkscrew or vortex-type path that could influence the makeup of the amino acids.

This information indicates that meteors striking Earth contain the basic building blocks for the beginnings of life, and we saw in the previous chapter that water was present from the very creation of our solar system. Apparently, all that is needed for life to arise is an environment warm enough to allow water to exist as a liquid.

This fact is further supported by the theory that the building blocks for life existed on Mars when its surface contained liquid water over three billion years ago. Giving credence to this theory was the August 1996 discovery relating to the 4.1-pound meteorite called Allan Hills 84001. This meteorite was found in Antarctica in 1984 and is assumed to have crashed to Earth about 13,000 years ago. The discovery of microscopic fossil-like remnants inside this meteorite became the topic of much scientific debate and speculation. This debate recently intensified further when NASA researchers identified the Allan Hills meteorite as being Martian in origin. Slices of the meteorite have revealed organic molecules that can be formed in only two ways, either by the biological activity of microorganisms or in the process that forms planets. Either way, water was identified as playing a key role in the formation of the organic molecules.

Complementing this NASA research is the independent work of Laurie A. Leshin of Arizona State University. Ms. Leshin studied the amount of a specific hydrogen isotope (deuterium) found inside the water-bearing crystals of the Allan Hills meteorite. By doing so, she determined that there is a high probability of significant quantities of water still existing as groundwater below the surface of Mars. Adding more excitement is the geological evidence provided by NASA in June 2000 indicating surface erosion on Mars due to once-flowing waters, as well as signs of present-day aquifers.

No matter where in the universe watery conditions do exist, electricity may be generated or enhanced by the constituents found within moving water. And, it is electricity that serves as a fundamental part in the creation and motion of life as we know it. Therefore we have the possibility, as suspected by Carl Sagan and others, that life exists elsewhere in our universe.

Scientists speculate that as life evolved, simple forms of green plants eventually provided the basis of the food chain to nourish all other life on Earth. Green plants living on land and in water have the ability to take energies from the cosmos (such as sunlight) and the surface of the planet and create food. Even though scientists have given this process the name "photosynthesis," and named the green pigment it creates "chlorophyll," there remains considerable speculation about how photosynthesis actually works.

In my search for the definition of life, my mind, spirit, and senses have continually guided me to see water as a loving, living, creative entity. Perhaps this is why many of us find ourselves experiencing certain emotions when approaching or passing near an ocean, a lake, waterfall, gurgling brook, or some other body of water.

It is water that dissolves stone to release the minerals and nutrients necessary for life. It is water in the atmosphere that shields us from the chilling death of outer space while filtering the heat and deadly rays of the Sun. It is water that absorbs and stores the Sun's energy. And it is water in plants that serves as the vehicle for photosynthesis—that mysterious process whereby solar energy, minerals, nitrogen, and various other elements and processes interact to create living chlorophyll cells.

Literally, indeed, water is the key that brings together various elements to form life. For without water, the elements would not have the opportunity to coexist in a way that would give rise to the variety of life forms we find on Earth. Hence, in this fashion, if you discover water in any shape or form, no matter where you are, you have discovered life.

Water is always working to create conditions conducive to life. It is unnatural for water to remain still. Water by its essential nature is always moving, and by constantly moving it serves to create, protect, energize, nourish, and sustain life.

Nothing is safe from being changed by water. Whenever water comes into contact with other molecules, it begins to assimilate them. Be it rock, wood, plastic, glass, or whatever—the molecules in water push apart the atoms, surround them, and then put them into solution. It is for this reason that seawater contains all the elements known to humankind. Scientists have also discovered that seawater contains only eleven elements in concentrations exceeding 1/100th of a percent and, not surprisingly, these same elements are the top eleven that make up the human body.

When water comes into contact with soils, metals, or minerals that are acidic, the water does its best to neutralize the acid. Why? Because acidic conditions are not conducive to abundant life of great variety. The same law applies when water comes into contact with anything that is too alkaline—water will try to neutralize the alkalinity so it too is conducive to fostering a healthy environment for many life forms.

Ancient wisdom about acidic conditions not being conducive to life can be found in early forms of birth control. The ancient Jewish sect of ascetics and mystics known as the Essenes practiced a form of birth control that was also used in ancient China. A woman's womb usually has an ideal acid measurement of about pH 5 or higher. (The pH scale ranges from 0 to 14, with 0 being the most acidic and 14 the most alkaline; a neutral pH is usually 6 to 7.) If the measurement is below this (more acidic), a woman will have great difficulties in conceiving. Therefore when fluids that are acidic are present in the womb, conception will usually not occur. For this reason, Essene women used the juice of rosehips (which has a pH of 2) as a form of birth control. Lemon juice (pH 2) or other organic liquids with a low pH could also be used. However, when such a method is used, it is important for the woman to douche with a liquid the following day or sooner with a soapy liquid that has a pH of 7 or 8. This will restore the acid conditions of the womb back to normal.

For whatever reason, according to the laws of water, life was meant to enjoy the greatest success and abundance when water is close to neutral. Evidence supporting this can found in lakes, ponds, and streams that suffer from acid pollution or acid rain fallout. The presence of acid in these bodies of water greatly reduces the variety and quantity of all life forms—insect, plant, amphibian, and fish.

Lake Baikal—The "Sacred Sea"

Many life forms occupying our planet at any given moment carry within their blood a chemical imprint of the place they were born as well as the environment with which they have intercourse. As an example, marine scientists now have the ability to identify genetic markers and other features on fish to provide information heretofore unavailable. For instance, as remarkable as it sounds, the stream where any salmon is born can now be ascertained by examining its scales for the water's unique characteristics. As reported by John Tierney in *New York Times Magazine* (August 27, 2000, p. 42), "marine scientists . . . have identified genetic markers and various features on fish that could serve as the equivalent of cattle brands. They can tell, for instance, exactly where a salmon spawned by examining its scales for the unique chemical signature of the stream where it was born."

Besides chemistry, there are also electromagnetic and cosmic influences specific to each body of water, all of which play into the makeup and evolution of every life form. Because of these and other advancements in understanding water, we are beginning to better appreciate the uniqueness of every life form, including prehistoric life. By studying one of Earth's most ancient bodies of water, Russia's Lake Baikal, we are beginning to gain some insight about how certain life forms evolved. This ancient lake is also known as the oldest and perhaps one of the strangest freshwater lakes existing on our planet today.

Lake Baikal, nestled within the steppes, mountains, and forests of southeast Siberia near the Mongolian border, is Earth's deepest (over one mile) lake, and one of the largest. Compared with other lakes, which die after filling with sediment, Lake Baikal is estimated to be 25 million years old—making it the world's oldest surviving lake. In a fashion, it therefore serves as a living museum for ancient life forms that have evolved without interruption for millions of years. This fact alone makes Baikal an ecological goldmine.

Fed by waters from hundreds of rivers originating in the nearby mountain ranges, Lake Baikal holds about 20 percent of the Earth's freshwater and harbors more local species of plants and animals than any other lake on Earth. There is so much water in Lake Baikal that it would take more than all the water contained in North America's Great Lakes to fill it; studies tell us that it contains over 5500 cubic miles of freshwater—60 percent of our planet's viable drinking water. It rests within a 12,200-square-mile basin. Although at least 336 rivers and streams flow into Baikal, only one, the Angara, flows out of it.

Why has Baikal not died from sediment deposits like other lakes? I asked this question of one of America's leading geologists, who has traveled to Siberia and studied Lake Baikal. According to Dr. Deborah Hutchinson, Team Chief Scientist for the U.S. Geological Survey's Coastal and Marine Geology Team at Woods Hole, Massachusetts, "From what my and other studies indicate, the plates located under Lake Baikal are pulling apart; which is the major reason why a rift lake like Baikal is so deep. The reason Baikal has not filled with sediment is due to its incredible depth as well as the lack of sediment transport from surrounding rivers. Most of the rivers flowing into Baikal are very short. The longest river, the Selenga, does carry a rather significant sediment load into Baikal—which is why we find the Selenga River delta in the shallow portion of the lake. It is in studying Baikal's ancient sediment deposits that we hope to learn more about climate change, since there are very few interior lakes in the world that have remained as undisturbed as Lake Baikal. As far as we can tell, Baikal's sediments were never scoured by overriding continental ice sheets, which is why Baikal's sediments yield such a rare glimpse into Earth's hydrological climate variations over a period of tens of millions of years."

In Baikal's waters there are about 1500 species of rare life forms that can be found nowhere else on the planet. What is even more surprising is that Baikal, a freshwater lake, contains species of life previously believed to live only in saltwater. Dr. Guy Fleischer, Research Fisheries Scientist at the Great Lakes Science Center, has visited Lake Baikal several times and has ongoing contact with Russian research scientists. When asked about the mystery of saltwater species living in Baikal's freshwater, Dr. Fleischer answered, "One of the theories is that when Baikal's deep rift occurred over 25 million years ago, it originally became flooded with salt or brackish water. Over time, with geologic shifts and as more and more freshwater filled the lake, the saltwater species became freshwater tolerant. Eventually, Baikal's saltwater species evolved into the unusual freshwater life forms we find today."

The sturgeon of Lake Baikal, for example, can weigh as much as 2200 pounds and, according to the annual growth rings found in their inner ears, can live up to 300 years. Dr. Fleischer, who studies the age of sturgeons, sharks, and other fish through a fin ray method, says, "Baikal's sturgeon can possibly live up to 300 years because of their slow growth and the fact that the lake offers them healthy cold water conditions." The sturgeon of Lake Baikal provide some of the world's finest caviar; however, due to human-made changes around the lake, there is the growing threat of pollution, as well as the potential of overfishing this resource.

Presently, scientists from around the world are also trying to understand how the lake has influenced the evolution of nearby terrestrial life forms as well as other life forms on lands and in waters around the world. This macro/micro approach is part of an ongoing effort by scientists attempting to unravel the mysteries of Baikal's unique ecosystem.

To many local people, the water of Baikal is known as "living water." The term "living water" is used because of the lake's unusual ability to support life forms from its surface down to its deepest depths. All other deep lakes of the world have lower depths that are mostly dead due to lack of oxygen and the choking presence of gases such as hydrogen sulfide. In contrast, Lake Baikal's deep waters are saturated with fresh oxygen. Only recently have scientists begun to understand how the underwater venting of hot, oxygenated water combines with the lake's horizontal and vertical currents. It is this unique combining along with other variables, known and unknown, that imparts special qualities to Baikal's water and contributes to its being so alive with aquatic life. And, even though Baikal is saturated with life, its natural water purity and its ability to self-clean are phenomenal. The waters of the lake are so clear that people prone to vertigo are cautioned; when taking a peek over the side of a boat, some have become nauseous at suddenly finding themselves looking down at what appears to be a drop of hundreds of feet into the depths far below the clear surface waters.

The water in Baikal has been known throughout the ages for its spiritual and healing qualities, qualities that have intrigued scientists and healers from around the world. It is no surprise to learn that Baikal's ancient name, the "Sacred Sea," is still used by people visiting and living around the lake today.

For the reasons expressed above and many more, it makes sense that we give priority to understanding Lake Baikal and other bodies of water and the life they hold. Dr. Robert Ballard, the scientist from Woods Hole Oceanographic Institute in Massachusetts who found the *Titanic* wreck says, "There is so much life that we have yet to discover in our oceans and other bodies of water, that we should allocate more resources and time to understanding what these life forms can offer humanity in medicinal and self-knowledge."

Protoplasm—The Water of Life

We as individuals are made up mostly of water. Water is constantly flowing through us. And, even though the water in our bodies is constantly changing, our appearance and organized shape remains somewhat the same. In a fashion, we can see the same phenomenon in a whirlpool of river water. The shape of the whirlpool retains its vortex shape even though the water forming it is constantly changing.

The physical reality of vortex energy manifesting in water is also related to another watery wonder—the spark of motion found in all life.

Where and how living things derive their energy to be "alive" is something that has befuddled the world's greatest thinkers. Where does the energy come from that gives something life? Where does the energy go when a living thing dies? These are perhaps two of greatest questions filling the drama of our human experience.

It is in dealing with the questions of the creation of life and the energy that gives it motion that we find the interface of matter with spirit. For it is in the watery creation of protoplasm that we have the world of life being born from the world of nonlife.

To define the watery realm of protoplasm with words is difficult. However, there are some things we know about protoplasm and the way we perceive it to behave in this reality:

- All living things contain protoplasm.

- Every cell in every living organism is filled with protoplasm.

- Protoplasm occurs only in living organisms.

- Protoplasm is made up of about 75 percent water.

- Protoplasm is what is "alive" in animals and plants—which means that it responds to stimuli; that it takes in and digests food, and discharges the waste; and that it grows and reproduces.

- Protoplasm is believed by most scientists to be the very first life form created on Earth.

- Humans and animals do not manufacture protoplasm; they must receive it ready-made from plants or from other animals that eat plants.

As expressed by Rachel Carson in *The Sea around Us*, "In what manner the sea produced the mysterious and wonderful stuff called protoplasm we cannot say. In its warm, dimly lit waters the unknown conditions of temperature and pressure and saltiness must have been the critical ones for the creation of life from non-life. At any rate they produced the result that neither the alchemists with their crucibles nor modern scientists in the laboratories have been able to achieve." In this book Carson also speculated about how some protoplasm floating on the ocean's surface developed the "magic of chlorophyll," while other protoplasm learned to eat these first plants. Thus we find the beginnings of the first plants and animals.

Echoing this thought is the renowned mythographer Dr. Joseph Campbell (1904–87), who was interviewed by Bill Moyers for a PBS television special toward the end of his life. In the final moments of this historic interview, Moyers asked Dr. Campbell a question about the purpose of human life. Campbell answered, "When you really think about it, life is a lot of protoplasm with an urge to reproduce and continue being."

Protoplasm was discovered in 1835 by the French zoologist Dujardin. Ever since then, scientists throughout the world have been attempting to understand how it was created and how it may have evolved into the various life forms created throughout time.

But why does protoplasm exist? Why does life exist in so many different forms? Why does life exist at all? What is the purpose or goal of life?

As part of the quest for these answers, our human ancestors have created religions and a substantial body of information that is known today as "mythology." This area will be explored below in Part Two to see what it has to teach us about water. But first we will look at more aspects of the energy found in water.

FOUR

Water Weather

Thus the Tao is the course, the flow, the drift, or the process of nature, and I call it the Watercourse Way, because both Lao-tzu and Chuang-tzu use the flow of water as its principal metaphor.
—ALAN WATTS

I BELIEVE THE EXPERIENCE of being raised on a farm with nearby wet-lands, ponds, and streams initiated me into appreciating the various dimensions of water. However, the local water knowledge I gained did little to prepare me for my two-year cross-country horseback trek, especially the challenges my horses and I would face early on in crossing the Southwest's Sonora Desert. What other knowledge I did gather came mostly from writings by Lewis and Clark, Henry David Thoreau, William Bartram, John Muir, and John James Audubon, and from the Western adventure tales of Louis L'Amour. These skillful writers filled my mind with thoughts of living outside while experiencing life on the trail. However, they did little to prepare me for what it would really be like to live outside while facing the day-to-day rigors of surviving the heat and dryness of a desert environment.

It was during this desert passage that I was to have my first of many earthshaking, hair-raising experiences with thunder and lightning. As I was to learn from local people as well as from a few close calls of my own, water in the desert can be deadly—either too little or too much will kill you. "Watch out for the chubasco," I was warned by some Southwestern ranchers and Native Americans.

During the desert's so-called wet season, violent storms called *chubascos* are known to suddenly appear. These surprisingly quick and deadly thunderstorms produce sizzling ground-level lightning, high-velocity winds, torrential downpours, and flash floods. The source of a chubasco's energy is the low-flying moisture coming up from the Gulf of California. When the moist Gulf air slams into the rapidly rising heat of the desert, it quickly spirals skyward, where it

33

forms into huge white cumulus clouds, which in turn become dark, towering cumulonimbus clouds. The dark, spiraling, moisture-laden clouds rapidly climb, cool, and then partially turn to ice before falling to earth with great speed. When the speeding ice and its surrounding cool moisture hit the hot air near the ground in the desert, a chubasco is formed. Which is why chubascos seem to magically appear where just moments before it was clear, calm, sunny, and 110 degrees.

I was about a four-days' ride into the Sonora Desert when I was hit by my first chubasco. At first, I couldn't believe the speed at which the awesome mass of dark clouds swooped down from the sky. The pulsing, churning darkness appeared like a huge dark spirit with wings stretching across the heavens. While I was watching this spectacle, a surprise welcome party of sorts leaped up from the ground as several spinning dust devils began dancing across the land. Slowly, long dark legs reached down toward the earth from the body of the monster storm bird—each leg flashing with talons of erratic lightning. As the storm got closer, I could see the lightning leaping in all directions—back and forth, sideways, as well as from the ground up into the roiling clouds. It was an awesome sight to behold. Besides being eerily beautiful, the chubasco's continuous flashes of lightning and pounding thunder had me throwing out my old survival rule for figuring the distance to lightning—"for every five seconds between a flash of lightning and its clap of thunder, the lightning is one mile distant."

By far the most horrifying aspect of watching the approaching storm was the way the distant lightning kept reaching down from the dark swirling mass of clouds and striking the ground below. With chills running down my spine from the electrified atmosphere, I dismounted and tied the horses to the bases of two large mesquite bushes. I then quickly removed and carried my pack gear and saddles to a nearby rise of land. I covered the gear with a big piece of green canvas, taking special care to tuck its edges beneath the pile to keep it from blowing away. A bolt of nearby sizzling lightning and a loud thunderclap had me thinking, "God! Will we live?"

The towering mass of wind, rain, thunder, and lightning made me feel like an ant. In awe, I stood mesmerized looking up at the swirling mass of electrified darkness. It appeared to have a life of its own! The sweet smell of wet earth reached my nose as the advancing winds and flying dust rapidly approached. Suddenly, I was shocked out of my reverie by the slap of something cold across my face. Helpless,

I was knocked to the ground by a dark wall of flying water filled with huge raindrops mixed with snow, sleet, and hail. The mothball-sized hailstones felt like stinging bullets hitting my shoulders and back. Ear-splitting thunder coupled with blinding flashes of lightning sent me crawling along the muddy ground toward the shelter of the green canvas. Along the way, the wind blew off my cowboy hat. The rawhide string tied beneath my chin kept the hat from flying away, but the blowing wind pulled so hard on the hat that the string almost choked me.

As surely as I see these words while writing, I saw a ball of lightning cross the distant landscape. It looked like a huge glowing basketball bouncing along the ground as if guided by an invisible hand. Whenever the ball struck the ground it got brighter. As it bounced, it threw off sparks in all directions until it exploded into nothingness. With the smell of sulfur in my nose, I took one last look at the horses. They appeared illuminated by a mystical yellow and blue strobe light. Their hindquarters were windward with their long tails blowing up between their legs against their bellies; their heads were down low to the ground with their ears back flat. I took one last look around before ducking under the green canvas. Like a pack rat, I curled up into the middle of the pile of pack gear and saddles. As the storm raged overhead, I felt like any other animal hiding from its fury. The noise from the hail and rain hitting the canvas was deafening. Soon, the sizzling lightning and pounding rain, hail and thunder built to a crescendo.

Then it was over. The entire storm lasted about ten minutes.

As quickly as it came, the rain, hail, lightning, and thunder faded away into the distance. "Hope the horses are all right," I thought while crawling from under the canvas. Lifting the canvas revealed a blindingly white sparkling landscape. The cool air was crisp and clear. Immediately, I looked for the horses. They were close together and throwing their heads up and talking to each other with throaty sounds. Like dandruff, large flecks of sleet and snow clung to their manes and backs.

As I stood up, my eyes seemed to go out of focus as the white ground around the horses began moving. At first I thought I was hallucinating. Or perhaps I was disoriented from being struck by lightning. Steadying myself, I squinted my eyes and walked slowly toward the horses. With each step I noticed that more and more of the glistening white ground was moving. I couldn't believe my eyes!

Soon, the ground in front of me began to move! To my surprise, I was soon standing in flowing water with hail floating on top. "Oh my God!" I thought, "What if a flood wall of water is on its way!"

I had heard and read stories of huge walls of water gushing out of nowhere into the quiet, sunny desert. These flash floods, sometimes originating from storms miles away, were capable of carrying trees, huge rocks, cars, and all else in their paths. Small towns and entire groups of people and livestock have been known to disappear.

I slushed my way to the horses. Reaching down into the icy water with both hands, I untied the ropes from the mesquite bushes. Quickly, I guided the horses to the nearest high ground and tied them again. Looking at the rising water, I judged there was enough time for me to make a running grab for the gear. The first run I brought back the pack gear. The second run found the muddy river current tugging at my legs as I grabbed the two saddles just as they began to float. By the time I rejoined the horses on high ground, I was cold, wet, dirty, and completely drained.

As flash floods go, this one turned out to be slow and gentle. Certainly not the most terrifying of desert floods ever recorded. With the return of the hot sun, it didn't take long for the river to magically disappear into the sand and air. After warming up and drying out a bit, I saddled up and rode northeast toward an outcropping of rock. With misty steam rising from the moist sands, the landscape took on mystical proportions. Wherever I looked, a misty, brilliantly colored rainbow greeted my eyes. Even the horses seemed to sense the magic. My skin tingled as the water droplets from the rainbows began kissing my face, the colors of the rainbows passing through my eyes and into my soul. A thought came: "If we respond to color energy, what do the colors of a rainbow do to us?" The beauty was so intense that it brought tears to my eyes.

As I rode into the waning hours of light and heat, I gave thanks for the blessing of water. My canteens needed filling and my body needed a bath. "Surely," I thought, "with this much rain, I'll probably be able to find a good quantity of drinking and bathing water in some deep water hole." Upon reaching the rocky plateau, my wish was granted.

After watering the horses and filling the canteens, I took a leisurely swim in the cool waters held in the palm of a deeply carved rock. Looking into the water, I noticed little bugs of various shapes and sizes swimming around with me. "Where did they come from?" I wondered. Afterwards, I stretched out nude on top of a large rock to watch the sunset. The radiant heat of the rock kept me warm as a cool breeze caressed my skin.

Watching the Sun and feeling the breeze, I thought of the wonder of living the day. Sparkles of reflected golden light played with my eyes as the wind touched the face of the nearby water. Near the edge where the water touched stone, I could see the continuous stirrings of little water bugs. I thought of the thousands of years it must take for the desert rains to carve water holes into solid rock. "Who knows?" I thought, "It could be ten, twenty, or even a hundred years before water reached this section of the desert again. But yet, at the very moment the rains blessed the scorched sands and weathered rocks—a world of life awakens."

Thor's Hammer

Certainly, for anyone who has camped outside, one of the most thrilling and frightening experiences is a thunder and lightning storm. The power and majesty of such a storm humbles the spirit and makes any human effort of fireworks appear a petty imitation.

In the old Nordic myth we have the image of Thor creating thunder and lightning by wielding his hammer while flying through the sky in a chariot drawn by two goats. From the Norwegian *Thordon*, we find the origin of the word "thunder." To the early Norwegians, thunder was created whenever Thor swung his hammer. In taking a close look at this image, I found it interesting that Thor's chariot is represented as being pulled by two goats. This intrigues me because the goat represents Capricorn in the tenth sign of the zodiac. And Capricorn, according to the mythological philosopher Joseph Campbell, is the sign "of the water god Ea, 'God of the House of Water.'"

In this fashion, we find Thor evidently relating to the god of water. Which, I assume, also helped early Norwegians to understand why thunder and lightning sometimes accompanies a rainstorm. If only we knew what Thor's hammer was made of, we could then solve the mystery of why and how lightning is created. It is a mystery that still befuddles our world's scientists.

Another take on the phenomenon of lightning is found in the ancient Vedas relative to the god Rudra. Rudra is the Destroyer and Regenerator, the one who transforms energy, and is known as the breaker of old molds with the power of will and vital force. Looking back even further, we find that the word *rudra* is derived from a

Sanskrit root relating to dynamic action and the electrical discharges released during atmospheric storms.

Thus, humankind through the ages has cast eyes skyward and pondered the powers of thunder and lightning. Perhaps giving names to these powers has lessened, to a degree, our fear of the unknown. And even though we may know a little more today than our ancestors, there remains much for us to learn about the phenomena of thunder and lightning. For example, in his book *Sacred Geometry*, Robert Lawlor states, "The morphic [physical] similarity between lightning and the root of a plant is also functionally accurate. Science now speculates that early in earth's evolution horrendous lightning storms in the atmosphere provided energetic ultra-violet light which transformed methane, hydrogen, nitrogen and carbonic gases into the proto-molecules for organic compounds. These molecules were deposited by torrential rains into the primal seas out of which life arose" (p. 30).

In this fashion, we begin to see how the physical form that looks like a plant root, such as lightning, a river's imprint with its tributaries, or the flow of water underground are all associated in some way with water, transformation, creation, and life.

One ancestor who gave thought to rainstorms was the Greek philosopher Thales (circa 600 B.C.). It was Thales who first coined the word "electricity." The word comes from the Greek word *elektron*, which means "amber." Thales came up with the word when he noticed that a strange thing happened when he rubbed a piece of amber with a woolen cloth. The amber, as a result of the friction, acquired the property of static electricity. Thus charged, the stone could deliver a small static shock. Besides delivering a shock, the stone could also attract lightweight objects such as particles of dust, straws, feathers, and small pieces of lint.

As mentioned in Part Two of this book, Thales was an influence on Aristotle and other Greek natural philosophers. As the renowned "founder of philosophy," it is fitting that Thales was the first human to observe and name the entity of electricity. When he observed the electrical energy of lightning created during atmospheric storms, he probably considered water to be its source, since in his mind water was the source of all things.

We know today that lightning and electrical energy are created by the natural motion of water in our planet's atmosphere. This natural motion of water is influenced by the spinning of the Earth on its axis; the influences of the Moon, Sun, and other planets; the flowing movement of water beneath and across the Earth's surface; and the evaporation and condensation that takes place in the natural cycle of water. As water moves, it creates a spinning effect called a vortex. Vortex energy, which is further explored in the next chapter, is a factor in the creation of electricity in nature. Lightning bolts flashing across the skies of Earth represent one of water's most profound expressions of its vortex energy.

In modern times, lightning flashes in the Earth's atmosphere about 6000 times a minute, strikes every commercial aircraft about once a year, wipes out power to entire cities, causes up to one-third of the power losses in the Northeastern United States, and hits an estimated 1000 people each year. According to the American Meteorological Society, lightning accounts for more deaths than hurricanes and tornadoes together. Also, more people are struck and killed by lightning in the evening hours during the month of July than at any other time of year. Lightning can be three to four miles long and an inch in diameter; can carry a charge exceeding hundreds of million of volts; travel at 100,000 miles a second; and has been estimated to be five times hotter than the surface of the Sun.

We also know that there is much we do not understand about the entity of lightning. For instance, to this day, humankind has little idea about what electricity actually is, and why and how our atmosphere becomes electrified. All one has to do is to go to any science book, dictionary, or encyclopedia to see that there is no definition of what electricity actually is and what gives it its living force. Electricity remains an energy form that defies definition. However, we do know that the atoms of which the molecules of matter are composed contain very tiny particles held together by electrical forces. In other words, without the force of electricity to hold things together, the reality we live in would break apart and go flying off in all directions.

One thing that humankind does know about electricity is that it is a source of energy that can be harnessed and manipulated to a certain extent, and to that end we have been most creative. The untold numbers of electrical gadgets that humankind has created are astounding, the computer being one of the most profound. Because of the sensitivity of many human-made electrical devices, it is often necessary to protect them from damage by lightning and static electricity.

Just as the Moon's energy is translated through tidal waves in our oceans, there are also waves of energy created when a vehicle such as a car, train, ship, or plane travels through our atmosphere. The same goes for a bolt of lightning. It is the wave of energy created by lightning as it travels as fast as 100,000 miles a second that we hear on our radios or telephones as static when an electrical storm is approaching. This static occurs whenever lightning discharges in the Earth's atmosphere. This discharge generates a wave frequency that vibrates on the common radio at 8 megahertz. This 8-megahertz wave of energy created by lightning travels almost instantaneously around the globe via Earth's watery atmosphere.

In my opinion, the purpose of lightning is something humanity is just beginning to fathom. What use the Earth makes of the waves of lightning energy we hear on our radios is a matter for speculation. Certainly, the waves of energy created and released by the estimated 6000 lightning flashes per minute in the earth's atmosphere don't just disappear. How these energy waves are absorbed and used by the planet remains a mystery. A theory proposed by some scientists is that lightning may be responsible for maintaining the electrical balance between Earth, its atmosphere, and the cosmos. The fact that lightning contains plasma similar to the plasma that permeates our universe in itself suggests a cosmic connection.

With a little stretch of our imagination, we can make the analogy that the electrical impulses within our brains are similar to lightning. Just as moving water creates lightning in our atmosphere, so too does moving water create electricity within our bodies. Brain waves created by electrical activity send electrical thought waves instantaneously throughout our bodies. On another note, it is the electrical impulses of thought activity that stimulate the synapses of the brain to store information and create ideas. With some speculation, we may think of our Earth as a large living being—with the ability to think and to constantly create our reality.

In the book *The Body Electric*, we learn that bioelectricity is now an evolving science. In the United States, the pioneering work of Andrew Marino, Harold Saxon Burr, and Robert Becker has shown how the shape and form of living organisms are influenced by their surrounding electrical fields. Research on using electricity for stimulating plant growth, healing body injuries, bone replacement, and regeneration of lost limbs indicates that body functions of living organisms are directly related to electrical currents.

Stating the obvious, as far as we know in the physical universe, there can be no thinking without water and electricity. Each of these entities—water, electricity, thinking—are distinctly different in some way, but they each play a part in the creation of intelligence. As far as humanity knows at this time, without water there can be no life; without electricity there can be no thought; without thinking there is no intelligence. Perhaps it is in the trinity of water, electricity, and thought that we may very well find the basis for the ongoing creation of the world we live in.

Red Lightning

Besides the earthly level of lightning that our eyes can see, there is another lightning—the recently discovered phenomenon called red lightning. Red lightning (also called red sprites) has been seen with long bluish tentacles flashing above storms up to sixty miles into space. The blood-red sprites travel away from the planet instead of toward it. The makeup and purpose of these red sprites and blue tentacles (called spouts) are anybody's guess. A U.S. Air Force investigation is underway, and scientists at Lawrence Livermore National Laboratory have been trying to photograph this strange energy high in the night sky over Colorado. Without much doubt, this is another manifestation of water's mysterious powers.

Researchers at the University of Florida's Lightning Research Laboratory are also doing their best to understand and learn about lightning. At this lab, Professor Martin Uman combined his talents with those of E. P. Krider of the University of Arizona to invent a nationwide lightning-detection system. Using a special computer program, every lightning flash over our country is recorded and plotted. This information has gone a long way in helping humankind to better understand lightning, but many questions remain. To date, the scientists have yet to figure out how and why lightning is created. At the time of this writing, the newly discovered red lightning is a dimension of storm activity not yet considered for study at this center.

Lightning discharges into our atmosphere when negative energy builds up in the layer between the Earth's surface and the top of a storm. There is positive and negative energy on the ground as well as in the storm atmosphere above. This causes the discharge of lightning to go up as well as down. Atmospheric researchers have yet to decipher this separation of positive and negative energy during a storm, or what causes a buildup of so much energy that it has to discharge itself as lightning.

We do know, however, that lightning helps to produce nutrients necessary for the existence of life. It is estimated that each year lightning converts more than 3 million metric tons of atmospheric nitrogen into nitrogen dioxide. Rainfall carries this nitrogen dioxide to Earth, where it helps give rise to the bottom of the food chain to support all life on Earth. Research on lightning's support of Earth's life systems has been conducted by Robert Socolow, a physicist at Princeton University's Center for Energy and Environmental Studies, along with Robert Ayres, a professor of environmental economics at INSEAD, the European Institute, and William Schlesinger, a Duke University professor of botany and geology.

The mysteries of electricity and lightning in living bodies and in our watery atmosphere may one day be fully understood by science. Or, it may be a matter of faith in the realm beyond the reach of ordinary science that truly provides the answers.

Weather Maker

The factors that seemingly create lightning are referred to by the all-encompassing term of "weather." And all weather is mainly the result of water's interaction with the powers of the Sun, the spin of the Earth, the pull of the Moon, the flow of ocean currents, and the motion of atmospheric winds.

Simply said, weather on Earth is created by water. Wind, rain, snow, clouds, sunny days, stormy days, humidity, heat, cold—all weather on the face of Earth is related to water.

As the Earth rotates, its surface waters and atmospheric waters interact with the Moon, Sun, and cosmos. Beyond gravity and the spin of the planet, it is the pull of the Moon and the heat of the Sun that exert the two greatest influences on the water cycle of Earth's surface.

The explosions of sunspots on the Sun's surface also influence our weather. Today scientists have found a direct relationship between the intensity and frequency of sunspot activity and the weather patterns on Earth. Only recently have scientists learned that sunspots contain water, as reported in a Reuters news release dated May 26, 1995:

> In research being released today in the journal *Science*, the experts report finding water not in the hot gaseous heart of the sun itself, but on somewhat cooler sunspots.

"It's really sort of interesting," said Peter Bernath, a chemist who was part of the research team from the National Optical Astronomy Observatories in Tucson, Ariz., and Canada's University of Waterloo. "One is surprised that water can exist on the sun because it is so hot."

Hydrogen and oxygen molecules both exist on the sun, which is about 10,200 degrees F. They apparently combine to form water in sunspots, which are about 5200 degrees F. Because of the heat, the water molecules form vapor or steam, instead of pools or puddles.

The water cannot be seen with the naked eye or even with an ordinary telescope. Bernath and his colleagues analyzed data from the sophisticated observation spectrometer on Kitt Peak in Arizona.

Finding water on the Sun may sound strange, but Thales taught over 2500 years ago that water existed in the Sun and stars and their "exhalations." He also taught that the stars were fiery bodies and that "the fire of which the Sun and stars are made is nourished by water exhalations—yea, and the world itself."

Now that we have confirmation that Thales was right about water being in the Sun and stars, is it possible that he was also right about all things finding their "original" in water? For certainly, without the presence of water on our Sun, there would be no moderating force to keep it from rapidly burning itself and us into nonexistence.

This moderating force of water on the Sun is mimicked in a fashion when humans create nuclear energy here on Earth with the moderating force of "heavy water." Discovered and named in 1932 by Harold Urey, heavy water is composed of certain molecules that are normally present in small quantities in water. Because of its special properties, heavy water boils and freezes at higher temperatures than ordinary water. This has made it most useful as a coolant in the creation of nuclear energy. This nuclear energy in turn helps us to create little weather systems inside our homes, since many of us use electricity for heating and air conditioning.

Since water is the key to weather, it is almost a joke to see the amount of time, energy, and money that is spent on trying to understand weather. In my opinion, humankind must first learn to understand water. The more we learn about water, the more we will understand weather and so many other aspects of our bewildering reality.

The rhythm of the Moon is expressed in the timing of the Earth's ocean tides. The high tides of our oceans come into shore roughly fifty minutes later each day. This is due to the fact that the Moon rises about fifty minutes later each day at any given location on the Earth's surface because of its movement in its orbit. Therefore, we see our ocean tides responding to the influence and timing of the Moon's cycle.

Our oceans make up Earth's largest sensory organs, for they respond to the rhythm of the cosmos and give life to so many forms. Filled with mystery since the earliest of times, the oceans of Earth still hold many secrets that intrigue and humble the minds and spirits of humankind. In all the known universe, there is no other known place with so much liquid water floating on its surface. Touched by the heat of the Sun, our oceans store warmth to protect Earth from overheating or freezing as it rotates. The moisture that evaporates from the oceans helps to shield life from harmful sunrays, cleanse the air with rain, and provide moisture for life on land.

Convention gives us four oceans: The Pacific (equal in size to the other three combined), the Indian, the Atlantic, and the Arctic. These oceans, with their adjacent gulfs and smaller seas, create a connected system through which an estimated 60×10^{45} water molecules intermingle and circulate in ways only to be imagined. There is so much water on the face of Earth that if the surface lands and the bottom of the oceans were flattened out, the entire planet would be drowned to a depth of about 12,000 feet. Can there be any doubt about water being a creative force we should take the time to understand?

It is because of the water on our Earth's surface and in our atmosphere that we live in a world of weather cycles. The movement of our oceans to the Moon cycle is obvious. Not so obvious is the greater influence the Moon has on the water vapor in our atmosphere.

Recently, "rivers" of water vapor have been found to exist in the atmosphere around the world. These concentrated streams of water vapor resemble rivers and flow from the equator toward the poles.

Reginald Newell at the Massachusetts Institute of Technology discovered these water vapor streams through his analysis of satellite data. Some of these water vapor rivers are up to 480 miles wide and can flow a distance of up to 4800 miles. Newell reported his findings in 1993 in *Geophysical Research Letters*, published by the American Geophysical Union. Prior to this discovery, water vapor was always thought to move in large unconcentrated masses.

At the time this book was being written, Newell said, "I expect it to take me another year or two to see if these water vapor flows remain constant." However, as reported in the April 1993 issue of *U.S. Water News*, "What the research has uncovered thus far is a huge amount of water in the atmosphere moving in a rather concentrated stream. One vapor river moves southeast from southern Brazil to the South Atlantic Ocean. This flow carries an estimated 165 million kilograms of water per second."

Since there is no landmass to restrict the flow of water in our atmosphere, the Moon truly has great influence on the flow cycles of the gases and particles that float in the air above us. These cycles have a rhythm in harmony with the cosmic influences reaching down to Earth from the Moon and the far reaches of outer space. This cosmic interaction probably played a large part in the evolution of Earth's watery surface and all the life it contains.

Who can witness the Moon tides of oceans, the following of the Sun by flowering plants, the opening and closing of plants to the cycles of Moon and Sun, the response of insects, fish, plants, and animals to the cycles of night and day, the migration patterns of insects, birds, fish, and animals, the change of seasons—and deny the interactions of life with water and with the cosmos?

An astounding example of how earthly life and our Moon interact can be found in Australia. Along the east coast of northern Australia is the largest living organism on Earth—the Great Barrier Reef. This reef is about 100 miles wide and 1500 miles long, and contains over 350 species of coral. Since the earliest of times, the native people of Australia have told stories about how the coral reef reproduces itself. Ancient oral history of the Aborigines tells of the Moon playing a spiritual part in the fertilization of the coral. This traditional story of the reef was passed off as "myth" until very recently. Scientists studying the reef have now discovered that there is a direct and mysterious relationship between the Moon and the reproduction behavior of the coral making up the Great Barrier Reef. For reasons still beyond our scientific understanding, we have learned that some 350 species of coral in the reef release their sperm and eggs between the third and fifth night after the first full Moon in October or November. No matter during which full Moon cycle this phenomenon occurs, the coral along the entire 1500-by-100-mile-wide reef release their sperm and eggs almost simultaneously. This synchronized release indicates a signal or communication of sorts takes place between the full Moon and the reef. What this signal is or what purpose it serves is beyond our present understanding.

What causes this orgasm of birthing material at some secret moment in harmony with the influence of the full Moon remains a mystery to scientists. Extensive research on the relationship between the Great Barrier Reef and the Moon is ongoing in Australia at James Cook University in Queensland. A similar phenomenon is found in many of the world's seaweeds, which release their sperm and eggs during a full Moon cycle.

With this in mind, can there be any doubt about the interplay of the cosmic influences of the Moon, Sun, and other forces of the universe with the Earth's weather and its water world of life?

FIVE

Vortex Energy

Scientists must be made to realize that water is not something to be handled carelessly, like an inanimate object. Water is not merely H_2O, but a living organism with its own laws commanding respect from mankind, if the consequences are not to be fatal.
—Viktor Schauberger

IT WAS MY FRESHMAN YEAR at the University of Corpus Christi, located on a small island off the coast of Texas. I was sitting shirtless on a rocky seawall looking east across the Gulf of Mexico. The day was sunny with hardly a cloud in the sky. A slight stir in the air rustled the leaves of some nearby palm trees. As I scanned the horizon, my heart beat with excited anticipation. I had just heard on the local radio news that a hurricane was approaching across the Gulf of Mexico and that Corpus Christi might be in its path. The tranquil beauty of the sky and sea gave no hint of this potential threat. "Maybe it won't come this way," I thought. Secretly, however, I was hoping it would. I was young and naïve at the time, without an inkling of the awesome destructive power a hurricane could deliver.

At the time, the island of Corpus Christi was connected to the mainland by a low-lying causeway with a narrow two-lane road. I wondered what would happen if the hurricane struck and we were cut off from the mainland. When I returned to my dorm room, there was a telephone message from my high school sweetheart; she was watching the television news and was concerned about my safety. Even though my phone bill was already breaking my meager budget, I welcomed any excuse to pick up the phone and hear her voice. "Don't worry, Judy," I remember saying in my brave voice, "the hurricane will probably miss us." Little did I realize that before too long it would be impossible for me to telephone anyone.

About twelve hours later, the hurricane struck with all its power and fury. We barely had time to evacuate our campus. The university

hastily arranged emergency housing for the students in a hotel overlooking Corpus Christi Bay. Between the hotel and the bay stood a
substantial seawall and a four-lane roadway with a wide divider in
the middle; certainly, the university's officials believed that our hotel
was out of harm's way.

In the beginning, it was party time in the hotel rooms. The Lone
Star beer flowed, and cheap food was abundant. Many of us students were thankful for the unexpected vacation from classes and
homework. The fact that we were all about to experience a major
hurricane only added more excitement to the party atmosphere.

Before long, the winds began to pick up and palm trees began
swaying back and forth as though waving a warning. Our view across
Corpus Christi Bay became a crazy show of choppy surf, bobbing
boats, and tall masts swinging in all directions as though in some sort
of duel. Looking off our fifth-story balcony, we also saw speeding cars
and people nailing boards over their storefront windows. I remember
someone jokingly yelling, "Hey, we better hurry up and do another
beer and food run before we get cut off."

Within a couple of hours we were cut off. Cut off from everything.
I watched with amazement as huge waves surged over the protective
seawall and washed across the four-lane roadway into the first-floor
lobby of our hotel; tornado-like water spouts whirled across the bay
waters; sailboats were literally picked up by huge waves and smashed
to pieces on tee heads. Some boats even managed to float across the
street and smash into buildings.

Soon, our television and lights went dead. The reality of possibly
being harmed began to suck the energy from our drinking, laughing,
and partying. Eventually, in quiet awe, six friends and I watched from
our hotel room as the world outside went totally crazy with howling winds, flying debris, animated sailboats, snapping palm trees, and
electric sparks flying from wires and poles. Still, we kind of felt in-
nocently safe in the gray darkness of our hotel room standing behind
our picture window with rain beating against the glass. But that safe
feeling quickly evaporated when the glass windows in our room began imploding. We ducked and covered our heads as glass shattered
and the crazy world outside quickly invaded our living room. Shouting, crying, and crawling, we struggled to open our room door being
held shut by pressing winds exceeding one hundred miles an hour.

For a second, the winds let up, the door yielded, and we were
propelled into the hotel's dark hallway—a hallway that was now

transformed into a wind tunnel with the windows on each end blown out. Clinging to the floor and walls, we made our way to the stair exit. The stairway door flew open with the help of the wind. In a jumbled fashion, we all fell onto the stair platform. It took the struggling effort of me and another male student to push the stair door shut behind us. With the sound of the howling wind trying to break down the door, we grabbed the cold slippery handrail and climbed down one flight of stairs. Feeling we were somewhat safe, we huddled together in a corner under a section of concrete stairs. It was dark and cold; we were wet, and there was water running down the stairs as though an upstairs bathtub was overflowing. We stayed huddled together for warmth and a feeling of safety. We now realized why animals gather together when frightened. Two of the girls were crying as we crouched and listened to the unrelenting pounding force of winds slamming and shaking the hotel.

Hours later, the monster would weaken and slowly go away, leaving behind a ravaged city and wounded populace, never mind some wet, shaking college students.

This was my first introduction to water's powerful vortex energy in the form of a hurricane. Eventually, I was to learn that the explosive power of a hurricane is equal to several thousand atomic bombs being exploded each second as long as the hurricane rages—certainly, a power that can quickly alter the fate of many life forms; a power that can drastically changing the face of our Earth; a power to respect and to try and comprehend.

Eventually, I would learn that the word *hurricane* derived from Huracan, an evil god recognized by an ancient aboriginal tribe named Tainos, in Central America. In time, I also learned that the vortex energy found in a hurricane is the same energy involved with creating and sustaining all life on Earth. In time, I learned to respect water's vortex power as well as its ability to dissolve, assimilate, neutralize, and nourish.

Spirals in Water and Stone

Just as the word "ecology" has come into common usage over the past thirty years, I believe the word "vortex," or some other word representing the vortex concept, will eventually come into common usage and understanding.

In Theodor Schwenk's *Sensitive Chaos*, we learn that all flowing water is divided into layers or surfaces that move against one another. As water flows down a slope, the surfaces of other water layers and of objects such as the streambed, rocks, and snags, create localized changes of speed. These varying speeds within the flowing water result in millions of vortices.

The same goes for standing bodies of water such as ponds and lakes. It is a known fact that lakes and ponds purify themselves through a process called "turnover." This happens when the surface water becomes cooler than the water beneath it. The cooler, heavier surface water will sink downward as the warmer bottom water rises toward the surface. Besides helping to distribute oxygen and nutrients throughout a body of water, the turnover phenomenon creates millions of vortices as the molecules of warm and cold waters flow by one another. In this way, energy is created from the vortices within a standing body of water, helping to vitalize the water and to keep the life it sustains in good health.

It is vortex energy that allows salmon to swim upstream, planes and bees to fly, galaxies to form, weather systems to develop, and life to be created and sustained. Even the seemingly playful antics of a water bird swooping in circles serves the purpose of creating a vortex that lifts potential food in the water to the surface. The existence of vortex energy was also recently found in radio waves traveling from galaxies one billion light years distant. These waves apparently make complete corkscrewlike turns as they travel through space.

To be certain, the concept of the spiraling vortex is not new. Throughout history the spiral symbol of the vortex has been expressed in many ancient forms of art. Some of the oldest representations of the spiral symbol in the United States can be found in ancient ruins of the Anasazi people in the Southwest. In Chaco Canyon, located in what is now New Mexico, the Anasazi developed an advanced system of roads and impressive stone buildings between A.D. 900 and 1250. These Anasazi constructs continue to exist today, along with the spiral symbol of the vortex found repeatedly in their art. Most impressive is the spiral that can be found in one of the most complex solar/lunar pre-Columbian calendars ever discovered. This Anasazi calendar was created by the purposeful placement of two large slabs of rock in front of a spiral carved on a stone. The openings between the rock slabs permit the Sun's rays to fall across the spiral as a narrow shaft of light. At the winter solstice, the shaft of light appears on both sides of the spiral; at the summer solstice, the shaft falls on the spiral's center; and at each equinox the shaft quarters the spiral. The fact that this complex rock calendar also depicts phases of the Moon adds another dimension to the mystery of its technical engineering.

The carved stone spirals in Chaco Canyon bring to mind similar carved spirals discovered on stones on the island of Malta and at another ancient site called Newgrange in Ireland. Malta, located in the Mediterranean just south of Sicily, is the site of what is sometimes considered the world's oldest remnant of ancient civilization. Who these people were and why they too carved spirals in stone is yet another mystery.

In similar fashion, at Newgrange and other ancient cairns (stone constructs) nearby, there are spirals of various sizes adorning many stones as well as the interiors and exteriors of ancient tombs and sacred places. The curious thing about Newgrange is that it predates Stonehenge, and is older than the pyramids by at least five hundred years. And, just as the Anasazi's stone vortex calendar is arranged by solar influence, so too is Newgrange arranged to a specific solar alignment. The difference at Newgrange is that the light penetrates into its passage chamber only at sunrise during the winter solstice on December 21. In the very rear of the passage is a chamber with a stone carved with three spirals flowing into each other. It has long been believed that only on rare occasions is sunlight capable of touching the three spirals. The present forecast is for sunrise sunlight to touch the carved tri-spiral circa December 21–22, 2007. Needless to say, there is a long waiting list of interested people who would like to attend this rare event.

I visited and studied Newgrange during March–April 1999. Besides exploring the inner and outer constructs of this cairn, I personally felt various forces at work. Most significantly was the orientation of Newgrange to the River Boyne, which flows in such a way as to form a peninsula around the cairn. When I walked over a bridge from the visitor's center, I couldn't help but observe the vortices created by the river's flow. The more I learned about Newgrange, the more I became convinced that these early people were in possession of incredible knowledge for their time, including the use of crystals enhanced by the river's energy. During one of the early excavations of the New-grange entrance, archaeologists discovered "607 quartz potato-sized water rolled pebbles" which for some reason were reported to be from the bottom of the River Boyne! In a 1996 monograph written and published by Claire O'Kelly of Cork, Ireland, we learn, "All along the front of the mound...was a layer entirely made up of pieces of white quartz and grey granite water-rolled boulders, the quartz by far the more numerous....The great mass of the cairn is composed of quite small water-rolled boulders [6 to 10 inches in diameter]....A surprising discovery made when the upper surface of the passage roof was exposed was that grooves or channels had been picked (by using a hammer and point, as for the execution of the ornament) on all the slabs of the front or first part of the roof so as to carry off the rainwater percolating through the cairn. By means of a most skillful arrangement, water was led away from one slab to another until it passed into the body of the cairn on either side of the passage." The stones topping off the Newgrange cairn were pitched in such a way as to shed water off the top of the mound and to keep the inside of the cairn completely dry. This engineering feat was done so well that Newgrange has not leaked from circa 3000 B.C. to the present.

Michael Poynder reinforces water's central role in the creation of Newgrange in his book *Pi in the Sky:* "Newgrange is considered to be the central 'bough' or 'mound' of ancient Irish mythology with its legends of heroic deeds and romantic stories probably reaching back into the Bronze Age community that lived around it. It is also the center one of three enormous cairns covering an area dotted with different Stone Age, Bronze Age and Iron Age structures that chronologically overlap each other. The cairn [Newgrange] is carefully positioned over a complex interconnecting underground water/energy flow."

Leonardo's Water Studies

In more modern times, about five hundred years ago Leonardo da Vinci (1452–1519) recorded ideas about vortices based on his experiments with water. In fact, the subject of water, hydrology, and hydraulics made up a large part of Leonardo's lifetime study. More of his writings were devoted to the subject of water than to any other subject. The existence of water vortices seemed to intrigue Leonardo, prompting him to speculate about the existence and behavior of vortices in the air and in the cosmos. The power and meaning of vortices in water also led him to closely study the behavior of water under different conditions. This fascination with fluid dynamics and vortices crossed over into Leonardo's art: the flowing motions of water vortices are expressed in his brush strokes and are obvious in his paintings.

The existence and behavior of bubbles in water was also of interest to Leonardo, since he noted from close observations that bubbles rise through water in a spiral motion. In his written notes in the *Codex Leicester* Folio 23V (now owned by Bill Gates), he observed that the "motions of waters always move in a circle from surface to bottom."

Leonardo spent many years in his makeshift laboratory and in the field observing the movements of water and air. To see the fluid dynamics of water at work, he did experiments using glass tanks so he could watch the motion of flowing water under various scenarios. During his field research, he maintained detailed notes and drawings to record his experiences and observations. He designed a water gate that utilized the pressure of water to create a tight seal, and his experiments and technical drawings of this were used in designing the lock gate system of the Panama Canal.

At times, Leonardo's mind would take off into other dimensions as his observations triggered ideas. Often, he would jot down or sketch these thoughts along the margins of his papers. One such series of notes in the upper right hand corner of one of his papers gives the outline for a proposed treatise on water. It was divided into fifteen books, with each book dealing with a different aspect of water, as follows:

1. Of Water in Itself
2. Of the Sea
3. Of the Veins
4. Of Rivers
5. Of the Nature of Bottoms
6. Of Objects
7. Of Various Kinds of Gravel
8. Of the Surface of Water
9. Of Things Moving in It
10. Of River Repairs
11. Of Conduits
12. Of Canals
13. Of Machines Turned by Water
14. Of Raising Water
15. Of Things Worn Away by Water

Given the numerous other activities Leonardo was involved in, he never found the time to complete the proposed treatise. His writings, especially the *Codex Leicester*, contain many references and brief notes to be included in the above books. An example of this can be found in his notes dealing with precipitation:

> Write how clouds are formed and how they dissolve, and what it is that causes vapour to rise from the water of the earth into the air, and the cause of mists and of the air becoming thickened, and why it appears more blue or less blue at one time than another. Write in the same way of the regions of the air and the cause of snow and hail, and how water contracts and becomes hard in the form of ice, and of the new shapes that the snow forms in the air.

Another of Leonardo's field observations dealt with the physical expression of the vortex principle on a grand scale. His written observations about a water spout he saw along the seashore were recorded on a page entitled "Of wind twists and eddies involving water." In his inimitable words:

> It often happens that, when one wind meets another at an obtuse angle, these two winds circle around together and twine themselves into the shape of a huge column, and becoming thus condensed, the air acquires weight. I once saw such winds, raging around together, produce a hollow in the sand of the seashore as deep as the height of a man, removing from it stones of considerable size, and carrying sand and seaweed though the air for the space of a mile and dropping them in the water, whirling them around and transforming them into a dense column, which formed dark thick clouds as its upper extremity.

Many people will probably never see a waterspout in their lifetime, but thanks to Leonardo and his detailed notes from long ago, we can at least appreciate the feeling of such an experience.

The Cosmic Vortex—Wheels Within Wheels

Even if we never see a waterspout, vortex energy is something that we cannot help but be familiar with on a smaller scale. Each time we flush a toilet or pull the plug in a water-filled sink, we witness vortex energy at work. As the water flows down the drain, it spins around and creates a visible vortex. If we look closely at water spinning down a drain, we will also see something that looks like a mini tornado. This is no coincidence, since a tornado is also vortex energy at work, except the vortex energy of a tornado is created by the water energy in the atmosphere. Recent studies have discovered that a tornado's center, which can produce winds exceeding 300 miles per hour with a 100-mile-per-hour updraft, is composed of supercondensed water vapor.

Another curious thing about vortex energy is that once we become aware of what it is and how it manifests itself in this physical reality, we begin to see it everywhere—a spinning hurricane; the small swirling whirlwind that picks up roadway dust or the leaves in our yard; the whirlpools of water created in rivers and streams; the circular motion of ocean currents; the hydrologic cycle; the spiral shape of seashells and the horns of certain animals; the water-induced shape of leaves; the contorted and twisted appearance of tree trunks and limbs, as well as countless other physical expressions visible and invisible to the eye.

On a macrocosmic level, looking far beyond our planet Earth, we see how entire galaxies in outer space are nothing more than swirling groups of planets and stars created by the same vortex energy. Our Milky Way has a spiral shape, as do black holes and quasars. Scientists have now documented that some black holes in outer space spin about like whirlpools, wrapping up the fabric of space. According to an April 30, 2001, NASA press release, "Dr. Tod Trohmayer of NASA's Goddard Space Flight Center, Greenbelt, MD, has studied one such black hole system . . . and found unique patterns in the X-ray radiation that have previously only been seen in spinning neutron stars." Getting back to Earth, the three-dimensional spinning vortex is the shape of the Van Allen belts hovering over our North and South Poles; the DNA in our bodies is based on the swirling "double helix" containing the genetic code that creates each one of us as unique individuals; even the umbilical cord that carries life to us from our mother is in the spiral shape of a vortex. The vortex is also found in various forms in the Earth's oceans. A particularly unusual example was reported in a Goddard Space Flight Center press release on April 13, 2001: "Scientists using satellite data discovered an unusual long-lasting, whirlpool-like ocean eddy that generated a dramatic increase in the marine food supply off the Hawaiian coast in 1999."

On a microcosmic level, we have the recent discovery of matter and antimatter. When energy is split into its basic constituents, it splits into matter and antimatter. Using special detection and photographic devices, the patterns created by matter and antimatter appear as spirals going in opposite directions. All these things, and so much more, are expressions of vortex energy within the physical universe.

Plain and simple, the vortex energy found in water may actually be the original creative force—the swirling mist of water that has always existed and is responsible for creating and continuing to create all things. As we are beginning to learn, this timeless swirling mist may also represent a form of intelligence. It is this source of creative energy that humans from the earliest of times have attempted to understand and relate to as they gave it a variety of names.

In Guy Underwood's posthumous 1969 work, *The Pattern of the Past*, we are provided with an all-encompassing answer to the spiral mystery:

> The philosophers and priests of the old religions seem to have believed that—particularly when manifested in spiral forms—it [the earth force] was involved with . . . the generative powers of Nature; that it was part of the mechanism by which what we call Life comes into being; and to have been the "Great arranger"— that balancing principle which keeps all Nature in equilibrium, and for which biologists still seek. Plato gave this force the name of "Demiurge."

This perception of the vortex can be traced back to oriental scripture, particularly the Hindu Vedas. The Vedas express thoughts about our universe being a huge spiraling wheel that contains an infinite number of wheels within wheels from the macrocosmic to the microcosmic. This early concept of the universe is now being corroborated by today's science, which, through the Hubble space telescope, has learned that there are billions of trillions of stars with planets of their own, all of them spinning in circles within circles. Another curious thing about the vortex spins of galaxies is that they all seem to have a rhythm, like a heartbeat. This rhythm can also be observed in hurricanes, tornados, oceans, rivers, and the pulse of our bodies.

This rhythmic beat or "pulsing" of a vortex can be visibly created at home. Simply fill a circular glass vase that is narrow at the bottom, wider in the middle and then narrow at the top. Fill the vase about three-quarters with water and use a wooden spoon to stir the water in one direction until a vortex appears in the center. Quickly remove the spoon and add a very small amount of diluted red clay. You will then see the vortex spinning in a bouncing fashion like a tornado. The vortex will go from a relatively thin tornado shape that spins deeply into the vase's center, to a more shallow vortex that is wider on the top. If you watch closely, when the vortex is shallow, you will see how energy is transferred to the top of the vortex—which will spin more quickly and widely across the surface of the spinning water. When the vortex again returns to spinning deeply into the center of the vase, you will see the surface waters of the vase slow down, while the deeper waters near the submerged vortex speed up. Thus will you see the ancient vortex principle expressed in the creation of our universe and of life.

The Sanskrit concept of the *chakras*, meaning wheels, has its foundation in the ancient Vedic healing arts involving the vortex principle. According to these ancient beliefs and practices, the human body is a reflection of the universe on a reduced scale. Being so, the human body has seven major chakra centers with twenty-one minor chakras and infinity of other spinning chakras within chakras. If our chakra centers are healthy, they will, according to healer Barbara Ann Brennan, all spin together in a clockwise direction as they absorb energy from the Earth's environment and the universe. According to Brennan in her book *Hands of Light*:

> Energy can be seen flowing into all these chakras from the Universal Energy Field [UEF]. Each swirling vortex of energy appears to suck or entrain energy from the UEF. They appear to function as do fluid vortexes we are familiar with in water or in air such as whirlpools, cyclones, water spouts and hurricanes.

Brennan believes that the energy from the Universal Energy Field maintains a healthy balance (homeostasis) of various parts of the fluid body as well as of specific psychological functions. It is the mysterious relationship of the body's seven major glands with its seven chakras and the endocrinal fluids produced by these glands that also provides a basis for "alternative" healing. According to Brennan, "the chakras appear to be vortices of energy made up of smaller spiral cones of energy.... In a healthy system these spiral cones spin rhythmically in synchronicity with the others, drawing energy from the UEF into their center for the body's use. Each cone is 'tuned' to a specific frequency that the body needs to function healthfully."

It is said in many ancient writings that one does not see something until it is time for one to see it. I firmly believe that a key to anyone developing new insight is to learn how to see the world with new information. With new information, we as humans can begin to see the world for the wonderful ongoing creation it actually is. More importantly, we may begin to see the role we as individuals and as a living species play within this water world of life.

In their book *Secrets of the Soil*, Peter Tompkins and Christopher Bird describe how they crossed paths with a water researcher named Dr. Patrick Flanagan. Christopher Bird (who died in 1996) was no stranger to understanding water, since it was his mind that brought forth *The Divining Hand*, a seminal work about the art of water dowsing. Bird's last book, *The Secret Life of Water*, was a work in progress when he died. It is my understanding that his widow, Shabari Bird, is now working on bringing this important book to print. I find it most touching that even after Bird was aware of his imminent death, he spent his remaining life energies schooling children about water.

The following is from a meeting that Tompkins and Bird had with Patrick Flanagan in Sedona, Arizona, as presented in *Secrets of the Soil*:

> In a monumental ten-volume work, *Wave Theory: Discovery of the Cause of Gravitation*, published in 1943, T. J. J. See, an American professor of mathematics who, in the 1930s was in charge of the twenty-six-inch Equatorial Telescope at the U.S. Naval Observatory in Washington, D.C., showed that the entire universe revolves around a geometric figure known as a rectangular hyperbola, which also defines the curve of the water vortex. This basic curve, says Flanagan, was discovered by See to represent many phenomena, including the universe-square law of electromagnetics; the laws of magnetism, gravity, and planetary motion; and—most importantly to the subject at hand—the surface-to-surface volume relationships and the structuring forces binding all matter.
>
> When Wilhelm Reich, the person once considered by Sigmund Freud as his most brilliant disciple, broke with the psychoanalytic movement to make his momentous discovery of a life energy called "orgone," related by some to [Rudolf] Steiner's "chemical ether," he found it to be made of *Kreiselwelle*, or spiral waves. In his book *Cosmic Superimposition* Reich describes

the creation of matter from the throat of cosmic vortices, such as nebulae.

In his laboratory, Flanagan demonstrates the cosmic properties of a vortex. Closer examination eerily reveals that the circulating water in its laws of movement is a miniature of the solar system, and, on a larger scale, is reflected in the great stellar nebulae, just as Reich already showed in *Cosmic Superimposition*.

Even though the above concept might be a little challenging for the layperson, it is a way of saying that vortex energy permeates all aspects of our reality—including matter, gravity, magnetism, planetary motion, time, electricity, light, and most importantly, that which causes matter to form our physical world. In *The Vortex: Key to Future Science*, David Ash and Peter Hewitt tell us:

> Just as the vortex creates space and matter, so it can be seen as creating time. Einstein believed that, in the absence of matter, there would be no space and no time either. He saw time and space as being inextricably linked, with time as a fourth dimension. We can see, through the vortex, why time is linked to matter.

Vortex Energy and Living Water

Dr. Patrick Flanagan, now in his early fifties, is an inventor and water vortex researcher. In the 1960s, he was listed by *Life* magazine as a prodigy for his work with Dr. Henri Coanda, called the "father of fluid dynamics." At the age of seventeen, Flanagan was listed by *Life* as one of America's top ten scientists.

In 1988 Flanagan was quoted in *Secrets of the Soil* as saying, "I read everything I could on water, only to discover it was one of the world's most mysteriously anomalous substances.... It is the universal solvent of chemistry, capable, with time, of dissolving any and all the elements, even gold.... In theory, liquid water, even when boiling, has microscopically tiny 'icebergs' of crystalline water within it, liquid crystals that retain their set structure, whereas the rest of the water is all randomly oriented, vibrating vigorously. Cooling water automatically creates more of the crystals until nearly the whole mass becomes crystalline ice."

The nature and behavior of the crystals found in glacial waters was one of the main areas of the research of Flanagan's mentor, Dr. Henri Coanda, who made water his lifelong study and is quoted by Flanagan in his *Elixir of the Ageless* as saying, "We are what we drink."

Dr. Coanda, a Romanian-born scientific genius, became renowned in certain circles for his discoveries in the 1920s of how watery substances "cling" to surfaces (known as the "Coanda Effect") and how certain waters hold the secret to long life. Coanda's research on water and longevity focused on the glacial water drunk by the people of the Hunza region of Kashmir, who were known for their long life spans and good health. To pursue his research, Coanda invented a machine to make snow from water so that he could study the properties of snowflakes created from different glacial water sources around the world. He discovered that the longer a snowflake survived after its creation by his special snowmaking device, the longer the life spans of the people who drank that water. As a curious aside, Coanda's snowmaking invention was used to make the first artificial snow for the ski slopes of France in the 1930s.

After extensive testing and research of the Hunza water with his snowflake and other methods, Coanda came up with the theory that the molecular structure of the Hunza water was in some way altered from that of other water. He never unlocked the mystery of why this was so, and Patrick Flanagan continued this research.

What Coanda did unlock, however, was the discovery that in the center of the frozen crystals making up each snowflake was "a circulatory system composed of tiny tubes in which still unfrozen water circulates like sap in plants, or blood in animals—water which he considered to be what dowsers characterize as 'living,' to distinguish it from its stagnant, lifeless counterpart" (*Elixir of the Ageless*).

As far as science can tell, no two snowflakes are alike. Why this is so remains somewhat of a mystery, since each snowflake is a result of crystallization, a process marked by growth. In the creation of each snowflake, variables such as air and temperature changes, cosmic sound and light influences, the special composition of the water at the time of freezing, and perhaps certain spiritual influences may all help to give birth to a unique snowflake. However, what all snowflakes share in common is that their crystals are arranged around a center at an angle of either 60 or 120 degrees, and all are invariably six-pointed (hexagonal). To me, this is curious, since we also find the hexagonal shape in the cells of bees and wasps, in petals of flowers, and in many other natural formations. It should also be noted that of all polygons, the hexagon is the only form in which the sides are equal to the radius of the circle that encloses it, therefore maximizing the space utilized.

Just as we have crystals in water forming snowflakes and ice, we also have rock crystals and minerals being assimilated into water under varying circumstances. These crystals and minerals can help to energize water through their electrical interaction. In researching Hunza water, Coanda discovered that certain particles are endowed with strong electrical charges and other special properties that make them colloidal. When particles are colloidal, their opposing electrical charge causes them to repel each other while floating in water; in this way they stay suspended as they keep bouncing off one another in water. Because of this, people who drink Hunza glacier water are drinking electrically charged mineral particles that otherwise would not be present. Without the electrical charge, the particles would settle out of the water or attach to other surfaces, and not be readily absorbed and digested by those who drink it.

Echoing this thinking was the late Dr. Charles Mayo, one of the founders of the renowned Mayo Clinic. Dr. Mayo stated the following about the mineral content of water relative to glacial water: "Most mineral-laden waters are constipating. Glacier water is supersaturated with dissolved oxygen and also carries the radiated energy of the sun—which we now understand to be natural atomic energy."

This information leads to the question of how minerals and other unknown particles get into Hunza water while being invigorated with electricity? To the best of my knowledge, the minerals in Hunza water come from the glacial grinding of crystals and minerals, and from the motion of water under pressure as it flows down from high altitudes. Because of glacial pressures and the accompanying high velocity vortex energy of the flowing waters, an electrical charge is imparted to the crystals and minerals and other substances. In this fashion, Hunza water becomes saturated with oxygen, contains the Sun's atomic energy, and contains a great number of ions (electrically charged particles).

Anyone who has seen a river flowing at flood level has certainly noticed the muddy color of its water. This color is derived from the increased energy present in the quantity and velocity of flowing water. Depending on the size of the water flow, this increased energy has the power to pick up soils, sand, gravel, rocks, trees, cars, and houses. The color of the soils, sediments and rocks of many waterways often end up providing their name—for example, the Yellowstone River, Black Brook, the Big Red. Regardless of the name, the ability of volumes of flowing water to create vortices of energy gives flowing water the power to lift and energize minerals and other particles. Our growing knowledge of this fact is now figuring into the management of the Colorado and other rivers.

Colorado River researchers have recently figured out that occasional river flooding is beneficial to the ecology of the river. The stirring up and cleaning out of the riverbed by flooding helps to loosen sediment while also helping the flora and fauna of the river thrive at different levels along the canyon walls. Today, thanks to common sense and the hard-fought efforts of many people, dam water is released in a way intended to mimic the Colorado's historic seasonal flows. Besides the obvious benefits, there are the subtle benefits of vortex energy charging the river water and its minerals with special healing and life-giving properties.

To take this thinking one step further, we have mineral waters in this world that have become renowned for their healing properties. In a way, we find that mineral waters and their salts share in the special electrical properties found in many glacial waters. Under close microscopic examination, we find that the salts in mineral water contain positively and negatively charged ions that repel each another—just like the minerals found in glacial water. It is in this way that we can view certain waters as fluid forms of life that are alive with energy—just as plants and animals are alive because of the electrical properties found in their watery substances.

Somewhat similar research to Flanagan's innovative use of crystals and water can be found in Lyall Watson's *Secret Life of Inanimate Objects*. Watson, who holds doctorates in anthropology and ethology, and additional degrees in botany, chemistry, geology, geography, marine biology, and ecology, has become renowned as the author of several books, including the best-selling *Supernature*. In *The Secret Life of Inanimate Objects*, Watson tells us:

> There are interesting parallels with tribal beliefs in the potency of water in which a crystal has been kept, but there is in the end just one attractive grain of science among all the crystal chaff. Marcel Vogel, for twenty-seven years a research chemist with IBM, has turned his attention to the question of crystal

energy. His careful experiments suggest that water, as long as it is not too pure, can act as an electrolyte and pick up charge from a crystal with which it comes into contact. Measurements by spectrophotometer, an instrument for comparing light radiation, show changes in the 'atomic fingerprint' of water before and after exposure in this way. It is impossible at this stage to be certain what such changes might mean, but the fact that they exist and can be monitored provides at least a possible mechanism for crystal influence on living things—which consist largely of water with a few added impurities (pp. 37, 38)....

Impure crystals, like badly designed tower blocks, soon come to throb with the strange music of these wild spirits which can be trapped and held captive for thousands of years. But they can also be persuaded, in certain circumstances, to release their energies and the information these contain, on demand.

This property in just one kind of crystal, that of silicon, is what lies at the heart of our whole electronics industry. It is what makes transistors and microchips and semiconductors possible (p. 31).

Silicon crystals are found in silica, a white or colorless crystalline compound that occurs extensively in the Earth's crust. Throughout the world, silicon crystals occur naturally, as they are continuously created by Earth's body. As humankind has learned, silicon crystals have the innate ability to accumulate and release data, a property now greatly used in silicon chips in computers. This may lead one to wonder about the religious and creative implications of silica as found in clay. Clay is mostly composed of hydrated (watery) silicates of aluminum. And, either by coincidence or by Divine design, clay is also the element from which most of the early writings and religious beliefs tell us that life was first created.

In *The Secret Life of Inanimate Objects*, Watson tells us more about clay crystals:

Crystals are regular geometric forms which seem to arise spontaneously and then to replicate themselves in a stable manner. Those in clay are even more lifelike, arranging themselves into complex layered structures which have the capacity to evolve. They grow and change, absorbing other molecules into their fabric, responding to changes in their environment by finding and using new patterns and ploys. They practise, in a very real sense, the arts of survival in which the 'fittest' go on to produce more of their own kind. Clays, in other words, are self-starting, self-assembling and self-replicating. Their crystals are tiny "naked genes" which are being churned out constantly by the earth machine and sorted into arrays with very different functions. Each patch of silt or sand, each kind of soil or stone, differs in porosity, transparency and conductivity, depending on its constituent clays. But all are simple membranes, rudimentary containers— a kind of "glassware," if you like—in which more elaborate chemistry can and does take place.

This is the missing scaffold. This is where amino acids got together, initially for purely structural purposes, as ways of holding useful metals in solution for a more "ambitious" clay, but later in their own interest. They became more and more independent of the relatively clumsy clays, evolving into what Cairns-Smith describes as a "slick super life made largely from air and sunshine."

Looked at in this light, the question of the origin of life on earth becomes a branch of mineralogy with pride of place, as our ultimate ancestor, going to a tiny crystal of clay. And the beauty of this insight is that it nicely bridges the gap between the inorganic and organic worlds, showing how organisms based on one genetic material can evolve into those based on another (pp. 23–24).

With the above-proposed scientific basis in mind, there appears to be credible support for the various ancient writings that tell us that an ancient power formed life from clay. Of course, clay itself is created from crystal deposits gathered together by water flowing across the face of the Earth. These deposits eventually accumulate in fine layers. Another thing about clay is that it cannot take on its lifelike behavior with electrical impulses networking the energies of its silicon crystals unless water is present. This fact may loan further credence to the speculation of how God and water may be alike in nature.

The trillions of crystals found naturally in any body of water are energized according to their environmental exposure. If a body of water is polluted, the crystals suffer an energy drain as they impart their power to remove or neutralize the pollutants in the water. Why water crystals naturally do this is unknown. Apparently the crystals found in water are empowered with the purpose of making sure water is as fit as possible for providing life with the energy to survive and prosper.

If a body of polluted water is stagnant without any fresh inflow of spring or surface water, it will remain polluted for a very long time. However, if there is an inflow of fresh water, vortices are created, thereby helping to energize the water crystals needed for altering, neutralizing, or removing pollutants.

From this thought it follows that water flowing from a pressurized source such as a glacier or underground spring fills itself with vortex energy as it flows over and mingles with clay, sand, rock crystals, and the calcified and petrified remnants of organic life. The vortex energy created from flowing mineral waters creates a mingling of crystal energies that generates electricity. This electricity in turn charges the large number of crystals found in cool water, thereby giving certain spring and glacier waters special properties for providing good health and extending life. If the grinding of glaciers is of significance, then places on the planet that received large quantities of glacial deposits during previous ice ages would tend to produce spring waters with special properties. There may also be some significance to how long the water remains in contact with the glacial minerals and sediments while under pressure beneath the ground.

The Creation of Matter from Vortices

Lord Kelvin (1824–1907) was the founding father of thermodynamics and also defined absolute zero by giving humanity the Kelvin temperature scale. He was also known for his studies of electricity and magnetism, which led to his invention of the magnetically shielded ship's compass. Throughout his life, Lord Kelvin was recognized and highly honored by society and academia as an enlightened man who was an original thinker.

If it hadn't been for his long list of accomplishments, Lord Kelvin might have found himself thrown out on his ear when he gave the scientific establishment a vortex spin with his new theory about matter. Based on some simple laboratory experiments with a box that produced smoke rings, Kelvin hit upon the idea that the properties of atoms and matter were creations of vortices, which led him to the concept that all matter is nothing other than an expression of vortex energy. Taking this concept one step further, he built upon the work of his friend, the German scientist Herman von Helmholtz (1821–94), which simply stated that vortex energy could live forever if it were to exist in a frictionless fluid.

Seemingly overnight, the entire scientific establishment of Europe was reevaluating its definition of reality. Support for the vortex theory was soon evident. James Clerk Maxwell (1831–79), renowned scientist and professor of experimental physics at Cambridge, jumped aboard and authored an article on the vortex atom in the 1875 edition of the *Encyclopaedia Britannica*. It was Maxwell who developed the electromagnetic theory that eventually led to the development of radio, television, and radar. Because of the vortex theory, the world was waking up to the fact that there was an invisible world of energy out there and that waves of sound and light could be projected and received.

Following Maxwell's lead in experimental physics at Cambridge, Sir J. J. Thomson (1856–1940) discovered the electron. Thomson's insight into electricity helped him see into the behavior of vortices and how they fashioned the reality of space, matter, and time, and he published scientific papers dealing with vortex mathematics and how chemical reactions could be explained in terms of the vortex atom. Supporting the idea that chemical reactions may be explained in terms of the vortex atom is the fact that almost all chemical reactions are dependent on the presence of water.

Taking the above into consideration, we see how modern science was beginning to redefine our worldly perception at the turn of the twentieth century. The idea of vortex energy lasting forever in the presence of a frictionless fluid established a new dimension of thought. This new dimension somewhat altered our view of the world. We were now looking at a world that was literally being composed second to second by chemical reactions taking place in water.

In the first half of the twentieth century, the same undying vortex energy was found to exist in the cell centers of living organisms. The French surgeon Dr. Alexis Carrel (1873–1944) presented proof of this and won the Nobel Prize in medicine in 1912 for revealing how living cells may be kept alive forever. According to Dr. Carrel, "The cell is immortal. It is merely the fluid in which it floats that degenerates. Renew this fluid at intervals, give the cells what they require for nutrition, and as far as we know, the pulsation of life may go on forever" (quoted in Patrick Flanagan, *Elixir of the Ageless*).

Since these cell centers contain vortex energy that seemingly spins in a frictionless fluid akin to water, it is here that we may find the secrets to death, birth, and infinity. This theory of an undying cell center was also proposed by the Austrian natural scientist, hydrologist, and inventor Viktor Schauberger (1885–1958), as described in Olaf Alexandersson's *Living Water*, and is supported by other research theory. Alexandersson tells us that the German scientists H. P. Rusch and Anto, in *Wiener Medizinische Wochenschrift*, Nos. 37–38, 1951, "presented proof that the cell center, the genes and chromosomes etc. do not die when the organism dies, but continue to exist by changing into other special forms" (note 18, p. 154).

Without saying so, Lord Kelvin, Schauberger, Helmholtz, Maxwell, Thomson, and many other scientists of that era were delving into water's vortex energy—the very energy that may be responsible for creating and sustaining our living reality.

Part II

MYSTERY

The author on his 7000-mile "Ride for Nature" across America, in Bowie, Arizona, with an extra packhorse given by rancher Ray Thomison for the desert crossing.

SIX

The Desert

DURING MY 7000-MILE HORSEBACK TREK across America, one of the most challenging territories was the Southwest desert. At the time of my passage, the Southwest was experiencing an extreme drought. By extreme, I mean the drought was so bad that several ranchers refused to give me water. "Can't spare any water," said one rancher, "Got to think of my family and animals first," said another. One time, while I was approaching a desolate ranch with a wooden shack, the owner burst out the door brandishing a pistol in his hand yelling, "Get the hell out of here!" amongst other things.

Perhaps the saddest and most heart-wrenching was the sight of cattle and sheep in various stages of body rot. Besides providing a gutsy feast for maggots and buzzards, the smell of rotting carcasses made my lead horse, Shalamar, and packhorse, Buck, get a little spooky. Every time they caught a whiff of a dead body, they would flare their nostrils, snort, prick up their ears, tighten their muscles, and quickly change direction to get away from the stink of death.

While crossing one section of desert we stumbled onto an entire cattle herd with a few horses and a dog lying dead around a dried-up water hole. The water hole looked like the crater of an exploded bomb. Inside the crater and around its fringes lay a bunch of contorted dead bodies. In my mind, a bomb killing would have been more merciful than the apparently slow and agonizing death caused by lack of water.

As reality would deliver, about five hundred miles into the horseback journey, Buck fainted from dehydration in the Arizona desert just north of Mexico. We had just finished traveling across miles of sand dunes and dry riverbeds, and the three gallons of water we carried had been consumed the previous day. As darkness arrived without our finding water, things became desperate. The horses' mouths were so dry that they had taken to licking the air with their swollen tongues.

71

When Buck fainted, we were traveling after dark to escape the blazing heat of day. It hadn't take me long to figure out that traveling in the cool of early morning and late day as well as the desert night was the only way to escape the sun's blistering heat. By doing so, we avoided searing winds, scorching heat rays, and sands so hot (up to 190 degrees F) that you felt as if you were taking an extended fire walk across a bed of hot coals. These desert elements dried my exposed skin so badly that my cheeks and lips became sore and started cracking, and the fingers on my swollen hands began bleeding from bending the dry skin at the joints.

At the start of our crossing, the desert made us pay a painful toll. I soon learned that the benefits of crossing the desert at night were offset by payment of a prickly price. Every desert plant has a thick rough skin to protect it from losing water to the sun. As a second line of defense, many desert plants also have a weapon system of needles, thorns, and barbs to protect from birds, rodents, and other mobile life forms that would cause injury while attempting to steal precious water.

After several sticking episodes of pulling barbed prickers from my skin and the horses' legs, I quickly learned to identify the shape of the plants that liked to "stick it to you" the most. Besides the barbed gauntlet, desert night travel offered other dangers. With nothing guiding your footsteps but the light of moon and stars reflecting off desert sand, an occasional rat, badger, or prairie dog hole offered a stumbling and sometimes spraining experience. After about two hundred miles of desert travel, however, the horses and I did gain a kind of oneness with the land, a "desert sense" that helped to guide and protect us over progressively dangerous terrain.

On the night Buck fainted, there was no moon to guide our footsteps. We were about six hundred miles into the journey and had just emerged from a section of deep desert. Fortunately, we found a narrow paved road and immediately traveled north toward some lights in the far distance. I say "we found a paved road" because there were many times when I would let the reins on my lead horse, Shalamar, dangle loose. With no guidance coming from me, Shalamar would make the decision of our travel direction. When Shalamar found the paved road, it gave me hope that we might soon get to water. After starting along the paved road toward the distant lights, I thought to myself, "Ah, yes, things are looking up. Soon we'll have water to take away the pangs of thirst." Yes, things were looking up. At least, that is, until my right arm was almost yanked out of its socket.

The lead rope for my packhorse, Buck, was wrapped around my right hand. Like a boat's plunging anchor line wrapped around an ankle, the lead rope suddenly grabbed my right hand and snapped my arm backward. A quick look behind revealed Buck fainting dead away in the middle of the road. Sensing something wrong, Shalamar abruptly stopped and backed up to give some slack to the lead rope pulling my arm. If he hadn't reacted this way, either I would have been pulled out of the saddle onto the hard pavement, or my arm would have been severely injured.

With Shalamar holding steady, I quickly dismounted and grabbed my flashlight. At first, I thought Buck was lying dead in the road, but a quick check of his nose with my ear told me he was breathing, although his breath was rapid and short. "Thank God, he's alive!" I thought as I kneeled beside him. "What should I do?" was my next thought.

But there was little time for thinking. As I was bending over Buck, I suddenly found myself being blinded by light as if a UFO had appeared out of nowhere. A loud blast of an air horn and the sound of burning rubber told me it was an unidentified flying tractor-trailer coming directly at us. I quickly fumbled around in my vest pocket and grabbed the tiny flashlight. I then pointed its tiny beam of light at the headlights and prayed. At the last second, the truck swerved around us. Soon, I found myself waving off all kinds of speeding traffic coming out of Mexico. It was a scary scene. Holding Shalamar's reins, I stood in the middle of the road lane between Buck and oncoming traffic. As the blinding headlights of cars and trucks raced toward us from out of the black night, I would shine my flashlight at the traffic hoping they wouldn't run us over. "What if my batteries die out?" I thought.

It was a nightmare out of "The Twilight Zone."

With horns blasting, brakes screeching, Shalamar rearing up in the air trying to escape the madness of blinding headlights, and hunks of speeding steel racing toward us, we shivered on the brink of annihilation. Then, just like in the eye of a hurricane, there would be moments of eerie stillness when the traffic was no more and the swirling air of its speeding passage disappeared into the darkness. During these brief breaks in the traffic, I would quickly pocket the flashlight, grab hold of Buck's halter, and try to pull him to his feet. Then, like a nightmare revisited, there would be the distant hint of lights as another wave of vehicles approached us at high speed. As they neared, I could feel the air they pushed as their tires slapped and roared across the hot black asphalt. All seemed hopeless. What I needed was a miracle.

After what seemed like several lifetimes, two young men had the good sense to stop their car and put on their hazard blinkers to keep the traffic off the horses and me. One of the men held Shalamar's reins while I cut the packsaddle and gear off of Buck's back. With me pulling on Buck's halter and the other man pushing, we finally got Buck to his wobbly feet. I put my face close to Buck's and called his name. Looking into his dazed eyes, I could tell he didn't hear me. The third time I called his name, Buck blinked his eyes and actually looked at me. I asked the two men if they had any water, so I could wet Buck's mouth. The answer was, "No. Sorry." With tractor-trailers and high-speed traffic rushing by us, the two men threw Buck's pack gear into their hatchback car and followed behind me along the shoulder of the road with their blinkers flashing. We headed toward the distant lights of civilization.

Fortunately, about a mile up the road there was a remote ranch that had some cattle, a couple of horses, chickens, and an Australian shepherd that barked and barked. Before long, an old cowboy named Steve Bains appeared from the trailer he lived in with his wife. Steve didn't seem to mind the ruckus his barking dog made. He was a lean and mean-looking man, with grizzled face, no shirt, stained denim pants, cowboy boots, and a gun on his hip. And even though Steve had just jumped out of bed, you could tell his cunning eyes knew what was wrong within seconds after he opened the trailer door. "Their bellies are tucked up," he said, looking at the horses. "Follow me and we'll get some water into 'em."

Steve was seventy-five years old and had been a cowboy all his life. Obviously he had seen horses in this condition before. "Can't let 'em drink too much too fast," he said as he took Shalamar's reins from my hand. At the watering trough, he taught me to carefully allow the horses to drink only small amounts of water at a time. To stop them from drinking too much too fast, we had to literally pull hard on the their reins to get them away from the water and then struggle with them a few minutes before letting them dive back in. Between drinks, Steve and I talked soothingly as we stroked the necks of Buck and Shalamar.

Once the horses drank their fill, I reached into the trough and pulled up a handful of the precious liquid to my mouth. What I remember most vividly is how the cool water felt going down my parched throat and hitting my empty belly. It gave me a sharp pain in my gut. Then, something strange happened—my mind suddenly went from being kind of fuzzy to a state of crystal clarity. It was as if I had just awoken out of a foggy dream. All of a sudden the Arizona night sky with all its sparkling stars came into sharp focus. So too did the scene with Steve and the horses. It was as if everything suddenly became clearly connected through that swallow of water—my mind, the universe, the struggling horses, the help of a stranger, the weathered tumbleweed resting against the barbed-wire fence, the smell of sweat steaming off the horses' backs, and the eerie distant howl of a coyote far off in the desert.

After thanking the two men who had saved me and the horses from becoming roadkill, I settled in for the night in my sleeping bag next to Buck and Shalamar. Over the next two weeks I camped at Steve's ranch and paid for our room and board by helping with chores. In those two weeks, Steve taught me the finer points of equine care and how to survive in the wilds of the Sonora Desert. One of the first things he had me do was to lighten my load and simplify my travel gear. This meant dumping my tent, miniature camping stove, goose-down sleeping bag, self-inflating air mattress, camera equipment, camping booties, aluminum mess kit, extra pair of boots, and other stuff that Steve kept referring to as "unnecessary luxuries."

"A piece of canvas and a wool blanket is all you need," said Steve, "and you can use your saddle blankets for a mattress."

To this day, I think of how Steve Bains taught me his tried-and-true methods of survival in desert cowboy country. He even gave me some pointers on wielding a gun and knife. "Most cowboys carried a gun on their hip to shoot their horse," Steve informed me. "More cowboys died from getting dragged to death by their horses than from snakes and mountain lions. Best chance you have when a horse is draggin' ya is to shoot it! Ya also may need a gun to finish a horse if it falls into a gully and ya can't get 'im free, or if it breaks a leg."

I have not forgotten Steve's advice. Nor have I forgotten how wonderful that mouthful of cool water felt at his watering trough. The moment the water touched my tongue there seemed to be an instantaneous clearness of thought and sight. And that instant clarity provided by a mouthful of water brought with it an epiphany that eventually led to the writing of this book.

It wasn't until many years after the horseback journey that I learned about water's magical and immediate effect on the mind of a dehydrated person. When you are in a state of dehydration, your body's survival mechanism is programmed to first send water to your brain and eyes. This makes a lot of sense, since thinking and seeing clearly are the two most important survival tools we as humans possess. Besides this, there are other physiological, biochemical, neurological, and spiritual connections between water and the brain, all of which help us to connect to and survive in the environment surrounding us.

As many of us know, you don't have to be in the middle of a desert to suffer from dehydration. There are many people today who have good drinking water readily available to them in their homes and offices and who lack the understanding and common sense to drink enough. As strange as it may seem, some people actually choose to live in a state of self-imposed dehydration.

I guess when it comes to living in a desert, it is all a state of mind.

SEVEN

Is Water Myth Water Truth?

Looking back into the distant past as far as our awareness reaches, we find that water was the object of human veneration, a veneration amounting to religious worship. Every great culture felt water to be connected with the loftiest gods. It was considered holy, an element not to be tampered with in its purity.
—THEODOR SCHWENK

OVER A TIME SPANNING THIRTY YEARS, I performed water research in the field as well as in my water-testing laboratory on Martha's Vineyard. The more I worked with the physical manifestation of water, the more I became intrigued about its mythological and theological aspects. At times in my life, I actually had a sense that I could hear water speaking to me as if I were having a conversation with an old friend.

Eventually, my research into water mythology revealed that I am not the first person on Earth to hear voices from water. There are and have been many other people throughout time who have felt some form of communication with water. The more I researched the history of water, the more I gained insight into the ancient belief systems surrounding this mysterious liquid substance. I have become so intrigued by this information that I felt I could not write this book without mentioning water mythology.

Before there was history (that which is recorded in writing), there was prehistory (that which was passed along orally). The so-called history of humankind began about 5000 years ago, while the "prehistory" of humankind (*Homo erectus*) began over 1,200,000 years ago. Ancient humans left behind chips of tools and weapons and cave drawings from about 750,000 B.C. to 15,000 B.C. From about 15,000 B.C. to 10,000 B.C. there is evidence of more sophisticated weaponry and cutting tools. Also, at about 10,000 B.C., we have the mysterious and ancient city of Jericho, with its evidence of an advanced and organized society. Finally, from circa 10,000 B.C. to 5000 B.C. we have the development of farming, irrigation of crops, pottery, and advanced stone implements.

Through all these various stages of humankind's early evolution, no evidence has yet to be discovered of any written form of communication being invented or developed. However, the prehistoric ceremonial reverence for water is well documented in many ancient sites studied in recent times. Ireland, as mentioned earlier, has many sacred spots that once were a part of a system of Celtic leys, water wells, and springs. Since the fourth century A.D. many Christian shrines have been located on these prehistoric sites, thereby providing a form of continuity throughout the ages.

When writing was discovered and inscribed on clay tablets about 5000 years ago, it was used to record some of the history that had been passed down orally through human evolution for tens of thousands of years. In these first writings we find references to water, which some people today refer to as "myth." These first writings provide us with some insight into the prehistoric knowledge passed down by our ancestors. Along with prehistoric pictographs and artifacts, these writings provide clues of how our ancestors lived for hundreds of thousands of years before the invention of writing.

Are these so-called myths true?

Could it be that information passed down orally from the beginning of human time represents only made-up stories?

What about the city of Troy and its discovery by German archaeologist Heinrich Schliemann in 1875? For thousands of years, the writings of the blind poet Homer immortalizing Troy were believed to be a myth. However, it was Homer's *Iliad* that literally gave Schliemann the geographical information he needed to rediscover the ancient city. In fact, Homer's descriptions were so accurate that once Troy was unearthed, all the landmarks in his writings were found to clearly describe the layout of the city. Could it be that the information about Atlantis in Plato's *Critias* is also based on fact?

Considering that early humans must have been greatly preoccupied with the business of survival, it is interesting to read the information they selected as being vital to future humans. Obviously our early ancestors thought it important for their children and their children's children to possess certain information about this world's beginning. In a curious but strange fashion, some modern humans have given the word "myth" to the information passed along so dearly by our ancient ancestors throughout human time.

Next to my writing desk I keep several dictionaries. One of the "big fat ones," *Webster's New Twentieth Century Dictionary* (Unabridged, Second Edition), defines "myth" in this way:

myth, n. [LL. *mythos;* Gr. *mythos*, word, speech, story, legend.]

1. a traditional story of unknown authorship, ostensibly with a historical basis, but serving usually to explain some phenomenon of nature, the origin of man, or the customs, institutions, religious rites, etc. of a people: myths usually involve the exploits of gods and heroes.

2. such stories collectively; mythology.

3. any fictitious story.

4. any imaginary person or thing spoken of as existing.

Syn.—fable, fiction, legend, falsehood.

So there it is. After using the tools of writing for only 5000 years, some modern humans have decided among themselves to label the information passed along by our ancestors as imaginary, fable, fiction, legend, falsehood. Information that survived as oral history for over tens of thousands, and perhaps up to a million years, is suddenly dismissed with words such as "fiction" and "falsehood."

Does this make any sense?

As far as we can tell from geological and archaeological research, the conditions our ancient ancestors lived under were very demanding. Just to survive each day was without a doubt an accomplishment to be proud of. Why then, while living under such challenging conditions, would parents waste their time passing along oral information to their children that was unimportant or useless or false? In response to this commonsense approach, more and more scholars are beginning to realize that these early writings and stories actually represent a lot more than myth or the wild imaginings of our early ancestors.

In support of this thinking is the work of the renowned scholar and author Zecharia Sitchin. Sitchin is recognized throughout the world as one of a handful of linguists who can read Sumerian cuneiform text, ancient Hebrew, and Egyptian hieroglyphics. After years of research, it is his firm belief that the early texts that first recorded the remnants of humanity's oral history should not be read as myths, but as a form of journalism that recorded true events. A sampling of Sitchin's books include *The Cosmic Code, The Stairway to Heaven,* and *Genesis Revisited: Is Modern Science Catching Up with Ancient Knowledge?*

Also supporting this position is the author Robert Bauval. In his book *The Orion Mystery* Bauval expresses the importance of the Pyramid Texts as the oldest extant religious writings on the planet. It is Bauval's belief that there is literal information in the Pyramid Texts that relates directly to providing factual information about Egypt's three pyramids of Giza. Bauval also infers that the texts contain important information passed down orally before being recorded for the first time on the walls inside the pyramids.

A Moment of Reflection

As far as we know, our early ancestors lived very intimately with nature. Each and every day they interacted with the weather and with the plants and animals of their surroundings. Without much doubt, they would have acquired a store of knowledge about nature and the world of life—knowledge that was passed along orally in the form of stories.

Considering this, let us take a moment and imagine how the urban life of a modern-day human might appear to a person living in a remote primitive environment, or to one of our ancient ancestors if time travel were possible:

A typical modern-day urban person awakens in a bedroom that is insulated from the outside world of life and weather. The air the person breathes may be "conditioned" by human machines, and the light in the bedroom may come from various human-made sources. There are probably very few if any living organisms in the home. At most, maybe a few plants; some insects; a dog or cat; perhaps a bird or a tank with fish.

Basically, the square spaces making up the rooms of the home are lifeless. And, just to make sure that there are no other living things in the home, insecticides are used with a passion. Certainly, no spiders, moths, ants, cockroaches, flies, or other insects are accepted without a battle. To keep the place "livable," dirt is vacuumed or swept up from time to time and removed from the home. If need be, poisonous chemical solvents are used to remove any stains or dirt marks that end up on some surfaces in the home.

Before going to work, the person may eat a breakfast without having any idea about where, how, or by whom the food was grown. While taking a shower, the person doesn't give a thought to the water's source. The person then dresses for work in clothes that have been made by strangers from materials of unknown origin. Periodically, the clothing is cleaned in a machine containing water and chemicals or by a chemical process called "dry cleaning."

Out the door goes this modern-day person into a car, bus, or train. There are no living organisms in the transportation machine. Arriving at work, the person then commences to pass the day in an office surrounded by nonliving things. This routine is repeated every day except maybe on weekends, when there may be a drive into the "country."

Modern-day people may work and live under such conditions most of their lives without ever thinking to question why they have accepted living this way. Rarely do people see that since the age of five years, they were taught that this is the way to live their life on Earth. By the time they graduate from high school or college, they have little information in their minds to cause them to wonder if the nonliving human-made reality they have been programmed to live and work in makes any sense.

Many people today, if they want to get a "feel" for the great outdoors, may take a vacation to the seashore, or take a brief hike along a human-made trail or country lane. Regardless of how adventurous and active modern-day people are, they rarely venture out into the wild untamed country without technological support. Such things as a four-wheel-drive vehicle, high-tech camping gear, a communication radio or cellular telephone, various weapons, ready-made foods, and other things help to make the brief wilderness experience reasonably safe and comfortable.

Each and every day the modern person sees, touches, hears, smells, and works with mostly nonliving, human-made technology of every purpose, shape, size, color, and sound. Such things as telephones, televisions, refrigerators, computers, typewriters, tape recorders, radios, cars, trains, subways, jets, buses, CD players, electric lights, cooking stoves, toasters, microwave ovens, soda machines, sound systems, paging devices, watches, clocks, construction equipment, sirens, and cleaning machines fill the modern world with their nonliving presence, motion, and sounds. And, it is with these nonliving things that modern-day people end up spending most of their lives.

Now let us go back to the so-called primitive person we have transported from a remote village, or via time machine, from long ago, to bear witness to the lifestyle of modern humans. Upon returning home, this primitive human sits down by the fire and tells the above story to friends and family. They would find it incredible that humans could just open a box and find food to eat; turn a handle and have water pour out; make fire appear by turning a round knob on a box; make light appear by touching a special place on a wall; see other people and places like magic from a box they sit in front of; fly into the sky and outer space inside the body of things that look like big birds. Without a doubt, upon hearing such fantastic stories, they would think that the things their companion was telling them were nothing other than a made-up story, a falsehood—a "myth."

Just as these ancient people would find it hard to believe such a story, so, too, do modern humans find it difficult to accept what they don't readily understand or witness firsthand. They don't trust the oral information passed down over tens and perhaps hundreds of thousands of years from humans who lived intimately with other life forms.

Astounding! Unbelievable! An amazingly creative story! Impossible! These are the terms some modern-day urbanized people apply to the information passed down to us from ancient humans— information that time and time again shows up not just in the ancient writings of one civilization from one part of the planet, but in the writings of many civilizations from every corner of the globe.

The First Sumerian Writings

Sumer was an ancient civilization located in the lower Euphrates River valley. This location is where some of the oldest written records have been discovered. These ancient texts were written on clay tablets in the cuneiform script (composed of wedge-shaped characters) used by the Sumerians.

The so-called Land of Sumer was a collection of city-kingdoms from the area of present-day Baghdad to the Persian Gulf. Gathered archaeological evidence tells us that this location was the home of some of the earliest humans. The fact that prehistoric humans lived in this region since the early dawn of humankind provides strong evidence that some of early humankind's oral information was also recorded in the writings of the Sumerians.

We discover, perhaps with interest, that from the very beginning these clay tablets contain writings about water and creation. Obviously, the Sumerians thought information about water was of such vital importance that it was one of the first things recorded with their new invention of writing. It is also obvious that what they recorded about water was based on an oral tradition that had been passed down from humanity's distant past. Because of this, it is no surprise to learn that the Sumerian word *mar* meant "sea" as well as "womb." The Sumerians believed that in the beginning only a vast swirling sea existed. All things of creation came from this sea after the storm god Huracan moved upon it.

As can be expected, interpretations of the ancient texts found in Sumer vary. However, one thing stands without question—"water" served as the source of creation for humankind and for many other things as well. The god Ea-Enki, the principal divinity of the liquid elements, especially the freshwaters, is written about most in the early Sumerian texts as the Creator. Ea-Enki is depicted as coming from the sea at the dawn of time and is said to be of "supreme intelligence, skillful, ingenious, He who knows all things." Upon arrival, Ea-Enki fertilizes the land and brings forth the plant world to produce food for the human beings he creates from clay.

The name "Ea," which means "House of the Water," makes up the first two letters of "Earth," the present name of the watery home to humans and all life. Ea's domain was the Apsu—all the waters that surrounded the planet and kept it afloat, as well as all the springs, rivers, and lakes. These fresh waters were also considered the source of happiness, knowledge, and wisdom. Ea is represented symbolically as a goat with a fish's tail, which is the sign of Capricorn, a point of interest expressed in Joseph Campbell's book *Occidental Mythology*.

The deity Ea is also mentioned in the world's oldest epic poem, *Gilgamesh,* a poem of love, death, and water.

In 1872 members of the Society of Biblical Archeology in London were shocked to hear from the archaeologist George Smith that he had deciphered a story written on ancient clay tablets in the Akkadian language in cuneiform writing. These tablets had been discovered in the ruins of the temple library and palace of Nineveh, once the ancient capital of the Assyrian empire. Since this find, older versions of *Gilgamesh* have been discovered, making it obvious that the poem was of Sumerian origin. It is now theorized that *Gilgamesh* was embellished upon as it was passed along from one civilization to another over thousands of years.

What startled the biblical scholars in 1872 was the fact that these ancient clay tablets predated the Bible, expressed a story about the "great flood," and contained information about the building of a ship to save people and animals. How could this be? How could clay tablets that were written around 3000 B.C. contain information that was thought to be specific to the teachings of the Bible? This discovery led to much conjecture about whether early biblical authors had used the Gilgamesh story as a source or had been influenced by it.

The following portion of the verse narrative, from Herbert Mason's translation of *Gilgamesh,* speaks for itself:

> There was a city called Shurrupak
> On the bank of the Euphrates.
> It was very old and so many were the gods
> Within it. They converged in their complex hearts
> On the idea of creating a great flood.
> There was Anu, their aging and weak-minded father,
> The military Enlil, his adviser,
> Ishtar, the sensation craving one,
> And all the rest. Ea, who was present
> At their council, came to my house
> And, frightened by the violent winds that filled the air,
> Echoed all that they were planning and had said.
> Man of Shurrupak, he said, tear down your house
> And build a ship. Abandon your possessions
> And the works that you find beautiful and crave
> And save your life instead. Into the ship
> Bring the seed of all living creatures.
>
> I was overawed, perplexed,
> And finally downcast. I agreed to do
> As Ea said but I protested: What shall I say
> To the city, the people, the leaders?
>
> Tell them, Ea said, you have learned that Enlil
> The war god despises you and will not
> Give you access to the city anymore.
> Tell them for this Ea will bring the rains (pp. 76–77).

Certainly, the parallel of the above section from *Gilgamesh* with the Bible cannot be overlooked. It is not surprising that this startled the Bible scholars around the world in 1872 and was the subject of considerable media attention.

On this note, Mason further informs us, "The *Gilgamesh* is unquestionably older than either the Bible or the Homeric epics; it predates the latter by at least a millennium and a half. The discovery of a fragment of the epic in Palestine suggests the existence of a version known to early biblical authors. Though we cannot know how widespread knowledge of the Gilgamesh epic was in the ancient Near East, we can say with surety that it is one of man's oldest and most enduring stories."

Such information now stimulates speculation about how many of today's religions are unknowingly practicing water beliefs and rituals passed down to us from the dawn of human history. Today it is generally recognized that the use of water in religious rituals had its beginning in ancient times long before the written words of recorded history. In the John Gardner and John Maier translation of *Gilgamesh*, we are informed, "The so-called Babylonian Creation Epic was recited during the New Year's Festival."

What I find curious in the translation of the ancient epic of Gilgamesh is that the old man who is telling this story is ordered by the water god, Ea, "Into the ship / Bring the seed of all living creatures." Could this be an overlooked clue about how the "seeds" of all living creatures were rescued by humans from the great flood? In lieu of bringing actual pairs of living creatures into the ark, perhaps somehow their seeds were harvested and rescued.

Will history repeat itself?

As humankind enters future time with our evolving genetic expertise, we are already setting aside small "arks" holding the foundation seeds of plants and creatures that are in danger of being destroyed forever. In this fashion, perhaps the seeds of many of today's endangered species may be set aside for reintroduction at some future date—when the Earth and its waters may once again be suitable for providing livable habitat.

Joseph Campbell, one of the world's preeminent scholars on religion and mythology, presented an enlightening viewpoint on the subject of the water god Ea in *Occidental Mythology*. On the subject of water and John the Baptist, Campbell writes:

And the rite of baptism that he preached, whatever its meaning at that time may have been, was an ancient rite coming down from the old Sumerian temple city of Eridu, of the water god Ea, "God of the House of Water," whose symbol is the tenth sign of the Zodiac, Capricorn (a composite beast with the foreparts of a goat and body of a fish), which is the sign into which the sun enters at the winter solstice for rebirth. In the Hellenistic period, Ea was called *Oannes,* which is in Greek *Ioannes,* Latin *Johannes,* Hebrew *Yohanan,* English *John.* Several scholars have suggested, therefore, that there was never either John or Jesus, but only a water-god and a sun-god (pp. 349–50).

Reading this passage, one is reminded that the god Ea is depicted in the early writings of the Sumerians as a water god who also brings forth the dawn of light. Could there be some truth in what, according to Campbell, some "scholars" have suggested?

The First Egyptian Writings

Egypt derives its name from the early word *Hat-kaptah,* one of the names for the ancient city of Memphis, which was located on the Nile River about two hundred miles south of Cairo.

Some of the earliest Egyptian writings, which tell about the creation of all things, can be found in the Pyramid Texts. What is curious about these writings is that the Pyramid Texts were not written specifically to pass along information dealing with water and creation, but to express thoughts about the kings of Egypt and their destinies after death. The information about water in the Pyramid Texts appears to express what was considered to be common knowledge at that time— that a primordial waste of water named Nun, which had no shape or order, was the beginning of all things. The Texts further express that from Nun emerged Atum with land upon which to stand, and then Atum masturbated and created the deities of air (male) and moisture (female). From the union of air and moisture came forth gods of earth (male) and sky (female), which in turn joined in a close embrace, and from this embrace, came the birth of the cosmos and the universe.

Again and again, throughout many ancient Egyptian texts concerning the origin of the universe, the "Primeval Waters" are said to be the source from which the world and all things were created. Any areas of

Egyptian mythology that one researches seem to express remarkably similar information about water.

Eventually, this information was made manifest by the construction of a temple in the Egyptian city of Heliopolis (today a suburb of Cairo) to honor Atum, the supreme Creator or Universal Lord. This temple is considered one of the most, if not the most, ancient and holy temple in the Egyptian world. In a way, it serves as a psychological bridge between this reality and that of the source of all things—the Universal Lord who was created by the Primeval Waters.

Another translation of the Pyramid Texts gives this definition of the Primeval Waters from which Atum came forth: "Where the Universal Lord dwelt when he was in the infinity, the nothingness, and the listlessness." Other terms that apply to the waters of creation are "nothing," "infinity," "inertness," "invisibility," and "darkness."

Today there are Egyptologists who believe that the priests of Heliopolis were the heirs to a powerful secret knowledge, and that this knowledge culminated in the building of the Great Pyramid and other forms of profound architecture. Supposedly, the priests of Heliopolis knew the secrets of the origins of humankind, and supposedly passed along secret knowledge through the pyramids themselves as well as through the Pyramid Texts, which were inscribed on the walls of inner chambers of several pyramids.

In the introduction of Idries Shah's seminal book *The Sufis*, Robert Graves gives another example of sacred knowledge being incorporated and hidden in architecture. Graves tells us (p. xix) that the Sufis "are an ancient spiritual freemasonry," and that the architects of King Solomon's temple at Jerusalem were Sufis, as were the architects who built the Dome of the Rock on the ruins of Solomon's temple. According to Graves, the architectural measurements chosen for these temples, as well as for the Kaaba at Mecca, "were numerical equivalents of certain Arabic roots conveying holy messages, every part of the building being related to every other in definite proportion."

In *The Sufis* we learn that Hermes Trismegistus, the Greek name for the Egyptian god Thoth, is the supposed author of works on alchemy, astrology, and magic. In *The Roots of Consciousness*, Jeffrey Mishlove says that many renowned Greek philosophers were initiated into certain mystery cults. Supposedly, the initiation rites into these cults induced a transformative state of being. According to Mishlove, "Pythagoras, Plato and other Greek philosophers were said to have been initiated into these cults—which are said to have originated in

Egypt. The tradition of Hermetic mysticism also claims an origin in the legendary Egyptian-Greek god-sage Hermes Trismegistus."

According to Shah and other great writers, Hermes left behind a mysterious riddle inscribed on an "emerald tablet." This riddle is sometimes believed to represent the key, the great inner principle, of the Great Work of alchemy. Here is Shah's rendering of Hermes' riddle on the *Emerald Tablet:*

> The truth, certainty, truest, without untruth. What is above is like what is below. What is below is like what is above. The miracle of unity is to be attained. Everything is formed from the contemplation of unity, and all things come from unity, by means of adaptation. Its parents are the Sun and the Moon. It was borne by the wind and nurtured by the Earth. Every wonder is from it, and its power is complete. Throw it upon earth, and earth will separate from fire. The impalpable separated from the palpable. Through wisdom it rises slowly from the world to heaven. Then it descends to the world, combining the power of the upper and the lower. Thus you shall have the illumination of the world, and darkness will disappear. This is the power of all strength—it overcomes that which is delicate and penetrates through solids. This was the means of the creation of the world. And in the future wonderful developments will be made, and this is the way.
>
> I am Hermes the Threefold Sage, so named because I hold the three elements of all the wisdom. And thus ends the revelation of the work of Sun. (p. 223).

The above mystical revelation from Hermes gave me chills when I first read it. As time went by, I returned again and again to contemplate its meaning. In reading Shah's translation of this riddle, it came to me one night that additional wisdom might be revealed by replacing the riddle's words *unity* and *it* with the word *water*. My personally revised rendering of the *Emerald Tablet* reads as follows:

> The truth, certainty, truest, without untruth. What is above is like what is below. What is below is like what is above. The miracle of water is to be attained. Everything is formed from the contemplation of water, and all things come from water, by means of adaptation. Water's parents are the Sun and the Moon. Water was borne by the wind and nurtured by the Earth. Every wonder is from water, and its power is complete. Throw water

upon earth, and earth will separate from fire. The impalpable
separated from the palpable. Through wisdom water rises slowly
from the world to heaven. Then water descends to the world,
combining the power of the upper and the lower. Thus you shall
have the illumination of the world, and darkness will disappear.
This is the power of all strength—water overcomes that which is
delicate and penetrates through solids. This was the means of the
creation of the world. And in the future wonderful developments
will be made, and this is the way.

I am Hermes the Threefold Sage, so named because I hold the
three elements of all the wisdom. And thus ends the revelation
of the work of Sun.

When reading this revised version with the word "water" so
placed, the riddle's hidden meaning suddenly seems to make a world
of sense. If this is true, I wonder why Hermes chose to hide the use
of the word "water" from his original composition of this passage.

Given the information passed down to us by Hermes, as well as
that revealed in the Pyramid Texts about the god Atum and his origin
from the Primeval Waters, I believe we have a clear message from
our Sufi and Egyptian ancestors—humankind was created by water;
humankind was created in the image and likeness of water.

I feel an important point to think about here is that with the creation of Atum by the waters of infinity and darkness came also the
creation of light in the form of the Sun. Atum, or "The Complete
One," was also worshiped as the Sun. The importance of this is found
in the creation of light from an entity (Atum) derived from the "waters of infinity." It is also significant that the god Atum was worshiped
as the Sun, because the physical entity of "light" cannot exist unless
there are physical "eyes" to see the light. And, eyes can only be created
and see through the presence of water.

Another aspect of this water and light relationship is that light is
created through the burning of hydrogen mixed with oxygen—both
found in large quantities in the entity of water. In a high school experiment, I learned about the explosive production of light from oxygen
and hydrogen. A simple laboratory test of filling an upside-down jar
with hydrogen and placing a match inside will produce a gentle pale-
blue flame before the match is extinguished. This pale-blue flame will
appear only at the opening of the jar where the hydrogen mixes with
oxygen and air. When the same jar is filled with two parts of hydrogen

mixed with one part of oxygen, they combine to create a watery vapor or steam, which will suddenly explode with a loud noise when a match is placed at the mouth of the jar. In this fashion, hydrogen and oxygen mixed together are capable of developing light and heat. Which makes one wonder, since recent studies have determined that extremely hot water vapor is present on the surface of the Sun, and is believed to be responsible for keeping it from overheating and destroying itself.

Such recent scientific research gives credence to the ancient belief that the god Atum, although created from water, was also a Sun god and the source of light and heat. The name Atum is also similar to the "atom" that plays a major part in the material existence of our reality. And, of course, much light and heat are created by the explosion of an atomic or hydrogen bomb.

The so-called mound that rose with Atum out of the waters was supposedly recreated in this earthly reality by the mound of Atum's temple built in Heliopolis. It is believed that this mound invested considerable power on many levels to the priests of the temple, and that the priestly knowledge about the origins of humans from water allowed them to transform the world through time. These priests of Heliopolis may have passed on knowledge about water and the creation of life that is being held in secret to this day by safekeepers awaiting the proper time to reveal this powerful information to humankind. Some people may believe that the principle of the "water vortex" may very well represent the secret source of existence and of all knowledge coming forth from Heliopolis.

The swirling energy of the vortex can be thought of as an expression of the swirling mist or waters from which all existence was born. We see the swirls of the vortex expressed often in various forms of early art from the Egyptians and other civilizations.

In my opinion, the source of the creation of "all things" from water is a significant contribution of Egyptian "prehistory" to understanding the world we live in today. I feel modern-day humanity is most fortunate that the wisdom of the Pyramid Texts is available to help us at this time in history.

Greek Philosophy:
The Bridge Between Myth and Science

According to the Greek biographer Plutarch (first century A.D.), the water nymph Egeria exerted her influence on the ways of humankind from a gushing spring beneath a great oak tree in Rome's legendary grove in Nemi. Egeria became the wife of the Roman king Numa Pompilius, who succeeded Romulus, and, when they met each evening at her clear spring, she gave him many suggestions about laws for governing Rome. Many priestesses of that time and since were believed to receive prophetic visions and oracles from Egeria's murmurings coming forth from flowing water.

Similar in a fashion are the visions received by the famous oracle at Delphi on the southern slope of Mount Parnassus in central Greece, where there is a groundwater source that has been held sacred since the Bronze Age and was originally dedicated to the worship of an Earth goddess. It was here that the legend of the Delphic Oracle arose over 2400 years ago and a temple was built dedicated to the god Apollo, who was believed to speak through the oracle. The priestess, Pythia (or Pythoness), would ritually bathe herself in a nearby stream before performing her duties as a seer. After bathing, she would seat herself on a stool over a fissure in the earth and inhale the magical vapors that arose and gave her special powers to speak for the god Apollo. It was believed that the watery mist rose from the womb of the Earth and captured the essence of the Earth's energy; the word *delph* in Greek means "uterus." This energy supposedly endowed Pythia with the ability to see future events.

Leaders would travel long distances to consult the oracle at Delphi; Socrates is known to have been one of the seekers. These answers were given by the oracle through sounds uttered by Pythia while in a trance; the sounds were interpreted by her attending priests and delivered in verse form to the seeker. The answers were ambiguous, and it was left to the seeker to determine the meaning. It should be noted that the famous inscription KNOW THYSELF was carved in stone above the temple's entrance. Over time, the term "Delphic" has come to mean answers that are ambiguous or obscure.

In a curious fashion, the use of water for prophecy is a theme that appears again and again in myths and religious traditions. In Donald Tyson's book *Scrying for Beginners* we read, "The ancient Greeks believed that nature spirits dwell in the bodies of fresh water, particularly in springs where the water wells forth out of the ground on its own accord. In Europe many of these famous springs were enclosed with stone and made into wells or fountains. The spirits of elemental water, which Paracelsus called Undines, are particularly fond of human beings and very willing to form close relationships with men and women who invoke and give offerings to them."

Over 2500 years ago, in the Greek territory known as Ionia, lived a man named Thales, who has since been described as "the world's first philosopher," "the father of philosophy," "the founder of philosophy," and, according to Aristotle, "the founder of Ionian natural philosophy." And it is in Ionia that we also find "recorded history's" first naturalists.

Thales, born in the Ionian town of Miletus, has forever left his imprint on the realm of human thought. His contributions were so profound during his time that he was canonized as the wisest member of the Seven Sages of Greece.

Most of what we know about Thales comes from the writings of Plato, Aristotle, Plutarch, and others. Thales was apparently an original thinker who must also have had a keen understanding of the myths of oral history from hundreds of thousands of years before. At the same time, he was a scientist, astronomer, mathematician, teacher, author, politician, and a "seer" who could forecast future events. For his time, Thales was considered well traveled. While living in Egypt, he is said to have calculated the height of a pyramid by measuring its shadow at the precise moment when the length of his own shadow was equal to his height. What he learned about the Egyptian tradition in his travels may have influenced his philosophy about water.

Thales was born into a world filled with the so-called mythologies and gods that were recorded in the first writings of humankind. He closely observed the natural world about him and seems to have had an unusual ability to synthesize mythology and natural science. Desiring to grasp the "first cause" of all things, he searched for a unifying hypothesis for the creation and sustenance of things both visible and invisible. This led him to the startling revelation that all things come from water, that the Earth floats on water, that water is the material constituent of all things, and that water is the cause of earthquakes. According to Plutarch's *Miscellanies Vol. III:*

> Thales the Milesian doth affirm that water is the principle whence all things in the universe spring. . . . He pronounced, that all things had their original from water, and into water all things are resolved. His first reason was, that whatsoever was the prolific seed of all animals was a principle, and that is moist; so it is

probable that all things receive their original from humidity. His second reason was, that all plants are nourished and fructified by that thing which is moist, of which being deprived they wither away. Thirdly, that the fire of which the sun and stars are made is nourished by water exhalations,—yea, and the world itself.

Today we know that continental plates float and crash into each other and that there are chemical and other changes in groundwater just before an earthquake.

From the little information that can be gathered about Thales, I found him to be a mysterious man who apparently introduced many new ideas and concepts that cannot be found anywhere before his time. Besides teaching people about water, he expressed practical knowledge of how the world worked through his mathematics, astronomy, and engineering. As Plutarch wrote in his *Lives*, "Upon the whole, Thales seems to have been the only philosopher who then carried his speculations beyond things in common use, while the rest of the wise men maintained their character by rules for social life."

One example of how Thales fostered new concepts was when he astonished the natives of Miletus by informing them that the Sun and stars, which were worshiped as gods, were merely gaseous balls of fire. Through such revolutionary revelations Thales is credited with ushering in a new era of Greek thought by daring to give natural explanations for cosmic complexities and mysterious events. Following his lead, later Ionian philosophers sought in physics for the natural causes of certain incidents, and in philosophy for a natural theory of all existence.

As is the case with many original thinkers who dare to share new thoughts with the world, Thales was held up to a considerable degree of public ridicule. According to various records, he counteracted the disbelievers of his time by doing two things that to this day remain quite inexplicable and impressive.

First, being an astute observer of the universe and its motions, he reportedly predicted a solar eclipse to his fellow Ionians in the year 585 B.C. Modern scientists have checked this event and generally agree that a solar eclipse did take place on May 28, 585 B.C., and that it was visible in Ionia. How Thales was able to perform this profound astronomical feat remains a mystery. According to the best of information available today no theory for predicting a solar eclipse existed in Thales' time, and his feat is all the more impressive because he had to take into consideration the influence of geographical latitude. This fact has led me to speculate that he may have gained his knowledge not just from observation of nature, but also from secret information connected with the pyramids of Egypt.

Second, in a story passed down to us from Aristotle, Thales found himself publicly humiliated for spouting thoughts that had little practical use in the day-to-day activities of humankind. Knowing that nothing in this material world makes people believe that one is something special more than making of a lot of money, Thales used his understanding of the natural world to show his countrymen how he could in fact make himself a wealthy man whenever he desired. To demonstrate this, he applied his knowledge of astronomy, weather, and, of course, water to foretell a large harvest of olives in the countryside surrounding Miletus. Knowing this fact long before the harvest season, he quietly went about Miletus and purchased time on many of the olive presses. When his predicted rains produced a bountiful olive harvest, to the amazement of his fellow villagers, Thales made a huge profit by having a monopoly on most of the presses for squeezing olives to make oil.

Needless to say, after the above two events, Thales' stature as a man who knew what he was talking about was greatly elevated. Another of his practical accomplishments was his recommendation that Milesian sailors use the starry constellation known as the Little Bear, also called Ursa Minor or the Little Dipper, as a navigational aide. He further helped sailors by developing a method of measuring the distance of ships out to sea. And, on an even loftier note, Thales is sometimes credited with introducing geometry to Greece. It is believed that it may have been Thales who gave us the concepts that the circle is bisected by its diameter, that the base angles of an isosceles triangle are equal, and that vertically opposed angles are equal.

Since Thales is credited as being the world's first philosopher, it naturally follows that he exerted a considerable degree of influence on many of the Greek philosophers and writers who succeeded him, including Anaximander, Socrates, Euripides, Plato, and Aristotle. On another note, we find passages in the tragedies of Euripides about the healing properties of the sea and how its waters could cure humankind of all its ills.

Of course, the most important thought left to us by Thales is that *all things exist because of water.* Our knowledge of this is based on Aristotle's passages in the *Metaphysics* crediting Thales with saying that water is the material constituent of all things. This thought reaffirms the earliest writings of humankind, which record again and again in different parts of the world that in the beginning there existed a watery mist from which all things were created. For instance, Old Testament writings tell a similar story about the Earth floating on water:

> The Lord's is the Earth and its entirety,
> the world and all that dwells therein.
> For He hath founded it upon the seas
> and established it upon the waters (Psalm 24:1–2).

Thales' idea that the Earth floats upon water is not that far-fetched. The more we learn about water, the more we realize that it is present in all places—even on our burning Sun and in the emptiness of outer space, albeit in its very basic form. What takes this thought one step further is the indication that Thales also looked upon water as a "remote ancestor." In other words, he considered water to be directly related to every human and every living thing that ever existed throughout eternity.

This idea of water being "related" to every human and every living thing cannot be overlooked. For thinking of water as an ancestor indicates a belief that water is a living being.

Further supporting this concept of a fluidlike substance permeating all things was the mathematician Helmut, who suggested in the 1800s that there was a "universal fluid" pervading all of nature which was not corporeal, but a pure vitalizing form of spirit continuously flowing through all bodies.

Also, we can see that Thales thought of water as both a principle and an element—meaning that the water we see, drink, swim in, and otherwise use in this physical reality also has a basis in realms beyond the senses.

Anaximander (c. 611–547 B.C.), who is thought to have been a follower of Thales, according to Plutarch "assigns the principle of all things to the Infinite, from whence all things flow, and into the same are corrupted; hence it is that infinite worlds are framed, and those vanish again into that whence they have their original." This concept of all things "flowing" from an infinite source was also put forth by another Greek philosopher, Heraclitus (c. 540–480 B.C.). Both of these philosophers assigned the principle of all things to the Infinite, and believed that "everything flows," from which it follows that one "cannot step twice in the same river."

It is curious to find that at about the same time the Buddha (c. 563– 483 B.C.) was setting forth a similar philosophy through his teachings in Asia. How appropriate for the name "Buddha" to have the Sanskrit meaning of "awakened." The fact that Heraclitus, Thales, Zoroaster, Confucius, Pythagoras, and Buddha provided life-changing philosophic or religious beliefs and lived about the same time makes one wonder if they ever met or heard news of each other. Or, perhaps their traveling devotees crossed paths and shared the teachings of their respective masters. Another interesting note is the fact that these great thinkers all lived along the 35th parallel of North latitude (J. Wright, *Scient. Monthly*, 1920, xi, 131).

Socrates (470–399 B.C.) expanded on Heraclitus' thought of all things "flowing" by teaching that all things flowed from "ideas" originating in a "source" that was unseen in this reality. This concept of flowing was further elaborated by Plato (428–347 B.C.), who created his academy as a center of learning to carry on the teachings of his teacher, Socrates. It is interesting to note that near Plato's school in the grove Academus flowed a gurgling stream of water. With a little imagination, one can easily envision the great philosophers sitting in the grove near the gurgling stream while discussing Thales' teachings about water. Perhaps they even heard voices coming forth from the stream. Of course, from the grove "Academus" where Plato taught, we have the origin of the words "academic" and "academia."

What Thales taught about the spiritual nature of reality during his lifetime seems to be reappearing in our own time, except in a slightly different fashion. The belief that science will provide us with all the answers of physical existence is slowly but surely being replaced with the belief that science will perhaps help lead us to the spiritual source of our existence. The world of human thought and belief is once again returning to the search for the spiritual within nature. People from all walks of life are once again seeing and believing in the presence of god and spirits in the natural world within and without. Truly there is great wonder in the ongoing creation and sustenance of humanity and the world we live in. Each day more people are awakening to the wonder of being human, this creation called "Earth" that we temporarily live on, the sharing of time with other life forms, and the endlessly fascinating expanse of cosmos surrounding us.

Nostradamus

Nostradamus (1503–1566), one of the greatest visionaries, used water for seeing the affairs of humankind across the span of time. While alone at night, he would sit on a "tripod stool of brass" and look deeply into a large bowl of water. With the special use of a branch, he would perform magical rituals to open the way for divine communication and visions of the future. This much we know from Nostradamus's own hand. The following two quatrains in his first Century (I.52–53) were published in 1891 by Charles Ward in *Oracles of Nostradamus:*

> Gathered at night in study deep I sat,
> Alone, upon the tripod stool of brass,
> Exiguous flame came out of solitude,
> Promise of magic that may be believed.

> The rod in hand set in the midst of the Branches,
> He moistens with water both the fringe and the foot;
> Fear and a voice make me quake in my sleeves;
> Splendor divine, the God is seated near.

Renowned as France's most famous seer, Nostradamus published his book of prophecies, *Les Vrayes Centuries* ("The True Centuries") in 1558. In it he seemingly predicted twentieth-century events such as the World Wars, the assassination of John F. Kennedy, humans landing on the Moon, the fall of Communism in Russia, the reunification of Germany, global pollution, and the human epidemic of a virus (AIDS). One of the prophecies yet to be fulfilled is the opening of the lost Hall of Records in Egypt near the Nile River. In this prophecy, Nostradamus says:

> They will come to discover the hidden topography of the land (at Giza),
> The urns holding wisdom within the monuments (the Pyramids) opened up,
> Their contents will cause the understanding of holy philosophy to expand greatly,
> White exchanged for black, falsehoods exposed, new wisdom replacing the established tradition that no longer work.
>
> (VII.14)

In ancient times, the term "urn" was used as a measure of liquids. An urn was said to hold about 3.5 gallons. It will be curious to see what "wisdom" will be revealed to us if this prophecy comes to pass.

Concerning other prophecies of Nostradamus that may touch our lives in the near future, Stephen Paulus gives us more to think about in his book *Nostradamus 1999*.

The Natives of America and Australia

Just like the Sumerians and the Egyptians, the American and Australian Indians also had a body of knowledge that was passed along orally for thousands of years before the written word. In what is now the United States, the Kwakiutl tribes of the Northwest, the Algonquin tribes of the East, and the Taos Indians of the Southwest all shared the similar belief that in the beginning of all things there was nothing but water.

From the Eastern Algonquin-speaking Cree Indians came the belief that before the Earth existed there was water, and from this water two ducks came into being. In turn, these ducks placed some floating sticks upon the water. Eventually other animals joined the ducks on the floating sticks and dived beneath the water to bring up more sticks to make the raft larger. Eventually the raft became very large to accommodate all the wildlife living upon it. Then came the Great Manitou who placed some sand on the raft—and thus the beginning of an ever expanding landmass rising out of the water.

In Massachusetts, the Wampanoag tribe on Martha's Vineyard has been recorded as believing in at least thirty-seven different gods. However, they also believed in the one Great Creator called Kiethan, whom they believed held the power of life and death over the entire universe. Kiethan was said to come from over the ocean to the southwest and was responsible for sending the warm rains in the spring that brought forth life.

The Taos Pueblo Indians of New Mexico to this day believe that Blue Lake is the center of the universe, the source of all created humans and the home of all departed souls. Blue Lake is an ancient spring-fed lake high in the nearby Sangre de Cristo Mountains. According to local mythology, the waters of Blue Lake are believed to possess mystical properties that sustain the well-being of the Taos Pueblo on many levels, as well as sustaining the ongoing reality of all of creation. Each summer for centuries beyond memory, every able-bodied person in the tribe has made a pilgrimage to the lake to give thanks and pray for the universe.

Holding a similar belief, several aboriginal coastal clans in Australia say they were led to their locations long ago by individuals called Wandjina. These clans believe that after death each Wandjina was represented by a painting on a cave or rock shelter in the clan's country and that the Wandjina spirits went into a "water-place." As a result, the Wandjina spirits are associated with coastal rains, the rainbow, the sky, and therefore the cycle of seasons. Every year as the wet season approaches, each clan retouches the rock paintings, thus making sure they continue to exist. In this way, the dream spirits that bring rain become operative, as they were in the days when the Wandjina lived on Earth, thus ensuring that the wet season will come, vegetation will grow, and animal and bird life will be plentiful.

Another living example of the passing along of ancient information concerning water is provided by the Kogi Indian tribe in Colombia. The Kogi live in the remote mountains and represent one of the few surviving pre-Columbian Native American civilizations. Due to the geographical barriers of the Andes on one side and the Caribbean on the other, the Kogi, until recently, had lived undisturbed for thousands of years.

Living high atop the mountains, the Kogi began to notice changes in the vegetation and wildlife, and in the snow and ice formations. It did not take them long to realize that these destructive changes were caused by modern human activities. For this reason, the Kogi decided to come forth from isolation to warn all humankind that the water of Earth must soon be nurtured back to health. They warn that humankind must change its ways, or else a great catastrophe will soon come to pass.

The Kogi's respect and love for water has been and is an integral part of their culture. For untold thousands of years they have lived their lives according to ancient customs. Is it any surprise that we learn from the Kogi, whose word for "water" is the same as their word for "spirit," that all of creation was born from "water thinking"?

Myth or Truth?

The above examples represent just a small sampling of what many of our ancestors believed to be truth for thousands to possibly tens of thousands of years before the invention of writing. Why would so many so-called myths share the belief about water being the source of creation?

Is there truth to these teachings of early humanity?

And, just what is "truth" when it comes to people and their beliefs about water and their interactions with each other in the natural world?

It is this thought that takes us into the realm of water in religion and its use in rituals.

EIGHT

Ritual

The spirit of God is like a stream of water and His disciples are like many beautiful fountains fed by this river of waters. Each one of us is such a fountain, and it is our task to keep the channel open so that God's spirit can flow through us and others can see His glory.
                                        —JOHN MARKS TEMPLETON

IN MY BOYHOOD YEARS I served as an altar boy in the Catholic Church. Even though I no longer follow the Catholic religion closely, I still recall with fascination the rituals and beliefs surrounding water. The "holy water" that we dipped our fingers into as we entered the church and blessed ourselves with by making the sign of the cross; the use of water in baptism; the sprinkling of water on parishioners during certain ceremonies; Jesus' miraculous transformation of water into wine—these are a small sampling from the Catholic water ritual and belief system.

Over the many years of researching and experiencing water on many levels, I have come to see and feel water as a religious experience. This feeling manifests itself in various ways at various times. For instance, each time I submerge myself into a hot tub of heated water with herbs and mineral salts, or into a body of healthy water in nature, there is a sense of well-being that emotionally moves me to quietly say "thank you" to God.

As I continue to evolve through this life's journey, I find it endlessly interesting to attend the various services of our world's different religions. As a result, I am constantly intrigued by the fact that almost every service I visit seems to offer something about water as a ritual or oral reference during the service. To me, it is no surprise to learn that many water rituals in use today have survived through changing times for thousands of years. "Why is this?" I ask myself. Over and over again the answer comes to mind that the common use of water in so many different religions probably has its origin in a single

101

source. Could it be that water, the common denominator connecting all life, is also the common denominator connecting all religions? And, if this is true, will we soon find new knowledge revealed to us through water about our spiritual connection to each other? Perhaps this will happen much in the same way as water has revealed and continues to reveal information to us about the interconnectedness of all life. I say this with the thought and hope that water may serve as an important factor in our finding a common ground to neutralize many ongoing religious conflicts. On this note, it is no coincidence in my mind that the sharing of water in the Middle East and elsewhere has impelled some warring factions to try and work out their historic differences.

In his book *Patterns in Comparative Religion*, Mircea Eliade explains how water "precedes all forms and upholds all creations." In exploring the religious use of various water rituals, Eliade tells us, "Immersion in water symbolizes a return to the pre-formal, a total regeneration, a new birth, for immersion means dissolution of forms, a reintegration into the formlessness of pre-existence; and emerging from the water is a repetition of the act of creation in which form was first expressed.... Water purifies and regenerates because it nullifies the past, and restores—even if only for a moment—the integrity of the dawn of things" (pp. 188, 195).

As I express elsewhere in this book, in almost every form of mythology, both recorded and oral, water is presented as a necessary ingredient for the creation of the world and of humankind. Recognition of this fact may be seen as the source or essence of many religious rituals involving water. For this reason, we find many gods and prophets being quoted as speaking with reverence about water. In this way, we see how water plays a vital part in many of the rituals and sacred writings evolving through time.

In the *Encyclopedia of Religion* we read that in addition to its generative powers water also possesses wisdom:

> There is a more enigmatic aspect of water: it possesses wisdom and knowledge. Water seeks the truth, we read in the Vedas. The Mesopotamian water god Ea, full of wisdom, dispenses counsel to the gods ... [and] resembles Proteus, who knows the present, the past, and the future.... But perhaps the wisdom of the water gods is a function of their age. In the Hellenic world, the wisest among them are called "the old men of the sea."

> Waters, which at one and the same time are sages and generative forces—to the point of symbolizing at times the creative power itself—are close to the word....In *Rgveda* 10.125, the ritual word itself, whose efficacy is cosmic, says of itself: "My origin is in the waters, in the ocean."

The thought of water possessing knowledge that can be transferred to humans is a foundation stone in the belief system of the Ijaw, a tribe that lives along the Niger River. These people have long held that the Niger transmits knowledge and information to their people in a psychic fashion.

Another aspect of how water can transmit its knowledge is found in the Sufi practice of "imitation." According to old Sufi teachings, there is a purpose to knowledge that is passed along by certain teachers, even though the teachers mostly imitate the words and rituals relating to water. This imitation of ancient worship was once commented on by the great Sufi Master Jalaluddin Rumi shortly before his death in 1273. One of his last messages was, "The imitator is like a canal. It does not itself drink, but may transmit water to the thirsty." Thus, we see how knowledge may be unwittingly passed along by those who are imitators of ancient water rituals, even though they lack the essential knowledge. In a way, these so-called imitators may have little or no idea of the original purpose of the water ritual they continue to practice.

There are many examples of the ritualistic use of water—John the Baptist cleansing people of their sins by baptism; Jesus Christ washing feet; Pontius Pilate washing his hands before turning Jesus over for crucifixion; a Greek Orthodox priest using an aspergillum to sprinkle holy water over the altar before beginning the ceremony; using water to exorcise demons; Japanese Kamikaze pilots using hand-painted cups to drink from a common bowl before flying off to their deaths; the blessing of wedding rings in a Catholic ceremony; the washing of hands by Moslems before reading the Koran; and the washing away of sins by millions of worshipers in the Ganges River each year, to name only a handful. The physical use and presence of water for washing, healing, sprinkling, drinking, pouring, anointing, sound effect, and worshiping is an ongoing practice in many religious ceremonies; as is the symbolic touching and blessing of oneself or of an infant with water believed to be "holy."

Today many people have lost touch with the original purpose of the ancient water rituals that remain as part of their present-day religions.

The sections below demonstrate how water flows as a common denominator through various religions and philosophies. Even though the reasons many water rituals were originally created may be forgotten, the fact is that they remain a vital part of ongoing worship. It is hoped that these examples will inspire readers to take time from their busy everyday lives to better appreciate the water rituals of their faith, as well as mention of water in their holy books. In this way, many of us may come to see the important role water plays not only in our physical life, but also in our spiritual and personal life.

Eastern Religions

The sacredness of water receives great emphasis in Hinduism. According to its teachings, the "waters of life" bring humankind the life force itself. The sacredness of water was expressed clearly in the early Hindu writings of India known as Vedas (*Veda* means "knowledge"). These Vedas were written in ancient Sanskrit and include the psalms, incantations, hymns, and formulas of worship practiced by the faithful. In the ancient Vedas water is called *matritamah* (most maternal).

An example of how revered water was and still is to the Hindu is shown in the following example of Vedic writing:

Neither Non-Being nor Being existed then.
Neither air nor the firmament above existed.
What was moving with such force? Where? Under whose care?
Was it the deep and fathomless water? (*Rgveda* 10.121.1).

Here, in my interpretation, we find that the image of water clearly represents the state of things prior to the distinction between being and nonbeing. What this ancient writing also illustrates is that water is a "force" with motion, that it has the intelligence to choose "where" it moves, and that it possesses the emotion of "caring." Finally, the last sentence tells us the water is "deep and fathomless." The understanding of what water actually is and how it creates life remains a mystery to humankind—thus on this level it is "deep and fathomless." On another level, the concept of being "deep and fathomless" can be associated with the infinite space of the universe.

In India, there is an extensive temple complex known as Rameshvaram. This complex is located near the seashore in Tamil Nadu in South India. Within this elaborate temple are twenty-two sacred bathing pools, known for their miraculous healings, which receive over ten thousand pilgrim visitors each day. The pilgrims immerse themselves in the water fully clothed, before going on to pray in another part of the temple complex. According to the explorer, environmentalist, anthropologist, and photographer Martin Gray, the Rameshvaram temple is one of the most visited and vital sacred sites of all of Asia. Gray has visited over six hundred sacred sites in forty countries around the world and will soon publish his book *Places of Peace and Power: Photographs of a Pilgrim's Journey.*

A major theme in Eastern thought is the concept that all things flow from a common or infinite source, and water is naturally seen as an image of this flowing.

In Hinduism, an example of this flowing concept can be found in the "Hymn to Goddess Earth" from the *Atharva Veda:*

> That earth which formerly was water upon the ocean of space, which the seers found out by their skillful devices; whose heart is in the highest heaven, immortal, surrounded by truth, shall bestow upon us brilliancy and strength, and place us in supreme sovereignty!
>
> The earth upon which the attendant waters jointly flow by day and night unceasingly, shall pour milk for us in rich streams, and, moreover, besprinkle us with glory!...
>
> Purified, the waters shall flow for our bodies; what flows off from us that we do deposit upon him we dislike: with purifier, O earth, do I purify myself!

Touching on the concept of yin and yang we have the book *Eastern Wisdom*, edited by C. Scott Littleton. In the section on Daoism, entitled "The Way and Its Power," yin and yang are related to water in the following fashion:

> Nature confirms the Daoist preference for the soft and hidden qualities of yin over the brightness and hardness of yang. Water in particular is considered to represent the Dao: "Nothing is softer than water, yet it is stronger than anything when it attacks hard and resistant things. Gentleness prevails over hardness; weakness conquers strength"; "The highest good is like water. Water benefits the myriad creatures without contending

with them and comes to rest where none wishes to be. Thus it is close to the Dao."

A variation on this watery theme can be seen at every Shinto shrine in Japan. Each shrine has a water bowl decorated with sacred images. Those who enter the shrine are required to dip water from the bowl and wash their hands and clean out their mouths. This ritualistic cleaning is an ancient practice of purifying the spirit and body before worship. Shintoists also believe that departed spirits return to the flowing water of rivers as a way of traveling home to the next world. On this note, it is curious that the Japanese also refer to the universe with the word *Ukiyo*, which means "the floating world," and that the ancient word *umi*, which means "ocean," is also related to the word meaning "birth." The Japanese are also known to use spring water for healing—as evidenced by their famous Moon Washing Spring.

Another form of mind, body, and spirit purification using water is, at certain times, practiced by Zen monks. These monks may sit under a chilling waterfall, sometimes for days at a time as they cleanse their beings of this world's defilements.

In India an ancient practice of Yogis is to dive into cold water, a practice believed to help induce wakefulness of the body, mind, and spirit. On a similar note, the Brahman rainmaker has to bring himself into union with water three times a day, as well as on various special occasions, to make himself an ally of the water powers.

In Tibet, Buddhist monks follow an ancient ritual of pouring water from a silver vessel to cleanse their mouths. After sucking in the water and swishing it around, they spit it out while expressing mantra. They also refill the seven water cups upon the Vajrayogini altar each day before proceeding with their chants.

In the far western region of Tibet, rising over 22,000 feet above sea level, is the holy Mount Kailash. This mountain with its sacred lake has been a site of holy veneration since before the dawn of recorded history. We know this because Buddhism, Hinduism, and Jainism have origin myths that include stories of this mountain and its holy water. The believers see the water on this mountain as the birthing place of all things and the ongoing center of the world. With its sacred water, Mount Kailash is recognized as a holy site by billions of people.

Each year thousands of pilgrims make the long and difficult journey to the peak in order to visit the highly sacred Lake Manosaravar.

The pilgrims drink of the lake's holy water fed from snowmelt, and many also take a plunge into its chilly waters. It is not surprising to learn that the word *Manosaravar* means "Lake of Consciousness and Enlightenment."

Native American Traditions

In Cuzco, Peru, the capital of the ancient Inca Empire, there was a system of "holy lines" directly relating geographical water features to human-made and natural holy places. These lines, known as *ceques,* were in evidence throughout the 2000 miles of the Empire that stretched from Colombia to Chile. In his book *Shamanism and the Mystery Lines*, Paul Devereux describes the system:

> Social or kinship groups called *ayllus* had the care of specified ceques. As the ritual year rotated through the symbolic landscape, each ayllu would be responsible for preparing the holy places along their line or lines for the appropriate observances when their time came around. The water theme was a prominent one amongst the various attributes of the ceque system, and this had genealogical and thus social correlates because the water came from underground, where the ancestors dwelt....
>
> The Cuzco ceques were multifunctional, but one of the key elements was that they related to water locations, because the Inca people "receive, by right of birth, the underground water directly from their ancestors who are believed to reside within the earth."

The Aztecs of ancient Mexico used water in purification ceremonies, as described by Arthur von Wiesenberger in H_2O: *The Guide to Quality Bottled Water:* "Water has also been used as a symbol for spiritual cleansing in purification ceremonies. Aztec midwives washed infants with this prayer: 'May this water purify and whiten thy heart: may it wash away all that is evil.'" The Aztec goddess representing the element water was named Chalchiuhcueye.

Along with the civilizations of the Inca and the Aztec located in present-day Latin America, there was also the Mayan. The Mayans apparently focused their religious worship on the rain god named Chac.

Native North Americans had their rain dances and sweat lodges. The sweat lodges, still very much in use today, are believed to purify one's body and spirit while also helping to induce visions and spirit quests. Native Americans to this day revere rivers, lakes, and oceans as though they were living entities with spiritual powers.

This reverence for water can also be associated with some of the most striking Native American constructions in North America. These constructions are massive serpentine terraglyphs found at the headwaters of the Little Arkansas River. As described by Arthur Versluis in *Sacred Earth, The Spiritual Landscape of Native America,* these serpentine figures are large engravings etched in the soils of an elevated land area. From the top of the high bluff where a serpentine terraglyph still exists, a person can see miles and miles of the massive watershed spread out below.

The metaphysical researcher Clark Millam spent a considerable amount of time in the Little Arkansas River area investigating the mysteries of these earthly snakelike intaglios (engravings). In Millam's opinion, the Native Americans of this region created these figures, which are sometimes two hundred feet long, because

> the intaglio is an early version of the "Giant Horned Serpent, Antlered Serpent, or Water Monster" so common in historic Native American beliefs. Its location on the southeastern margins of the headwaters indicates a "guardian" role for the source of life—water.... [The serpent] signified...through its placement and orientation, the natural and cyclical process of death, rebirth, and the regenerative power of life.... Cross-culturally, the serpent represents... "disruption, disharmony, and dissolution," and continual life renewal through annual shedding of its skin and hibernation. It is often associated with earth openings and springs and frequently viewed as the "Chief of the Under (water) World," the "guardian of life-bestowing substances."

In his book, Versluis corroborates Millam's comments by writing, "The serpentine form in Native American traditions, as in Hindu, Buddhist, and other religious traditions, is identified with water. Indeed, in Buddhist tradition, as in that of Native Americans, there are said to be serpentine creatures in springs, rivers, and bodies of water."

From the small sampling above, we have an idea of how Native Americans respected water on many levels. And, as stated earlier, these beliefs by Native Americans reflect a reverence toward water as an entity to be respected on many levels. Moving onward, let us

take a look across the ocean at another belief system and its reverence
of water.

Islam

Today Islam is the fastest growing and one of the most influential
religions in the world. One who believes in and practices Islam is
called a "Muslim," which means "one who submits." To the Muslim,
there is only the will of Allah, which influences all of life, be it family,
politics, business, or faith.

Islam began in the seventh century A.D. It was then that Islam was
first proclaimed in the Arabian Desert by the prophet Mohammed. As
such, it is one of the youngest of humankind's great religions. Today
it is estimated that about 1 billion people worldwide practice Islam.

The sacred book of the Islamic religion is the Koran. The Koran is
accepted by Muslims to be the infallible Word of Allah as revealed to
the prophet Mohammed by the Archangel Gabriel. The Koran was
written nearly 1400 years ago, and to this day provides the rules
for moral and social conduct fundamental to the Islamic way of life.
The Koran also expresses the oneness of all things with God and
emphasizes divine mercy and forgiveness.

In my mind, Mohammed was a realist as well as a visionary when
he established water rights for his followers. He envisioned water as
an object of religious charity and declared that free access to water
was the right of every Muslim community. The statement in the Holy
Koran that "No one can refuse surplus water without sinning against
Allah and against Man" laid the foundation of a body of social traditions and regulations governing the ownership, use, and protection
of water.

One of the supreme experiences of any Muslim is to visit Mecca
and to touch its Shrine of the Black Stone, the place where the Prophet
and his companions walked, toward which hundreds of millions of
Muslim souls around the world daily turn five times in prayer. Overlooking Mecca is Mount Arafat, where Mohammed gave his last
sermon.

One aspect of Mecca's Shrine of the Black Stone is the granite
building from which Mohammed cast out the pagan idols of the
pre-Islamic Arabs. Together, the Black Stone and the granite building to which it is attached at a corner make up the cubical temple
called the Kaaba. Also near the Black Stone is a cupola covering the

sacred well Zemzem, which reputedly nourished Hagar, mother of Ishmael, when she was wandering in the wilderness long ago. As part of the sacred ritual of walking seven times counterclockwise around the Black Stone, pilgrims drink the miraculous well water of Zemzem. The water is believed to be most holy, and many pilgrims take some of it with them to share with others upon their return home.

As with other religions, Muslims hold a strong belief in life after death. In the writings of the Koran (or Qur'an, "The Recital"), it is the holy presence of water in life after death that accentuates much of the material.

The Koran was revealed in Arabic. It is a matter of faith in Islam that this book is of Divine origin, and therefore any translation is often viewed in certain Islamic circles with skepticism. In past times, it was prohibited to render the Koran in any other language, since any translation was thought to be lacking in the message as presented in the Arabic tongue. With this in mind, I refer to the translation offered by the eminent Koran scholar N. J. Dawood in the edition published in 1990 with parallel Arabic text. I am grateful to Mr. Dawood for his kind permission to quote.

For the uninitiated person reading the Koran, it should be noted that God speaks in the first person plural, which often changes to the first person singular or the third person singular in the course of the same sentence. No matter what language the Koran is read in, one thing is obvious: heaven abounds in running rivers and streams of cool, crystal water. The following words are quoted from the Koran:

> When Moses requested water for his people We said to him: 'Strike the Rock with your staff.' Thereupon twelve springs gushed from the Rock, and each tribe knew their drinking place. We said: 'Eat and drink of that which God has provided and do not foul the land with evil.'

> But those that give away their wealth from a desire to please God and to reassure their own souls are like a garden on a hillside: if a shower falls upon it, it yields up twice its normal produce; and if no rain falls, it is watered by the dew. God takes cognizance of all your actions.

> Would any one of you, being a man well-advanced in age with helpless children to support, wish to have his garden—a garden planted with palm trees, vines and all manner of fruits,

and watered by running streams—blasted and consumed by a fiery whirlwind?

Thus God makes plain to you His revelations, so that you may give thought.

Such are the bounds set by God. He that obeys God and His apostle shall dwell forever in gardens watered by running streams. That is the supreme triumph. But he that defies God and His apostle and transgresses His bounds, shall be cast into a Fire wherein he will abide forever. A shameful punishment awaits him.

As for those that have faith and do good works, we shall admit them to gardens watered by running streams, and there they shall abide forever. Such is God's true promise: and who has a truer word than God?

He sends down abundant water from the sky for you and bestows upon you wealth and children. He has provided you with gardens and with running brooks. Why do you deny the greatness of God when He has made you in gradual stages? Can you not see how He created the seven heavens one above the other, placing in them the moon for a light and the sun for a lantern? God has brought you forth from the earth like a plant, and to the earth He will restore you. Then He will bring you back afresh. God has made the earth a vast expanse for you, so that you may roam its spacious paths.

With the above in mind, can there be any doubt about the writings of the Koran expressing a reverence for water in this life as well as the afterlife? Let us now take a look at the role water plays in the holy books of some other great religions.

Judaism and Christianity

One of the greatest influences on Western thinking is the Hebrew creation story as expressed in the Book of Genesis. Without a doubt, the following words sound familiar and resonate as true within many people:

In the beginning
God created the heaven and the earth.
And the earth was without form, and void;
and darkness was upon the face of the deep.
And the spirit of God moved upon the face of the waters.

Even though the date the Book of Genesis was written remains a mystery to us, the creation of the world by a god finds many believers throughout ancient and modern history. What can be found in the writings of the Bible is that the Creator of the Savior of humankind is never mentioned by name.

In Genesis 2:10 (the Ephraim Speiser translation), it is written, "A river rises in Eden to water the garden; outside it forms four separate branch streams. The name of the first is Pishon; it is the one that winds through the whole land of Havilah."

Today it is generally recognized that many influences of earlier writings inspired the writers of the Bible. This account of creation indicates a strong Mesopotamian influence, especially in the words about the original watery chaos: "And the earth was without form and void; and darkness was upon the face of the deep." That the story line of Genesis is similar to that of the epic Gilgamesh poem of early Sumerian origin is widely accepted, as discussed in the last chapter, and Sumerian loanwords are in evidence, such as the term "Eden," which in Sumerian meant a geographical location such as a plain or steppe, or the word for "flow," which represented an underground swell of water from below. This passage tells us that there was an underground spring that flowed to the surface in Eden to water the garden of life; giving us another example of water energy rising from below to create a holy place on the surface. And, it is at points where spring water emerges that we historically find many healing shrines and places of worship around the world.

In Genesis 7:11, the Hebrew term *Mayanot Tehom Raba* is translated as "the fountains of the great deep," which burst forth at the same time that the "windows of heaven" were opened at the beginning of Noah's flood. The Hebrew word for "deep" is *tehom*, which is derived from the word *Tiamat*, representing an ancient goddess of the heavenly waters and the waters of the deep.

In later times, the Hebrew term *Tehom Raba* lost its connection to the goddess Tiamat, but remained in use to represent a body of water. What I find curious about some ancient terms referring to water flowing from the ground is that they imply that the water flows from the eyes of the goddess Tiamat. The thought that the eyes of Tiamat are the source of spring water naturally figures into recorded Middle Eastern beliefs that the Tigris and Euphrates Rivers also came from the eyes of Tiamat. This makes me wonder, since in reality we find the Tigris and Euphrates Rivers emerging from large springs in the foothills of the Zagros Mountains along the border of Iraq, Iran, and Turkey.

The fact that all living beings that see the physical world have eyes that require a constant bathing of water is something most people take for granted. That our eyes were created so we may see the created world revealed to us by light is rarely given much thought. So, too, is little thought given to the fact that our eyes cry tears when we are emotionally moved. The flow of water from our eyes is a form of emotional release of which we have little understanding. Why our eyes were created and constantly washed by water is something we understand as a "given" on a functional basis. However, we have no idea about why the creating Power selected water that is akin to seawater to wash our eyes. Why not air, oil, or some kind of tree sap? From what we understand of the physical principles that rule our bodily health and living reality, water in our eyes makes sense because it has always been a part of our thoughts from the very beginning.

The close relationship of water with eyes bestowing the gift of sight is something that seems to come up time and time again in ancient writings. There appears to be a natural relationship between water, seeing with the eyes, and light. In many ways, these ancient beliefs and early words were carried over into biblical writings. If we believe the thought that water is the Creator and Knower of all things, then it naturally flows that the familiar phrase "God sees and knows all things" makes sense, especially, when we find that some of the earliest writings of humankind associate water with eyes and the ability to "see."

In *Mystical Christianity: A Psychological Commentary on the Gospel of John*, John Sanford provides the following analysis about the biblical concept of living water:

> [In the words of Jesus]
> They have abandoned me,
> the fountain of living water,

> and dug water-tanks for themselves,
> cracked water tanks
> that hold no water (Jer. 2:13, NJB).

There is a reality within us that we can directly experience and that is analogous to the spring of water of which Sanford says Jesus is speaking. We noted earlier that Etty Hillesum knew of this and spoke of "a deep well inside me, and in it dwells God." It is this source of life within us, for instance, from which our dreams well up, an unending source of life from and for our souls.

The early church psychologist-theologians did not hesitate to identify this water with Christ, whom they termed "the fountain of life." (This and the following quotations are from Clement of Alexandria's *Discourse on the Holy Theophany*, Part 2.) Speaking in his inimitable mystical, psychological way, Clement of Alexandria writes of water that not only is it the natural source of all life, so that "without the element of water, none of the present order of things can subsist," it is also a spiritual element without which the life of the soul cannot exist. In fact, this water is none other than "Christ, the maker of all," who came down as the rain and was known as a spring (John 4:14), diffused himself as a river (John 7:38), and was baptized in the Jordan. Christ is the "boundless River that makes glad the city of God..." (Ps. 46:4), the illimitable Spring that bears life to all men and has no end, who is present everywhere and absent nowhere, who is incomprehensible to angels and invisible to human beings. He concludes with words that could well have been spoken to the Samaritan woman: "When you bear these things, beloved, take them not as if spoken literally, but accept them as presented in a figure."

This is the healing water that comes up within, heals the weary ego, and replenishes the soul. This water was also known to the Greeks, who built their healing shrines, homes of the god of healing, Asclepius, over or near sources of water, particularly springs and running streams, shrines that were taken over by the church and rededicated to various healing saints when Christianity replaced paganism in the Graeco-Roman world. It is a water that was also known to the Greek playwright Sophocles. In his play *Oedipus at Colonus*, the stricken Oedipus asks the Greek chorus how to make atonement to the deities he has offended. They answer him:

> Make a libation first of water fetched
> With undefiled hands from living spring.

The water, then, of which Jesus speaks has the following characteristics: First, it is a special water, not earthly water, but spiritual water. As such it is, as noted, often represented in our dreams, sometimes appearing as a water that is of unusual clarity. One man, for instance, dreamt of a service of Holy Communion in which he participated with a companion: "We have regular communion wafers that we dip into some incredibly clear water from a tiny mountain stream. This water is so clear that it is most marvelous." Another man dreams of arriving in a certain city and coming upon a remarkable body of water: "It might be part of the sea, or maybe it is a river that goes through the city. What makes the water so amazing is its remarkable clarity, which gives it a most unusual quality. It might also be salt water, which, combined with the clarity, adds to its unusual and inviting quality."

Second, we are told that Christ is the source of the water. This is the water that he will give us, and is to be contrasted with the ordinary water that one receives from a well or municipal water supply. As we noted, Clement of Alexandria is of the opinion that Christ not only gives the water but is, in a mystical way, the water itself.

Third, we are told that this water will be like a spring of water welling up from within ourselves; as such, no one can ever take this water away from us.

From the above words, we can see what an esoteric and mystical document the Gospel of John actually is, and that has to do with the mysterious entity of water. In many ways, the Gospel of John and the writings of Clement of Alexandria serve as wonderful sources for exploring the many religious and spiritual aspects of water and its meaning to humankind.

Of course, the above references to water are but a mere fraction of water-related expressions that occur in the Bible. Any student of the Bible will find an abundance of passages dealing with water in all its various manifestations. A study of these would be a challenge unto itself. As an example, let us now take a brief look at a key concept of the Bible and religious writings.

Baptism with Water

The ritual of using water for the spiritual cleansing and rebirth of a person is a mysterious and ancient custom. The widely accepted belief that water plays a significant role in the cleansing of sins and evil spirits from the presence of humans is something that remains mysteriously with us.

In his book *A Treatise of the Compendium*, the Reverend G. H. Kersten teaches about Holy Baptism with a series of questions and answers numbered 53 to 56, with each question and answer followed by some commentary. Presented below are two of the questions with answers and a selection of material that follows each:

Qu. 53: *Which is the outward sign in Baptism?*

Answer: The water, with which we are baptized in the name of the Father, and of the Son, and of the Holy Ghost.

What does the water signify?

The water represents the cleansing by Christ's blood. . . . It is with this that we cleanse our body, and in baptism it signifies the blood of Christ that cleanses from sin.

In this manner did John baptize in Jordan, and thus also was the eunuch baptized in the water, which was along the way that goes down unto Gaza (Acts 8:36–39).

In baptism, the water is administered either by immersion or sprinkling. . . . In the Old Testament, therefore, sprinkling was used as well as immersion in the ceremonial cleansing. Moses sprinkled the blood of the covenant upon the people (Ex. 24:8). In Ezek. 36:25, the Lord says, "I will sprinkle clean water upon you"; and Paul speaks in Heb. 12:24 of "the blood of sprinkling."

Now the *Compendium* asks about the significance of Baptism.

Qu. 54: *What doth that signify and seal?*

Answer: The washing away of sins by the blood and Spirit of Jesus Christ.

But why then does Ananias say to Paul, "Be baptized and wash away thy sins" (Acts 22:16), and how then can baptism, in Titus

3:5, be called, "the washing of regeneration," if the water does not cleanse and regenerate?

That is very simple, because the places mentioned speak not only of the sign, but of the thing signified; not of the water, but of the baptism of the Spirit, which regenerates and assures of the cleansing of sin by the blood of Christ.

The above two questions with answers and commentary help to provide a basic view of the practice of baptism. From the second century forward, the value of the baptismal act was widely recognized and practiced in Christianity. Even though there are many meanings and beliefs on the ritual of baptism as practiced by Catholics, Protestants, and many others, water in some form is always seen as the common denominator for the cleansing of the body and regeneration of the spirit.

The relationship of Moses to water harks back to his earliest beginnings. Besides his sprinkling of the covenant upon the people, as depicted in the commentary above, we learn that the name *Moses* means "the water-drawer." Also not to be overlooked is Moses' origin from the Nile River. Exodus 2:1–10 tell us that as a baby, he was discovered floating in a basket by the Pharaoh's daughter. The word *tebah,* used in the Old Testament for the basket carrying Moses, is also the same word used to describe Noah's ark.

Besides Moses, there are other great people who had their origin in water. The god Akki, "the water carrier," rescued Sargon, the founder of Babylon, from water. Karna, the icon of an early Indian epic, was found floating in the Ganges. And, just as there are many historic figures having their origins in water, many also find their way through various forms of water baptism.

The early "mystery" religions (Eleusinian, Orphic, Mithraic, Egyptian, Syrian) required baptism for the washing away of evil in preparation for the rites of communion with the god whose mastery of death assured immortality. These baptisms sometimes symbolized the dying of the old life and rising again to the new. A similar idea underlies the baptism by immersion that is part of the initiation of proselytes to Judaism.

After centuries of widespread disuse, the Roman Catholic religion is now bringing back the Rite of Christian Initiation for Adults. This rite takes place the night before Easter Sunday. Following a sequence of ceremonies embellished with prayer, song, incense, and candlelight, the white-robed initiate kneels in a shallow pool of water and, in the presence of other believers, is fully immersed for baptism.

Of course, the installation of a water facility to allow for such baptisms can be a challenge. According to a *New York Times* article on March 23, 1997, "The growing popularity of the initiation rite has wrought physical changes in individual churches, many of which are installing shallow pools of granite, marble or fiberglass for dramatic full-immersion baptisms. At Our Lady of Good Counsel Church in Staten Island, for example, portions of four rows of pews were removed last year to make room for such a pool, in the center of the church." Other churches have created a see-through glass or Plexiglas tub beneath the elevated altar in front of the church. For normal ceremonies and mass, the altar is covered with linen and the tub cannot be seen. On the night of initiation, the linens and the top of the altar are removed, and the initiates step into the tub one by one for full immersion baptism.

In a way, baptism with water can be seen as a washing away of sins as well as the renewal or rebirth of a person on many levels. Because of this, it does not take too much of a leap in faith to see how water washes away the sins (pollution) of humankind from the environment. At the same time, I believe it is palpably clear in nature how water serves as a source of renewal and rebirth. From phenomena such as the hydrologic cycle, the cosmic connection of the tides, and the flow of water through all living things—there exists a holy connection of water through all things.

Religions and the Environmental Movement

I have already mentioned the repetitive biblical references to "living water." Common sense, science, and religion inform us that it is living water that truly brings life to all things—both physiologically and spiritually. And, this water cannot be water that has been contaminated by pollution; rather it is water that is teeming with life, that contains the pulse of electrical energy created by flowing vortices that imparts the life force into all things. Whether it is water we catch fish in or water that we drink from the earth, it is the partaking of "living water" that provides good health to all things that live. In drinking water from a pure mountain stream or from an unpolluted source from beneath the ground, we truly imbibe in the remarkable source of life.

Somewhere, somehow, along humankind's evolution, there appears to have been a departure of respect for upholding various religious beliefs associated with water. As people stopped respecting and caring about the common subject of water, perhaps, too, they also began losing their shared purpose and vision of the journey through life.

Thus we find today the manifestation of many conflicts, including religious conflicts, which are destroying the living world. This departure from common reverence and respect for water may also be associated with disrespect for the entity of life itself. The needless destruction of the living world "just because it is there" is an indication of how lost the human race has become. Besides the destruction of forests and other groupings of plant life, there is the even more frightening and ruthless slaughter of animals and other humans. The needless capturing and killing of wildlife for mere entertainment or sport is a sad statement unto itself.

Certainly the killing and eating of an animal by people who require it to survive can be understood. The same goes for killing an animal in self-defense—which is extremely rare since most animals will wisely run and hide from the presence of a human. Perhaps it may be wise for humankind to recall its early stages of survival when other life forms were actually looked upon as living beings that were placed here to help us survive.

Without respect for water, there cannot be respect for the forms of life it creates. Without respect for life, I believe the human race will not survive to evolve to its fullest potential. It is as simple and as complex as that. In time, we may learn that it is in the sharing of common beliefs about water that hope for all life on Earth springs.

The writings of many religions have carried forth through time the message that there is a sacred nature to all of creation. I believe the environmental movement is now flowing as a spring of sorts from these writings. In fact, the environmental movement is finding considerable support from various religions. In great part, this support is legitimized by the writings found in the holy books of various faiths.

This religious awakening is in part the outgrowth of the Joint Appeal by Religion and Science for the Environment. This group was set up after a meeting of over fifty religious leaders and fifty Nobel laureates and other scientists in Washington, D.C., in May 1992. Working together with a spectrum of political representatives, this organization started the work to awaken as many people as possible to begin taking action to save the Earth's environment.

The potential for the religious movement to preserve our environment and reawaken respect for water is awesome. One can get an idea of the millions of people an environmental/religious coalition can reach from a list compiled by the national Religious Partnership for the Environment in New York. This list contains hundreds of participating congregations in *A Directory of Environmental Activities and Resources in the North American Religious Community.*

The role of religion in saving our environment is likely to grow. Hopefully, this movement will lead most of the religions of the world to work toward a common purpose of living in harmony with life on Earth. Of course, the common denominator shared by all these religions is their ritualistic use of water as well as the writings of their holy books referring to this divine substance.

Part III

CRISIS

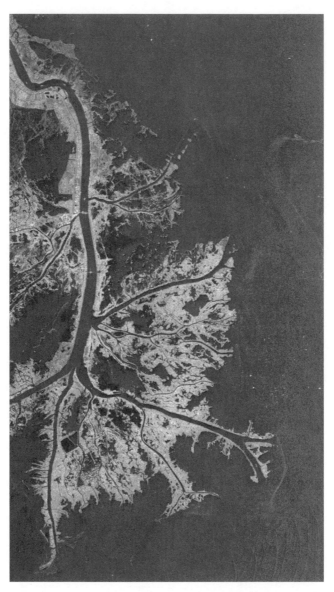

Radar image of the Mississippi River Delta along Louisiana's Gulf of Mexico. This image reveals a physical formation created by water's energy similar to the shape of a tree trunk with branches, a plant with stems, the veins of a leaf, or an animal's blood circulation system with a main artery and smaller veins. (Photo: NASA).

NINE

Dead Fish

ONE SPRING MORNING, I was riding my motorcycle to a morning college class, enjoying the open air. As I was crossing a bridge over the Whippany River, like most people, I couldn't help but look down at the flowing water below. That's when I saw something horrible—hundreds of dead fish floating belly up. Obviously something was amiss.

Shifting the motorcycle into low gear, I pulled off the road on the other side of the bridge. After a short hike, I slid down an embankment to the river's edge. Something looked very wrong. The river water was brown and muddy, and its currents seemed sluggish. I got a sense from the water and the air and light bouncing off of it that something was actually stealing the life force out of the river.

At the time, I was twenty years old and working my way through college. I was also coming close to being late for my classes. I thought to myself, "Surely something like this is being looked into." However, my inner voice, which I was just beginning to appreciate, guided me to look further. "Take a short hike and see what you see," said the voice.

After about a half mile of trudging upstream through mud, trees, and prickly briars, there was still no end to the floating dead fish. Nor was there yet any sign of what killed them. By then, sweat from my forehead was burning my eyes, and the rising Sun and humidity forced me to stop for a moment. In order to continue, some equipment adjustments were necessary. Off came my Asbury Park Lifeguard jacket and the neckerchief tied around my neck. For a fraction of a second, I had an impulse to dip the neckerchief into the cool water before wiping my face.

The hour was now such that I knew I was going to miss my morning classes. In a way, I was reminded of my childhood, when my brother Lefty and I would cut grade school to spend the day fishing and exploring. "Thank goodness I wore my boots," I said as I continued hiking up the river.

After about another mile, I came across a huge industrial complex. Smoke was billowing out of tall smokestacks and steaming effluent was flowing into the river from large discharge pipes. "Surely," I thought to myself, "this is what is killing the fish." To make matters worse, the air was so putrid and acidic that it made me feel like puking.

Continuing along the riverbank, I hiked through the noisy complex and its buildings located on both sides of the river. About one hundred yards upstream of the industrial discharge pipes, I could still see dead fish floating in the river. I was now fully committed to following the trail and finding out what was killing the fish.

The Sun was rising higher in the sky, making it feel like a hot summer's day. Unbuttoning my shirt, I continued hiking up the river. Along the way, the movement of various birds, rabbits, mice, or hawks would grab my attention, and I tried to observe every detail. I was beginning to feel like Sherlock Holmes on a quest to unravel a murder mystery. Something was killing those fish, and I wanted to find out what and why.

After about two more miles, I could see the river was muddier than ever. "What is making the river so muddy?" I wondered. Rounding a nearby wooded bend, I found the answer. There, in a cleared opening, was an assortment of heavy equipment—bulldozers, backhoes, dump trucks, and some huge earthmoving rigs. The rigs were sitting idle while their operators ate lunch. It almost looked as if the men had gotten carried away at creating a huge picnic spot for themselves. There they were, music playing as they sat basking in the sun or tucked away in the shade of their pickups.

Not wanting to give myself away, I climbed a sturdy oak tree to capture a bird's view. Much to my surprise, these men were in the process of literally changing the course of the river for a new highway. A large section of forestland had been leveled and excavated to create a new channel for the river. Apparently the old riverbed had been recently dammed to divert the water into the new channel. Like a dying body, the old section of the riverbed lay partially filled with stagnating water.

I daydreamed about all the life forms dying from this act. Not only the obvious dead fish, but all the other life forms in and out of the water that had established, over thousands of years, an interdependence with each other and the waterway.

Since I was born and raised in the general area, I knew that these river valleys were historically fertile with wildlife and vegetation, so much so that evidence of large Native American encampments has been discovered in many places. Along with plenty of fish to eat, there would also have been deer, beaver, rabbit, muskrat, woodcock, raccoon, bear, fox, weasel, squirrel, mink, hawks, owls, and many other life forms, including many herbs, berries, nuts, and roots.

The sound of roaring diesel engines awoke me from my reverie. In disbelief, I watched as the men drove their heavy machines back and forth through the new river channel, stirring up the unstable sediments below and along its banks. "This is the kill zone!" I said to myself. Climbing down from the tree, I circled around the construction crews and renewed my contact with the river. I was not surprised to find no dead fish floating above the construction site.

With common sense and knowledge taught to me while fishing with my father, I theorized about how the fish were killed. For thousands of years, fish born and raised in this river were nurtured by clean, cool, running water. Over time, an entire food chain evolved in and along the river. Insects, frogs, deer, fish, and many other life forms made up an interconnected network. The health of all these interconnected life forms centered on the health of their river.

When I was a boy, my father told me on our fly-fishing expeditions about how he recognized a good place to fish. "Fish like to hang out along stream banks where there are overhanging trees and bushes," he would say. "Besides being a place where they find insects, there is also more oxygen in the cool shaded water. And, if you look closely, you'll see how the water kind of circulates in a lazy circle in some of those places. All these things make it a nice place for the fish to hang out."

My "kill zone" theory went like this: It was springtime, and the fish were spawning and very sensitive to any change in the water they lived in. When the old river channel was dammed, they were suddenly forced to swim through the new channel. This new channel, in my mind, was the initiating shock or kill zone. This killing shock was created by several factors. First, the silt-filled water could clog the gills of the fish and cut off their oxygen supply. Also, since the riverbank was no longer covered with overhanging vegetation and the floating mud sediments captured the Sun's heat, the water itself would become warmer than usual. This warmer water could shock the fish while also providing less oxygen. Also, the warmer water would cause the heart rate of the fish to increase—therefore calling for more oxygen.

As any fisherman knows, any and all of these factors could result in the death of fish, especially trout, which are extremely sensitive to change.

By the time I arrived on campus, I had already missed my classes for the day and was late for lacrosse practice. Already, I was paying the price for my little Sherlock Holmes adventure. That evening, while doing homework and calling friends to get copies of the class notes I had missed, my mind kept returning to the smells and sights of the muddy river and the dying fish.

The next day, as usual, was filled with a heavy class load, homework, and lacrosse practice, allowing little time to think of dead fish. While studying late that night, I got a case of the munchies. So, off I went on my motorcycle to the local Seven-Eleven. While I was waiting in line to buy my armload of junk food, my eye caught the front-page news of Morris County's *Daily Record*. There, under a bold headline, was a story about all the dead fish collecting behind a dam located in a town several miles downstream from the bridge I crossed on my motorcycle. The story repeated several times that the cause of the fish kill was a mystery to the local board of health, and that the state's Department of Environmental Protection was sending a water expert to investigate that very day.

I couldn't wait to read the next day's newspaper. "Surely," I thought, "they will see what I saw and come to the same or a similar theory. Besides, the state's water expert can test the water for oxygen." To my disbelief, the next day's newspaper quoted the state's water expert as saying that he too was completely bewildered about what was causing the fish to die. By now, the small town with the dam was being overwhelmed with the stink of dead fish. The bellies of the dead fish were bursting open from the hot sun and, to make matters worse, rats were coming out of sewers and other places to feast on the bloody mess.

With the newspaper spread out on my kitchen table, I reached for the phone and called the news reporter who wrote the story, Helene Kingsland.

At first, Helene found it difficult to believe that some college student would telephone her out of the blue and claim to know the cause of the fish kill. I guess she thought it was one of those prank calls. I remember her asking me, "What makes you so sure that you know what killed the fish when the water experts who do this for a living don't know the answer?" I told her the story about riding my motorcycle over the bridge and my hike up the river. For some reason or other, she began to believe in me. "Can you take me on a hike to the same place tomorrow?" Helene asked.

After the news story and photographs broke with my homegrown theory, my telephone got very busy for a couple of days. By the time all was said and done, the local health agent and the state water expert ended up being very embarrassed.

Building on my initiation into the way the system worked, I began expanding on my knowledge of waterways and the legal system. Also, along the way, the media exposure grew. For instance, besides national television and radio, there was continuous reporting by Gordon Bishop, the prize-winning environmental editor of New Jersey's largest newspaper, the *Newark Star-Ledger*. Before too long, there was so much work that I enlisted the assistance of a college friend named Paul Lander. For a couple of years we worked as team, going up and down various rivers in my father's small fishing boat, looking for sources of pollution.

This fateful beginning led me to many other waterway adventures and pollution investigations. My alma mater, Fairleigh Dickinson University in Madison, New Jersey, was most supportive in allowing college credits for my extracurricular water activities, and the Conservation Law Foundation gave me a grant to research and learn about new water laws. Just imagine the fun I had as a college student! There I was going up and down rivers in a boat on beautiful days, taking photographs and water samples, and receiving college grant monies and credits for being outside communing with nature.

Much water has flowed under the bridge since my college days. Since then, my travels in this and other countries have taught me much about the history of water pollution. The more I learn, the more I realize that we, as a living group of beings, can actually be taught through our interactions with water. As the former owner/operator of a state-certified water-testing laboratory on Martha's Vineyard for over fourteen years, and the founder of an environmental research institute, I continue to learn about water and the impacts of pollution.

Along this trail of life, I have seen pollution rear its ugly head in various manifestations. Each time I witness pollution of any kind or scale, I ask, "Is this really necessary? Do we really need these pollutants to survive? What are the trade-offs? How much life is sacrificed in the name of this pollution? Is there a better way?"

The one thing I have come to know without doubt is that polluting our planet's water is the same as poisoning the blood in our bodies.

TEN

A Brief History of Water Pollution

Due regard for the health of the inhabitants not only means that their place of abode should be in healthy locality and should have a healthy exposure: it also means that they should have the use of good water. This is a matter which ought not to be treated lightly. The elements we use most and oftenest for the support of our bodies contribute most to their health; and water and air have both an effect of this nature. It should therefore be laid down, in all prudently conducted states, that if all the streams are not equally wholesome, and the supply of wholesome streams is inadequate, the drinking water ought to be separated from the water used for other purposes.

—ARISTOTLE

IF HUMANKIND HAD FOLLOWED Aristotle's advice from over 2300 years ago, think of the world we would be enjoying today!

Certainly, common sense tells us "the elements we use most and oftenest for the support of our bodies contribute most to their health." In order to stay alive, we must take in a certain amount of water and air (which contains water vapor) each day. If our bodies take in polluted water and air each day, what does common sense tell us the consequences will be?

It is almost a joke to see some modern-day medical doctors walking around scratching their heads and wondering where some of humankind's diseases are coming from. The grossly polluted water and air found in many of the world's major urban centers continuously flow through the bodies of every person living and working there. With over 70,000 human-made chemicals in daily use, and with an estimated 1000 new chemicals being developed each year, we are living today in a chemical bath of our own creation—a bath that saturates our planet's air and surface waters above and below ground. A recent study by the Clean Water Network reports that one-third of our

129

rivers, one-half of our estuaries, and more than one-half of our lakes are not fit for fishing and swimming—never mind drinking.

According to the Center for Disease Control, every year an estimated 120 million Americans drink tap water contaminated with waterborne diseases and known cancer-causing chemicals. In 1993, after undertaking one of the most comprehensive water studies ever conducted, the Natural Resources Defense Council found that each year more than 900,000 people in the United States become ill, and as many as 900 die from waterborne diseases. On a similar note, the United States Environmental Protection Agency (EPA) lists over 700 toxic chemicals that may be found in tap water. Since 1976 the EPA has monitored the amount of toxins in the fat tissue of Americans; on a consistent basis thirteen highly toxic compounds are found in 100 percent of all samples taken. The EPA continues to carry out this study each year.

The EPA and other governmental agencies state that they only permit chemical levels that are considered "safe" in our public water supplies. Such regulatory thinking leaves much to be desired. I find it curious that at every urban EPA office I have visited there is always bottled water available for drinking. The fact that our governments cannot adequately protect everyone who drinks publicly supplied water is one major reason that bottled water and in-home water filters have become such booming businesses. The residential water-treatment market alone is expected to exceed $3.5 billion in 2001.

Dwarfing this $3.5 billion figure is the $460 billion estimated by the Water Infrastructure Network as necessary to repair and maintain public drinking-water systems throughout the U.S. over the next twenty years. As reported on the front page of *Water World,* April 2001 (www.waterworld.com), this $460 billion will be needed "to upgrade and replace aging drinking water treatment facilities and distribution systems and also comply with EPA rules."

Recently, some of my friends were discussing the threat of human-made chemicals to life. During the conversation, I heard comments that reflect a misunderstanding of nature's way. One comment especially seemed to serve the ongoing prolific use of human-made chemicals. "How can chemicals be bad? The entire world is filled with chemicals found in nature," was one statement I clearly remember.

This statement is a half-truth.

Yes, the world is filled with chemicals that occur naturally in our environment. However, the natural world contains chemicals that have been filtered and tested for over three billion years as the world of life evolved. Through the seemingly intelligent efforts of water and its living organisms, many harmful chemicals not conducive to life have been washed from the atmosphere and buried beneath water-washed sediment, soils, and vegetation. With these nasty chemicals safely removed from the Earth's surface, life has evolved and prospered.

All life forms contain a flow of water in which chemical reactions take place. The digestion of food can be likened to a mass of chemicals reacting with one another in a watery soup. Living things are made up of thousands of different organic compounds. Organic compounds are basically combinations of chemicals made by living organisms. When the chemistry of a human-made product is said to be biodegradable, it means that *the product can be easily reduced by chemicals occurring naturally in the living world.*

Over the billions of years that life has evolved on Earth, it has more or less time-tested the chemicals that are helpful or harmful to its survival. This is why the chemistry of life is such that it is capable of breaking down, in a relatively brief time, every organic substance and waste product produced by life. In this fashion, life itself creates only those substances that can be broken down to nourish other life forms.

Humans are now deviating from evolution by bringing forth, through our industries, sciences, and technologies, new chemicals that living systems on the planet cannot live with or easily break down. Chemicals mined from beneath the Earth's surface and chemicals created in laboratories are often alien to the living environment. When they are introduced to the water world of life, life systems cannot cope with them and end up mutating, becoming unhealthy, or dying.

When human-made synthetic chemical compounds are used in the manufacture of detergents, insecticides, herbicides, and consumer products such as plastics, nature does not possess the chemistry to break them down; these types of substances are considered as nonbiodegradable. The evidence of nonbiodegradable plastic can be seen along our coastal shores, floating in our oceans, in landfills—everywhere. And just as plastics accumulate on the planet's surface, nonbiodegradable chemicals accumulate in water, soils, and the bodies of living organisms.

It is with this in mind that Theo Colborn and his coauthors of

Our Stolen Future suggest it may be necessary in the interests of life on Earth to stop the manufacturing of synthetic chemicals altogether. The authors of this timely book seemingly provide us with an update of Rachel Carson's *Silent Spring*, published in 1962. Besides informing us that it may be our human-made chemical bath that is causing worldwide reproductive problems, it also tells us that the United States alone created over 435 billion pounds of synthetic chemicals in 1992. According to the November 1993 special edition of *National Geographic* on water, "One billion pounds of weed and bug killers are used throughout the United States each year."

Certain chemicals are now believed to contribute in the reduction of sperm counts. Since World War II, the sperm count of men in industrialized countries has dropped nearly 50 percent. Besides impacting sperm, the chemical revolution of the 1940s may also be contributing to the soaring rate of other human reproductive ills such as breast, testicular, and prostate cancers. Such, too, is the case of degenerative diseases such as heart and liver disease.

In the September 1996 issue of *Discover*, a research article entitled "Hormone Hell" by Catherine Dold educates us about the impact of these chemicals on reproductive organs. Dold quotes Linda Birnbaum, director of experimental toxicology at the Environmental Protection Agency, as saying, "We have no evidence that there are any populations that don't have these chemicals—fish, wildlife, or people." The chemicals Ms. Birnbaum is specifically referring to are human-made chemicals that mimic hormones. This is of particular concern because hormones travel throughout the human body and tell cells what to do and when. Dold also discusses how hormones affect the development of the fetus:

> In the fetus, however, hormones do more than orchestrate activity. They perform complex developmental tasks, tasks that require precise dosage and exquisite timing. They tell tissues whether they should become female or male reproductive organs, nerve cells, muscle cells, and even eyelash cells. Hormones set off this differentiating process by binding to a specialized molecule—a receptor—on the surface of the interior of a cell. The hormone-receptor complex then informs the cell's DNA which genes need to be turned on, and the genes, in turn, tell the cell which proteins and other substances it needs to make to take on the structure and function of the cell it is fated to

be. Hormones are what tell the fetal cell what it will be when it grows up.

But what if chemical impostors interfere with these carefully articulated messages? Many researchers now believe that a small army of common chemicals can somehow imitate natural hormones, binding to receptors on fetal cells and scrambling genetic instructions. By causing a cell to turn on the wrong gene, or effectively turn off the right one, or even turn up the "volume" of a gene, these mimics can derail an animal's development, permanently distorting its reproductive, immune, and neurological systems.

Other information in Dold's article graphically depicts field research about sexual organ abnormalities in fish and animals that feed in areas where these "hormone-like" chemicals exist.

On a similar note, while doing research, I came across mention of a study linking DNA damage and cancer to the emissions of burning fossil fuels. This study provided proof that living in areas polluted by factories and vehicles burning fossil fuels can alter our DNA. The study was conducted in Poland by a research team led by Columbia University's Dr. Frederica P. Perera. I exchanged e-mails with Dr. Perera, who is a molecular epidemiologist. Her e-mail indicated that her team studied two separate populations in Poland. One population lived in an industrial region with high lung cancer, and the other lived in a rural region. Perera's research discovered that certain fossil fuel pollutants harmed the genetic material by binding to the DNA. Other research has linked DNA to mutation and cancer, but Perera's study in Poland established a molecular link between certain fossil fuel chemical pollutants and DNA damage.

How do chemical pollutants alter DNA?

In *The Elixir of the Ageless*, Dr. Patrick Flanagan expressed how water plays a part in the DNA coding process: "Recent discoveries by Dr. Fritz Popp of Germany indicate that the DNA molecule transmits its blue-print information to other cells by means of an encoded burst of coherent ultra-violet laser light. The optical pathway that transmits this information consists of highly structured cellular water" (*Fusion Magazine*, Sept./Oct. 1985).

With this in mind, could it be possible that cellular water contaminated by harmful pollutants will alter the DNA code of life?

It is a well-known fact that many of the world's urban centers suffer from air pollution in the form of smog. Polluted air is defined as having more than 2000 particles in a volume about half the size of a sugarcube. According to Dr. Patrick Quillin, an internationally recognized authority on nutrition and natural healing and author of four books (including *Healing Nutrients* and *Safe Eating*), many of today's cities average 15,000 particles of pollutants in this volume of air. Just as the presence of pollutants in water causes harm to life, so too does the presence of pollution in the air we breathe. It is now estimated that most children raised in polluted urban settings will lose 10 to 20 percent of their lung capacity by the time they are adults as a result of tissue damage from smog.

On certain smog-alert days, the very young, elderly, and those suffering from respiratory and heart problems are advised not to go outside. In cities such as Beijing, China, there are now places called "oxygen bars," where people seeking a break from the city's polluted air can stop in and inhale pure oxygen for about six dollars an hour. Special herbs and spices containing health-enhancing medicinal qualities can be mixed in for a higher price.

People dwelling in urban centers of the world are now waking up to the importance of breathing clean air for their survival. A case in point is a February 1996 Reuters media release concerning smog in Mexico City:

> Thousands of Mexicans have fallen sick with breathing difficulties, eye problems, headaches and nausea as Mexico City's smog emergency entered its third day, authorities said yesterday. Despite Draconian measures including curbs on factory output, gasoline sales and car driving, smog levels in the city were still above World Health Organization safe limits yesterday. Authorities appealed to residents to stay indoors. Environmentalists and church leaders attacked the government for failing to tackle the crisis.

The same goes for other places throughout the world, as expressed in this Associated Press world news release from France in May 1996:

> *Paris*—Roller skaters, bicyclists and pedestrians rallied yesterday in major cities to protest France's worsening air pollution, blaming the problem on people's reliance on cars. "It's the fault of people who use their cars too much," said Lyne Rossi, one of about 750 bicyclists with surgical masks who gathered on

Paris' Place de la Bastille for a two-wheeled protest. Similar demonstrations yesterday drew hundreds of protesters in cities including Bordeaux, Lille, Lyon, Marseille, Metz, Nice, Rouen, and Toulouse.

Not too long ago some 1580 scientists, including 101 Nobel Prize winners, signed a "Warning to Humanity" appeal that was sent to hundreds of world leaders. Some of the items listed were: stopping the environmental damage caused by oil and coal use, mining, deforestation, and bad farming practices; stabilizing the world's population; reducing poverty; giving women equality; and reducing violence and the threat of war. The warning also expressed concern for how environmental damage is actually causing large numbers of people to relocate from their destroyed homelands. The flow of environmental refugees from Eastern Europe and the Soviet Union, and emigration from North Africa and other countries were given as examples. Much of the environmental damage prompting these migrations of people and loss of wildlife was attributed to humankind's mismanagement of water resources. This group also noted that the loss of natural resources, especially water, combined with growing Third World populations, creates an environment ripe for war.

How Sewage Came to Be Accepted in America's Drinking Water

As colonial American cities and industries grew, sewage, chemical wastes, garbage, and dead animals were dumped without thought into nearby streams and rivers. This was a practice carried over from England and Europe. Most people in the eighteenth and nineteenth centuries had little inkling of how the pollution of water would affect their lives or the lives of other living organisms. At that time, the human mind was still in the "dark ages" in its understanding of life-giving water.

As dense populations grew with the Industrial Revolution and urban centers of commerce, the streams and rivers became open sewers of foul-smelling, nasty-tasting water. Eventually, these streams and rivers were covered over to reduce the offensive odors—thus the creation of our first sewers.

Most of the early settlers of America's Northeast came from England and were no strangers to the stinking rivers of their homeland.

The appearance and smell of the River Thames had become so putrid that in 1865 the Royal Commission on the Pollution of Rivers was created by the British Parliament. At the time the Thames stank so badly that even during the heat of summer Parliament held sessions with closed windows. Sheets soaked in disinfectant were sometimes hung inside the windows to curb the odor and to try to protect the members from disease. It was about this time that some thinkers were beginning to sense possible links between polluted water and human illnesses.

Such news from England about the Thames, coupled with the gross pollution of local waterways, prompted the Congress of the United States to attempt legal remedies. In 1899 Congress passed the Refuse Act, which made it unlawful to "throw, discharge, or deposit any refuse matter of any kind or description whatever, other than that flowing from streets and sewers, into any navigable water of the United States or tributary thereof."

The fact that "sewerage" was allowed to flow into the streams was not an oversight at the time the 1899 Refuse Act was written. In the 1870s, the United States government had undertaken studies on filtering sewage prior to its discharge into streams and rivers. It was also in the 1870s that the federal government funded the Lawrence Experimental Station in Massachusetts to develop the "trickling filter" method for "cleaning" raw sewage. Little thought was given at the time to treating heavy metals and industrial chemicals. It was assumed that these pollutants just dissolved in water and became "safe."

In the late 1800s and early 1900s, the government started to classify American waterways by use. It was hoped that by classifying rivers and streams, some could be used for carrying wastes and others protected for public water supply. This is exactly what Aristotle advised us to do about 2300 years ago.

In August 1912, Congress authorized the Public Health Service to conduct Ohio River studies to "provide data that will eventually be used as a basis for framing the necessary laws for preserving interstate rivers of our country as a safe source of water supply for the large cities located on them."

Coincidentally, it was also in 1912 that the Public Health Service undertook a pilot study of using liquid chlorine to purify a number of public water supplies. Waterborne cholera had begun killing people by the hundreds in local epidemics, and experiments had shown chlorine to be effective for killing off bacteria in water.

Chlorine had been discovered in the late 1700s as a by-product resulting from intensive industrial soap making. According to Ivan Illich in *H₂O and the Waters of Forgetfulness,*

> Industrial soap making led to the first public recognition of the environmental dangers represented by the chemical industry. Large amounts of hydrogen chloride gas were produced and dispersed in the air through tall chimneys. Widespread devastation of vegetation and even forest resources ensued. In 1828 the first lawsuit was initiated against the factory... in order to obtain protection against environmental damage. By the end of the century hydrogen chloride found industrial applications not only in bleaching but also in the chlorination of drinking water (p. 60).

In 1925 the Ohio River studies for classifying rivers by use were reported to Congress. However, by that time the chlorination of public water supplies had proven successful in hindering cholera, typhoid, and other diseases. Thus, the use of chlorine quickly became widely accepted and practiced. Ironically, the Public Health Service ended up being the political instrument responsible for having American rivers and streams used for both sewage and drinking water. For this reason, we have the present-day situation, which, for better or worse, has many Americans and other people around the world drinking chlorinated water derived from waterways carrying sewerage.

At the time, the United States Congress thought it was acting responsibly in allowing treated sewage to be discharged into our rivers. Congressmen believed the chlorine treatment of drinking water taken from these rivers rendered our drinking water safe. With the development of trickling filter treatment for sewage and the chlorination of drinking water, it was believed that technology had truly given humankind the answer for providing safe drinking water. It also represented a political and economical quick fix for convincing people that the government was doing something to ensure that the country's swimming and drinking waters were safe.

Little did anyone know in 1925 how inadequate the trickling filter technique for cleaning sewage would eventually prove to be; the same goes for the chlorination of drinking water. In fact, a significant quantity of bacteria, pathogens, disease-causing organisms, heavy metals, and life-damaging chemicals were still making their way into America's drinking water. However, these shortfalls were not understood in 1925, and it was believed that human health could be protected through sewage filtration and chlorination.

Even with this belief, the expense and effort to install and police the use of such technologies made their implementation slow. Rapidly growing industries and cities, underfunded governments, and lack of regulatory power prevented the problem of pollution from ever being adequately addressed. This is why these problems remain with us to this day. As reported in the March 1997 issue of *Water World*, "America's 55,000 community water systems must invest a minimum of $138.4 billion over the next 20 years to install, upgrade, or replace infrastructure if they are to continue supplying safe drinking water to their 243 million customers."

As for the River Thames, there is somewhat of a happy ending. In the early 1950s England undertook a major cleanup of the river. Industries and towns along the Thames were required to filter and treat their wastes with the latest technologies before discharging into the river. Forty-five years and almost a billion dollars later, the Thames is practically free from odors and once again plays host, albeit on a more limited basis, to an increasing variety of fish.

DDT: Did Rachel Carson Waste Her Time?

Humankind is playing with newfound knowledge like children with unknown lethal toys. We dig up a chemical from below the ground or create a new one in a laboratory, test it to see what purpose it may serve, and introduce it into the environment as safe—only to learn years or decades later that it destroys life in ways never dreamt possible. One example out of many is the DDT/pesticide/herbicide debacle exposed by Rachel Carson.

Ironically, when DDT (dichlorodiphenyltrichloroethane), a synthetic chemical compound, was first introduced to the world in 1940 by Paul Hermann Müller of Switzerland, he was awarded a Nobel Prize in medicine. Müller had discovered that DDT could serve as a powerful insecticide, and at the time it was believed to be a godsend to help rid the world of insect problems in agriculture, farming, and the home.

DDT was considered so safe that during World War II it was applied liberally on the bodies and in the sleeping quarters of the armed forces to control lice. After the war, farmers used DDT to control flies around the farm—including spraying or wiping DDT directly onto the bodies of milk cows so flies would not bother them during milking. Soberingly, some pesticides that were originally developed as nerve gases during World War II ended up being marketed domestically as insecticides for use around the home.

From after World War II to the early 1960s, DDT was routinely sprayed from trucks and planes as a thick fog near wetland areas, ponds, crops, and places where people lived. These applications were an attempt to control mosquitoes and other pests. At the time, people thought nothing of inhaling the chemical mist or leaving the windows of their homes open to allow the DDT fog in. I remember how on summer days when I was a child a small truck would suddenly appear and spray the chemical fog into the air near our home. I also remember my mother opening the front door and yelling for us to come inside away from the fog. With no advanced warning, it was sometimes difficult to get indoors before being surrounded by it. So too it was a real chore to try and close all the windows before the fog penetrated through the screens and entered the house.

On this note, there is actual film footage of park and picnic areas being sprayed with DDT fog while people just continue with their activities, relaxing, playing, and eating. To me, the real irony is to see children playfully running into the fog as their parents watch and laugh. Such was humanity's state of mind just decades ago. As absurd as it sounds today, people back then thought the DDT chemical fog was actually helping to protect them from the diseases that mosquitoes might carry. Little did they realize that they were inhaling a toxic chemical that could damage their nervous system and cause cancer, cell damage, and harm to the brain. The same can be said of the application of DDT to farm plants and food crops to control insect damage. Because of the long life of the chemical, it eventually passes into humans via their intake of food and water.

In September of 1962, Rachel Carson's *Silent Spring* was published. Velsicol Corporation of Chicago had attempted to prevent its publication, claiming that Carson's book contained incorrect information about one of their main products, chlordane, and threatening legal action if the book was published. Rachel Carson's publisher, Houghton Mifflin, took the position that her information was correct and went ahead with publication. Velsicol never followed through on the threat after *Silent Spring* came out, and poetic justice was served the following year. In 1963 several massive fish kills in the Mississippi were traced to the deadly chemical endrin, which is thirty times more deadly to fish than DDT. Further investigation discovered endrin thickly caked inside the sewers of Memphis. Velsicol was the only manufacturer of endrin in Memphis.

When the case to ban DDT was made in the United States during the 1960s, it was proven that DDT can accumulate to toxic levels in the human body and in the bodies of animals and birds. DDT was proven to cause damage not only to those exposed to it, but also to future generations of life. One of the prime examples is the impact on various bird species as a result of accumulating DDT from food, water, and air. DDT was found to change the behavior of enzymes in the liver of birds, causing thin eggshells, low birth rates, and fragile or impaired offspring.

Even though DDT has since been banned from use in this country, it is still being manufactured in large quantities in America and shipped to other countries for use in agriculture and mosquito control. In this fashion, DDT and other pesticides make their way back into the United States in imported fruits, vegetables, meat, and livestock feeds, and in atmospheric fallout. According to the Worldwatch Institute's 1993 *State of the World,* "Export of pesticides banned or restricted for domestic use is also big business in many countries: the U.S. General Accounting Office (GAO) estimated in 1989 that 25 percent of the pesticides exported from the United States were unregistered there. The banned pesticides sometimes return on imported food, a phenomenon known as the 'circle of poison.'" This "circle of poison" remains very much a part of our living reality today.

DDT and its successors—dialdrin, aldrin, heptaclore, and many other "unnatural" chemicals—often find their way into the water cycle of the planet. I recall reading a few years ago that about 25 percent of all the DDT ever produced is now in our oceans—the eventual destination of all atmospheric and surface waters.

In the May 1994 issue of *Discover,* Yale biologist William Smith reported that DDT is still widely used in Mexico, India, Eastern Europe, and Asia. Such ongoing use has impacts far beyond the borders of these countries. Smith and his research team found traces of DDT and its more toxic breakdown products in conifer needles and dead leaves of two remote forests in New Hampshire. According to Smith, "The atmosphere knows no political boundaries. If you introduce something into it, it can come down anywhere. That's been shown with the chlorofluorocarbons that deplete stratospheric ozone. Anything that circulates globally reminds us of how small the world really is."

Like many other toxic chemicals that are water-soluble, once created and released into the environment, DDT is transported throughout the world by air and water. When DDT is applied to a site, it can be carried by water to wherever flowing water goes, eventually reaching streams and oceans. Besides having a tendency to suspend in water, DDT also suspends in air when applied as droplets of spray, and can travel great distances from the site of application. It can also attach itself to dust, be picked up by the winds, and enter the Earth's atmospheric circulation system. DDT also enters the atmosphere by the process of codistillation with water; as the water evaporates into the air as water vapor, DDT is carried along with it.

Additional evidence that DDT is carried around the globe with water vapor and dust was discovered by scientists studying snow and ice deposits at the North and South Poles. Layers of snow and ice deposited around the time when DDT was first introduced into the world's environment have tested positive for the presence of DDT, proving how one chemical that was originally considered "good" for humanity has ended up touching and possibly injuring life forms on every part of the planet.

The rise of breast cancer since the dawn of the chemical revolution in the 1940s provides another warning. As reported by Cynthia Washam in the December 1995 issue of *Food & Health:*

> Researcher Mary Wolff of Mount Sinai School of Medicine found that the tissue of women with breast cancer had unusually high levels of DDE, a breakdown product of DDT. A German study reported elevated levels of PCBs in women suffering from endometriosis.... Many of the chemicals that concentrate in breast milk—including DDT, some PCBs and dioxins—are among a growing list of pesticides and industrial chemicals that mimic the hormone estrogen. These synthetic hormones disrupt the development of the immune, nervous, endocrine, reproductive and digestive systems. The reproductive system is particularly vulnerable.... Since World War II, the sperm count of men in industrialized countries has dropped 50 percent.... Reports of undescended testicles, prostate cancer and testicular cancer rose sharply in males. In the last three decades alone, the rate of testicular cancer tripled.... Each year, billions of pounds of these chemicals are dumped over America's croplands and waterways.

If Rachel Carson were alive today, she probably would be fighting the ongoing battle to prevent DDT and other deadly pesticides from being used throughout the world. This likelihood was related to me by my 96-year-old friend, the photographer Alfred Eisenstaedt, before he died in August 1995. Eisenstaedt, who was called "Eisie" by his friends, met Carson several times while photographing her for *Life* magazine. Eisie held a deep respect for Rachel Carson, especially since he considered himself first and foremost a nature photographer. Spending over fifty consecutive summers walking and photographing tidal areas along the beaches of Martha's Vineyard, Eisenstaedt possibly reflected on how Rachel Carson was at one time only seven miles away wading in tidal pools doing research at the Woods Hole Marine Biological Laboratory. It was because of this perceived relationship between Eisie and Carson that the Limited Editions Club in New York published Carson's *The Sea around Us* with photographs by Eisenstaedt in 1980.

When Rachel Carson died from breast cancer at age 56 on April 14, 1964, it was probably in her mind that her efforts in life had not been wasted. Little did she realize that DDT and many other poisonous chemicals would end up being banned from use only in the United States, and would continue being manufactured in America and transported around the globe.

Regardless of today's reality, Rachel Carson's spirit and thoughts live on in the minds of many people who otherwise would not think of the threat of DDT and other deadly chemicals.

Through Rachel Carson's efforts, and today's science and technology for chemical testing, we are more aware of how easily chemicals can end up in our air, water, and food. Little was known in the 1940s and 1950s of how toxic DDT was to the world of life—today, we know. This is probably why we see such a tremendous growth in the organic foods industry. According to the United States Department of Agriculture (USDA), retail sales of organic foods in 1999 totaled about $6 billion, and the number of organic farmers in the United States, which is currently about 12,000, is increasing by approximately 12 percent annually (see USDA website http://www.arms.usda.gov/nop).

According to the "briefing" section of the USDA website, "Organic farming became one of the fastest growing segments of the U.S. agriculture during the 1990s. U.S. producers are turning to certified organic farming systems as a potential way to lower input costs, decrease reliance on nonrenewable resources, capture high-value markets and premium prices, and boost farm income. Organic farming systems rely on ecologically based practices, such as cultural and biological pest management, and virtually exclude the use of synthetic chemicals in crop production and prohibit the use of antibiotics and growth hormones in livestock production."

Curiously, as the new standard for defining "organic" agricultural products was being composed, certain sewage treatment interests attempted to have the regulations allow the use of sewer sludge as a fertilizer. However, due to the outcry of many enlightened organic farmers, researchers, and consumers, the new "organic" standard prohibits that.

Some other heartening news is that the United States Environmental Protection Agency (USEPA) is in the process of banning two popular pesticides for residential use. Both of these chemicals are products of World War II nerve-gas research. As reported by LeAnn Spencer in the May 2001 issue of *Good Housekeeping*, "the oldest and most popular organophosphate pesticides: chlorpyrifos (often sold as Dursban) and diazinon... poison insects and mammals by attacking their nervous systems. But in spite of the ban, you might be exposed to the chemicals and not know it. Through December, you will be able to buy chlorpyrifos (an ingredient in more than 800 products, from gardening aids to flea collars) at your local home or garden center. Diazinon will be on store shelves until 2004."

The above information now begs two questions—why are some manufacturers still creating DDT and other deadly chemicals? And, why do certain industrial interests continue to encourage and educate developing countries to continue using DDT and other poisons?

Obviously the answers can be found in the realms of money and power.

The Choice We Must Make

The above example of DDT explains the brief history of only one toxic chemical that has been thoroughly studied. There remain the tens of thousands of other toxic chemicals we use daily and yet know very little about. Perhaps, at some not-so-distant future time their environmental consequences will manifest themselves in ways unimaginable today.

To complicate this further, many of the estimated 70,000 chemicals humankind releases into the environment end up mixing with each other or with preexisting chemicals on our planet's watery surface and inside our watery bodies to form new and unknown chemical compounds. There is no way to know what new compounds will be created and what their impact will be on life.

Such is our present plight and, if we choose—such is our future challenge.

But, one may ask, how does this information about DDT and other toxic chemicals relate to water? As expressed elsewhere in this book, almost all chemical reactions take place in the presence of water. We also know that as the water content of a group of cells increases, so does their chemical activity. The nutrient elements that plants need are brought to their roots in water. The nutrient-loaded water then enters the living tissue of the plants and causes swelling. When plant cells are full of water, the chemical activity from photosynthesis and other life-giving processes increases. It is therefore vital that the water flowing through the living world be as free of poisonous chemicals as possible. In this way, the cells of the living organisms remain clean and healthy.

But what about water itself? Is it injured by the presence of toxic chemicals such as DDT? The long-term answer to this is no. Water itself cannot be killed or injured or destroyed by toxic chemicals. It will continue to exist as it always has since long before humankind came into being, no matter what we do to it. However, the life that water supports may be altered or destroyed by the chemicals finding their way into water, and therefore eventually endanger the human race.

The reality of water is that over time, even if takes thousands or millions of years, polluted water will always purify itself. In this fashion, the renewed and purified water may once again play host to creating life and fostering its evolution. Because of this, it is important that we try and learn as much as we can from water, for it holds the key to our survival.

Looking at the world we live in today, humankind has a choice—either to live in a world where we continue to destroy the living world created by water, or to create a world living in harmony with water. If we choose the latter, we will play a profound role in the sharing of this beautiful Garden of Eden with other living beings.

Let us take a moment to picture in our minds the situation as it is today. Present knowledge tells us that it may have taken water billions of years to clean the air, land, and waters of chemicals not conducive to life as we have come to know it. After that was achieved, it took water hundreds of millions of years to create a variety of life forms, forms that further helped to clean the Earth of poisonous chemicals. As time passed, water was able to eventually bring forth more complex life forms—such as humankind.

This is the way of water. Upon observation, it appears as though there is a purpose to water and the way it behaves when it interacts with life. In my mind, this purpose is to create new and varied life forms that interact and evolve with each other. As many of us know through reading, observing, and working with nature, when water is unpolluted, it brings forth life abundantly. In this fashion, we can say that water has established certain laws for life. If these laws are heeded—life flourishes; if they are violated—life rapidly disappears.

Where life goes when it dies is a great mystery. Therefore the questions: Why do certain humans cause living things to disappear from Earth when we have no idea how to bring them back or to recreate them? Could our destruction of other life forms impact the quality of our life here? Out of all the Earth's living creatures, why have we developed the intelligence, science, and a communication system to make us aware of the loss of other life forms?

The way I see it, our intelligence is unique in having the awareness of how our actions are destroying other life forms and making them extinct. The choice is ours—either we care for water so we may share this place with the delight, wonderment, entertainment, and support of other life forms, or we continue polluting and abusing water, and in so doing, cause other life forms to no longer be here with us.

The loss of biodiversity is occurring more rapidly each passing day as our human populations and economies continue to grow, pollute, and place demands on Earth's ecosystems. The preeminent biological theorist and author E. O. Wilson—winner of biology's highest honors and two Pulitzer Prizes—has focused much attention on our loss of biodiversity. In Wilson's words, "The loss of biodiversity is the folly our descendants are least likely to forgive us."

ELEVEN

Deforestation and Dams

Water must be a basic consideration in everything: forestry, agriculture, and industry. The forest is the mother of the rivers. First we must restore the tree cover to fix the soil, prevent too quick run-off, and steady springs, streams and rivers. We must restore the natural motion of our rivers, and, in so doing, we shall restore their vitalizing functions. A river flowing naturally, with its bends, broads, and narrows, has the motion of blood in our arteries, with its inward rotation, tension and relaxation.

—RICHARD ST. BARBE BAKER

The Tree of Life Endangered

ANCIENT MYTHOLOGY and religious traditions through the ages consistently refer to the "Tree of Life." What is the Tree of Life? Is it a literal or a figurative reference? Does the Tree of Life have several meanings on different levels?

In her book *The Mystical Qabalah,* Dion Fortune expresses it this way: "In brief, the Tree of Life is a compendium of science, psychology, philosophy, and theology.... Each symbol upon the Tree represents a cosmic force or factor. When the mind concentrates upon it, it comes into touch with that force; in other words, a surface channel, a channel in consciousness, has been made between the conscious mind of the individual and a particular factor in the world-soul, and through this channel the waters of the ocean pour into the lagoon."

In a literal sense, trees have much to offer in the way of shelter, food, shade, flood and wind control, and a place of refuge. On another level, writers, naturalists, thinkers, and spiritual leaders understood the value of trees to life and the soul. All one needed was to take a walk through a forest, and behold—an entire world of interconnected life would reveal itself. The world of trees provides a support system for many life forms.

147

The intimate relationship between trees and water has evolved to the point where our remaining rainforests contain about 90 percent of Earth's terrestrial species. In the PBS companion book, *Water: The Drop of Life,* we discover, "as civilization encroaches on the wilderness, an estimated 49 million acres (20 million hectares) of rainforest are wiped out each year." This loss of millions of acres of rainforest is the result of humans slashing and burning the trees so farmers may make money from raising cattle or some crop that rapidly destroys the thin soils. After destroying the fragile soils in one spot, the farmer again burns down more of the rainforest.

As much as water is the essence of all living things, it is the world of trees through which water nurtures the terrestrial world of life—which is why I believe trees evolved to be some of the longest-lived living plants on the face of the Earth.

As I researched the world of trees, I found trees to be like us. Trees and humans are made up of about the same percentage of water. Like humans, trees have individual cells for carrying out different functions necessary for their health and survival. And, even though each cell performs it own unique function, it works in unison with all other cells in the tree through the network created by water. Every new cell in a tree is composed mostly of protoplasm and, except for the cell wall, is similar to the first single-celled plants created on Earth long ago. Science tells us that Earth's original one-celled plants contained mostly protoplasm and a nucleus or "heart"—just like the cells found in our trees of today. And, just as in humans, water moves through and around these cells, carrying nutrients and unknowns in and out.

Imagine a tree that is almost four hundred feet tall. Imagine a tree almost 5000 years old. Imagine a plant living longer than 11,000 years. Imagine a shrub living 40,000 years.

Fortunately, we do not have to imagine such living things because they really do exist with us at this time. H. G. Deming tells us in *Water, the Fountain of Opportunity*, "The tallest known tree (a redwood, 367.8 ft high) is probably 400 ft from root tips to the topmost leaves." But the tallest tree is not the oldest tree on Earth. That distinction is held by a bristlecone pine in the Great Basin National Park in Baker, Nevada, which was found to be about 4,950 years old.

However, this oldest tree is not considered the oldest living thing on the Earth's surface. According to the *Guinness Book of World Records*, the plant believed to be the oldest is a creosote plant clone in California named King Clone. Its estimated age exceeds 11,000 years. However, King Clone doesn't come close to the recent discovery of a Stone Age shrub living in Australia's Tasmania region with an estimated age of 40,000 years! As reported in the *New York Times* on October 20, 1996, this shrub, named King's Holly, is now believed to be the oldest known living organism on Earth. Imagine, 40,000 years old!

What I found curious about the long life spans of some trees is that even though a tree may be thousands of years old, the oldest living cells found within the tree are not more than thirty years old! How and why this happens remains somewhat of a mystery. Just imagine if this gift of long life could in some way be transferred to humans.

But imagine destroying these and other species of plants and trees, destroying life forms that we have no understanding of—what use they can have for humanity, or what life forms they feed and protect. In a fashion, the remaining ancient plants and trees still surviving today are the only "living" connection we have with our early ancestors of life from long ago. For humans to destroy such ancient living things without thoroughly considering the consequences is a practice I believe to be quite foolish.

A case in point is the attempt to save a giant redwood tree named Luna in Stafford, California. On December 10, 1997, a young woman named Julia Butterfly Hill climbed up Luna onto a platform 180 feet high. The platform was built to be occupied on a temporary basis to prevent Luna and other nearby redwoods from being cut down. This technique of temporary platform building has been and is still being used with considerable success in other areas.

The big difference with the Luna occupation by Ms. Hill was that she lived in the tree for two years, after which, with considerable hoopla, she climbed down from the tree and rejoined the world to pursue her environmental conservation efforts via the Circle of Life Foundation.

However, on the Saturday following Thanksgiving Day in November 2000, it was discovered that a sneak attack had been made on Luna with a chainsaw. This attack came after Ms. Hill, Sanctuary Forest (a land trust that is the holder of the deed of covenant), and Pacific Lumber Company/Maxxam Corporation had signed an agreement to create a protected sanctuary of 200 feet surrounding Luna. After learning of the potentially fatal chainsaw cut in Luna, Julia Butterfly Hill appeared on *The Today Show* on November 29, 2000, and made the following statement: "Luna is the greatest teacher and best friend I have ever had. I gave two years of my life to ensure that she could live and die naturally. But two years is nothing compared to the thousands of years she has lived, providing shelter, moisture, and oxygen to forest inhabitants. It kills me that the last 3 percent of the ancient redwoods are being desecrated. I feel this vicious attack on Luna as surely as the chainsaw was going through me. Words cannot express the deep sorrow that I am experiencing but I am as committed as ever to doing everything in my power to protect Luna and the remaining ancient forests."

As of this writing, the Circle of Life Foundation and Sanctuary Forest are working to try and save Luna's life from the critical chainsaw cut.

Throughout time, there have been people who saw how the destruction of forests would disrupt the water cycle and lead to dire consequences for humankind and all other life on the Earth. In the words of Richard St. Barbe Baker, "If a man loses one-third of his skin he dies.... If a tree loses one-third of its bark it dies.... Would it not be reasonable to suggest that if the Earth loses more than a third of its green mantle and tree cover, it will assuredly die?"

Plato (427–347 B.C.) warned the people of Greece about the folly of destroying trees. He warned that as forests were cut down, there would be drastic changes in the water situation and an adverse impact on the future for the land and the people it supported. It is no coincidence that the demise of Greek civilization began at about the same time its forests were decimated.

In 1936, the renowned Austrian naturalist-forester Viktor Schauberger wrote:

> The people who love it should only care for the forest. Those who view the forest merely as an object of speculation, do it and all other living creatures great harm, for the forest is the cradle of water. If the forest dies, then the springs will dry up, the meadows will become barren and many countries will inevitably be seized by unrest of such kind that it will bode ill for every one of us (*Tau mag*, Vol. 151, Nov. 1936, p. 30, as translated by Callum Coats in *Living Energies*).

It is estimated that the soils of America's primeval forests contained 137,000 pounds of humus per acre. Today, after the cutting of most of our forests and the following erosion of humus, we find our once-forested soils contain about 20,000 to 70,000 pounds of humus per acre, and sometimes almost none. Without the ongoing creation of rich humus deposits by trees, life on the Earth's surface will slowly diminish, for it is in water-holding humus that the alchemy of life takes place, in the microorganisms that create protoplasm. One pound of humus will store two pounds of water in the wet season, providing natural flood control and releasing water gently into plants and streams as it is needed during the dry season. As humus releases its stored water, it also releases vital nutrients derived from rotting vegetation broken down by the atmosphere, bacteria, and insects.

Over time, humankind has learned that air pollution and the use of chemical fertilizers, herbicides, and pesticides has an inevitable impact on the "balance" and health of soils. We have also learned from studies that without forests, soils are no longer "created" at a rate suitable for providing for a myriad of life forms. As we suffer the demise of our world's life-supporting soils, we also see the demise of many of Earth's life forms.

Historically, the rise and fall of every civilization throughout time seems directly related to the health of its water and forest resources. However, the ruling nations at this time have learned the trick of sustaining themselves by pillaging the natural resources of other, less powerful countries. Given this modern era of worldwide communications, commerce, and transport, it is now possible for a country that has destroyed its own natural resources to survive off the resources of others. Many Third World countries are now seeing their forests destroyed and their waters polluted to feed the demands of the more powerful.

In his book *Living Energies,* Callum Coats advises us, "Replanting of trees and global reafforestation on a massive scale is therefore imperative at this late hour if humanity is to be saved from disaster. As for the necessary work-force, there are millions of people available for such work. In actual fact there are not enough unemployed at present to do all that needs to be done" (p. 236).

As Bill Mollison of Australia points out in his groundbreaking books *Permaculture One* and *Permaculture Two,* "The real risk is that the needs of those 'on the ground'—the inhabitants—are overthrown by the needs (or greeds) of commerce and centralized power; that the forest is cut for warships or newspaper and we are reduced to serfs in a barren landscape. This has been the fate of peasant Europe, Ireland, and much of the third world."

Indeed, the prevailing powers of the human race in recent history seem to give little if any thought to the long-term consequences of destroying the world's water, soil, and forest resources. It is the short-term economic fix, the short-term profit, the short-term vision that has prevailed. And, as a consequence, the world of trees is slaughtered like an army of helpless innocents.

Today there is a big movement afoot to save the world's rainforests. What remains is a mere fraction of the rainforests of old. Millions of years ago, before the ice ages, a large portion of the planet was covered with forests similar to today's rainforests. These ancient forests helped to create a worldwide climate that was warm and humid, which was a key factor in the evolution of many life forms. There are currently about 3 million square miles of rainforest existing along the planet's equatorial belt. This remaining rainforest plays host to about half of all the animal species on Earth—an estimated 5 million life forms. The equatorial rainforests receive between 100 and 400 inches of rain each year, which is rapidly absorbed into the trees' root systems and foliage. The rainforest therefore acts as a flood prevention mechanism while also protecting its thin layer of soil. Unless protected by overhead foliage and plant root systems, rainforest soils would easily wash away during the heavy rains.

Rainforest soils contain only 5 percent of the nutrients necessary to sustain the lush vegetation of the forest. The other 95 percent of the nutrients are held in the vegetation. Due to ever present rainfall, the damp conditions on the forest floor rapidly rot and recycle nutrients from plants and trees.

Thus plants and other life forms in the rainforests act as a subtle governing device to prevent water from getting out of control and harming the surface of the Earth, while at the same time giving water the freedom and time to manifest itself in a variety of life forms. As we destroy our trees, we also destroy the homes of other life forms—forms that enrich our lives with their presence while helping to provide for our health and our future.

The destruction of trees has the potential of unleashing the destructive powers of water. There is a tremendous quantity of water and other energies held within the bodies of trees. Besides the large quantity of water held in trees, there is also a large quantity of water held in the root systems and spongy soils they create. Trees also help to tame the Earth's winds by causing a drag effect; they help to regulate the release of water vapor into the atmosphere by slowing evaporation through their leaves (transpiration); and, finally, trees provide shade to cool the air and soils and allow for moisture to soak into the earth.

Water gets into the atmosphere as a result of evaporation from surface water, soils, and plants. Plants take in water through their roots and by absorbing moisture through their skins. Water evaporates from plants through the process called transpiration, literally the exhalation of water vapor through the pores of the skin or from the undersides of leaves. The transpiration of water from plants has been estimated to produce more water vapor than is produced by evaporation from all of the Earth's land surfaces and their water bodies of streams, rivers, and lakes.

An acre of corn will transpire about 4000 gallons of water each day; a large oak tree will release about 40,000 gallons of water vapor in a year. When one stops and looks at a forested area and sees all the trees, underbrush, grasses, weeds, mosses, and other growth—surely one's mind has to also see that these different plants hold considerable quantities of water. This water serves the purpose of life; as it flows through plants it converts carbon dioxide into oxygen and creates food and shelter for innumerable forms of life.

As a regulator of water's power, we can view trees as a partner in the game of survival. Without the preparation of our Earth by trees, humanity probably never would have had a chance of surviving.

At today's rate of destruction, the world will lose most of its rainforests in one human lifetime. It is roughly estimated that 3000 acres of rainforest are destroyed each hour. And it is the rainforests that capture the heavy rains along the equator and put them to use for the creation of the most varied forms of plant and animal life on the planet.

Where the rainforest has been destroyed, the rainwater falls uncontrollably, eroding the soils and flooding the land. And instead of the water serving the purposes of life as it flows through plants and is gently released back into the atmosphere through transpiration, it evaporates rapidly, violently filling the atmosphere with more water vapor.

Water released into the atmosphere does not escape into outer space, but hugs the Earth instead. Therefore, the more water that is not stored underground, in vegetation polar ice caps, icebergs, running streams, lakes, and oceans, the more water there is in the atmosphere.

Water falls from the air in the form of fog, rain, snow, sleet, and hail. Collectively, these different forms of water that fall from the air are known as "precipitation," a word derived from the Latin, meaning "to fall headlong."

Since the water cycle on the surface of the planet is the key to our weather patterns, it would be foolish to believe that humankind's behavior has no influence on weather. For we as humans are manipulating ever greater quantities of the planet's water with each passing day. As humankind alters the flow of water on Earth's surface and in its atmosphere, we are also altering the interaction of cosmic forces that influence Earth's world of life.

All over the world there are ever increasing incidences of violent weather. Besides the ecological upset caused by weather extremes such as hurricanes (also called typhoons), tornados (twisters and water spouts), floods, tidal waves, Nor'easters, etc., there is also the human impact of weather on our personal lives and local and national economies.

Water, in the forms of rivers, oceans, underground water, ice, water vapor, rain, snow, sleet, hail, frost, mist, fog, clouds, and in all living things, is the most important element on the Earth's surface that impacts climate. We cannot escape the fact that human interaction with and impact on these various forms of water ultimately influence the planet's overall weather.

Humankind does have the power to force water to assume different forms through building dams, altering the course of rivers, destroying forests and other vegetation, pumping underground water, and many other activities. However, it is beyond our limited powers to control water once it is released into the atmosphere.

Herewith is the key. When water is contained beneath the surface or slowly flows through vegetation, it is somewhat manageable and tame. However, when the powerful energy of water is released from beneath the ground and from within vegetation, it becomes a power to be reckoned with.

It is a recognized fact that the world's desert areas are on the increase at this time in history. Study after study has shown us how humankind has destroyed systems of trees and vegetation that created and nurtured topsoil and many other forms of life, and how, once these living systems were altered, the soils have eroded away, and the rivers and surface waters disappeared.

In 1964, a civil engineer named Frank D. Steiner of Moraga, California, wrote a pamphlet called *Bio-Technology: A New Approach to Our Water Problems*, based on his lifetime study of humankind's destruction of forests as watershed land. In Steiner's words:

> When a watershed is subjected...to paving, draining, and urban sprawl, excessive terrestrial heat plays havoc with established climates.... Terrestrial heat engenders atmospheric dryness, which in turn causes failure in the rain cycle. A Senate document published in 1936 shows that the precipitation curve in California between 1850 and 1934 underwent "a downward trend of eight inches..." during the eighty-five year period. In other words, the annual average precipitation in California dropped one tenth of an inch each year. The downward trend did not stop in 1934.

Steiner believed that humanity's destruction of forests had greatly contributed to the creation of dry areas on the planet. In his mind, the only way humanity could slow down the expansion of deserts throughout the world was to use "bio-technological means, i.e., all the means modern technology can offer plus massive forest shelterbelts." In many ways, thirty years after the fact, this is the very thing that is being attempted in many parts of the world today.

In America it took the farmer's plow less than fifty years to turn almost 100 million acres of the richest soils on the planet into a dust bowl. Today, because of human activities like overpumping of the aquifer, the midwestern region of the United States will never again return to its original splendor of lush plains graced with waving grasslands. So easily and quickly did humans armed with technology forever alter the form in which water may reside there. The grasslands are gone, so too the rich topsoil, along with the streams and the dense animal life that once roamed the Great Plains.

Besides the dry areas of the planet created through humankind's interference with the water cycle of life, we also find that other areas of Earth are experiencing increases in flooding and violent weather.

According to the National Weather Service, the United States, due to its geographical location, topography, and water resources, experiences more violent storms than any other country in the world. In a given year, the United States can experience 10,000 violent storms, 5000 floods, and 1000 tornados. The American Midwest is known as "tornado alley," due to the tornados created when the warm, moist air flowing north from the Gulf of Mexico meets the cold, dry air flowing down from the Rocky Mountains.

In South America, the Amazon River basin receives more than half of all tropical rainfall on the planet. It was discovered in 1499 by a Spanish sea captain who was still far from the sight of land when he realized that he was sailing in freshwater. By sailing west he discovered the awesome river.

This 4000-mile-long river system holds about two-thirds of all the river water on Earth. At its mouth it is over 200 miles wide. The flow volume of the Amazon is so powerful that its freshwater reaches 100 miles beyond the continental shelf before it begins to succumb to the salty ocean. If the forests along the Amazon continue to be lost to present cutting practices, who knows what impact the uncontrolled river will have on the Atlantic Ocean and the planet's weather?

Global Warming

The buildup of carbon dioxide in our atmosphere from human-made emissions is now considered one of the major contributors to global warming. In a study published in the July 1996 issue of *Nature*, researchers claimed proof that the effects of carbon dioxide buildup in the Earth's atmosphere were directly linked to increased global warming.

According to the study's coauthor, John F. B. Mitchell of the British government's Meteorological Office in Bracknell, England, "One temperature pattern was cooling in the upper atmosphere and warming in the lower altitudes, an apparent result of carbon dioxide buildup." Agreeing with this assessment is Kevin Trenberth, a scientist at the National Center for Atmospheric Research in Boulder, Colorado. Trenberth sees a relationship between humankind's activities, global warming, and extreme weather events around the world: "If Earth's atmosphere heats up, there will be a corresponding increase in evaporation of moisture from the planet's surface. If you increase evaporation, you will also increase the moisture content in the atmosphere, which increases precipitation.... The extra moisture gets caught up in precipitating systems and produces heavier rainfall and snowfall than would otherwise occur."

To further complicate the problem of global warming, we have the escalating destruction of vegetation throughout the world—the cutting down of forests; the clearing of lands for buildings, highways, and strip mines; the loss of wetlands; and the removal of vegetation for agriculture. This destruction of Earth's forests and vegetation contributes to the release of more carbon dioxide into the atmosphere, as well as other impurities that would be filtered out by healthy forests. Besides the loss of vegetation from land surfaces, there is also the killing off of nitrogen-holding algae from the world's surface waters due to pollution.

All of these factors influence the behavior of the Earth's surface waters. As the Earth experiences temperature change, no matter the cause, there will be inevitable alterations in the forms of life that can continue to survive. Whether human-induced or not, a temperature change in the Earth's atmosphere will alter the behavior of water and determine whether it nurtures or harms life.

The Power of Water Unleashed

In my opinion, humankind at this time in history is playing roulette with the innate powers existing within water. As the water-holding systems of living animals, wetlands, forests, foliage, roots, and soils are destroyed, more water is released into the air and onto the Earth's surface. Think of all the water that was once held by forests all over the globe. These forests are now cities, suburbs, farms, roads, garbage dumps, graveyards, and deserts. The destruction of forests continues to release huge quantities of water into the water cycle.

When heavy rains fall on a densely populated region, flooding usually occurs. Rooftops, roads, and parking lots cannot control or hold water like the root system of a forest. Such human-made surfaces cannot soften the impact of rainwater before it hits the ground. But leaves of living trees and other foliage protect the ground and help create living soils. Runoff from a forest carries life-supporting nutrients and microscopic life into the food chain of streams and rivers, while runoff from human-made surfaces usually carries pollution.

Instead of being held in plants and filtered beneath the ground to nourish life, rainwater is more and more being sent directly into streams, rivers, oceans, and the atmosphere—completely bypassing its purpose of serving life. Water falling on human-made surfaces tends to run wildly across the landscape, creating flash floods. Flooding also occurs in areas along waterways where forests have been destroyed and the waterways "straightened out."

Since less and less water is being stored by living systems on the surface of the planet, the water that does fall on densely populated regions is subject to rapid evaporation from wind and sun. Such rapid runoff and evaporation of rainwater also results in less freshwater being stored in our planet's underground water table. The net result is that the quantity of water in the atmosphere is increasing. This rapid movement of water across the surface of the planet and into the atmosphere is placing greater amounts of unchecked energy into the planet's water cycle.

Further exacerbating the increasing water load in our atmosphere from the loss of vegetation is humankind's management of surface and subsurface waters. In order to provide for irrigation, hydropower, recreation, flood control, and drinking water for populated regions, a large system of dams continues to be built around the world. According to the magazine *Audubon*, May/June 1996, the worldwide number of dams higher than fifty feet increased from 5000 in 1950 to nearly 40,000 by the mid-1980s. At this time, there are about 75,000 dams in the United States alone.

The damming of rivers cuts off the flow of fresh water to our oceans. Flowing water is a powerful energy source. A flowing river supplies energy to a myriad of life forms that evolved with the river over eons. The damming of a river redistributes this energy and is a death sentence for much of the life downstream. Without water to feed the downstream vegetation and wetlands, these ancient living systems are weakened or destroyed.

In her book *Against the Tide, New York Times* science editor Cornelia Dean documents the many impacts human interactions have on America's beaches. Of course, many of these interactions deal with rivers, wetlands, and the ocean coastline. On the impact of river dams on America's beaches, Ms. Dean quoted Douglas Inman, who prepared background papers for the California Academy of Sciences on the subject. In Mr. Inman's words, "Dams provide water and intercept the normal flow of sand to beaches. Dams benefit cities, industry, and agriculture and damage beaches, coasts, and coastal communities. We must reconcile this inequity to coastal communities and beach users. The cost of nourishing beaches with the same amount of sand that is intercepted by dams would be a legitimate part of the cost of using water. The cost of replenishing beach sand should be borne by the [upstream] water users [who benefit from the dam]."

The damming of a river creates a deep and expansive surface area of stagnant water that releases additional energy into our atmosphere through evaporation. Other energy may be released through the production of hydropower, or the use of water for irrigation or public water supply. Regardless of what is said—a dam creates a huge energy shift on many levels across the face of the Earth. Once a dam is installed, the energy of moving water is no longer released to serve the many life forms that live in and along downstream river valleys. This stagnation of water behind river dams is also adding to our human woes by helping the spread of disease from mosquitoes. Stagnant water provides a wonderful home for mosquitoes, so they may proliferate and increase their geographical territory for spreading diseases into areas that once limited their reproduction.

Since the energy on Earth's surface is finite, the powerful energy of our flowing rivers is a major contributor to Earth's energy budget. The damming of a river causes its flow water energy to go elsewhere. And, guess where it goes? It certainly doesn't just disappear. It has to go somewhere else in our Earth's biosphere. And that place is into the atmosphere via evaporation and across the surface of the planet via gravity.

In the past forty years, over eighty-eight large dams have impounded huge quantities of water in the temperate areas north and south of the equator. As this book is being written, some of the largest dams in history are being built in China and other countries.

Besides changing the water and atmospheric flow patterns in Earth's biosphere, big dams place an incredible amount of stress on the continental plates of our planet. So much so that the use of large dams is altering Earth's orbit in our solar system. According to a *New York Times* article published on March 3, 1996:

Although Earth's rate of spin is gradually slowing because of the tidal drag of the moon, the slowing would have been measurably greater if it were not for the influence of 88 reservoirs built since the early 1950s, said the scientist, Dr. Benjamin Fong Chao, a geophysicist at the Goddard Space Flight Center. . . . Each of the reservoirs contains at least 2.4 cubic miles of water weighing 10 billion metric tons. The reservoirs contain the bulk of the world's impounded water.

The shift in the distribution of Earth's water caused by the reservoirs has tended to speed the planet's spin. . . . Moreover, Earth's axis is being slightly tilted by the weight of water that has collected in the 88 reservoirs, Dr. Chao found, and the shape of the planet's gravitational field has been altered.

Dam building in the former Soviet Union, Canada, Brazil and other mid-latitude countries has been rapid in the last four decades, and fresh water collected from rivers and other terrestrial sources has increased in this period by 10,000 cubic kilometers, or 10 trillion tons, an amount equivalent to all the moisture in the Earth's atmosphere. This water accumulates from rain, which in turn comes from clouds that draw their moisture largely from the evaporation of ocean water....

Geophysicists have little doubt that dam building will continue rapidly until all sources of recoverable water have been exploited, a time some scientists calculate will come in the next century.

The above documentation should give some pause for thought about the impact of large-scale water projects. What this article does not mention is how this relatively sudden shift of ten trillion tons of water is impacting the stability of Earth's continents. One would think that there would be an obvious connection of such shifting of water weight with earthquakes and other cataclysmic events.

The same article also mentioned that scientists were bewildered by the fact that global sea levels continue to rise. In some minds, large-scale damming of river water should result in stable or decreasing sea levels. Obviously the writer of the article and the scientists he interviewed lack vision in seeing the big picture of humankind's manipulation of Earth's water.

Sea levels continue to rise for various reasons. First, as mentioned earlier, the worldwide release of water into the Earth's atmosphere by the destruction of trees and other vegetation, the ever-increasing removal of groundwater, the loss of humus in topsoil for storing water, and the rapid evaporation of rainwater from human-made surfaces such as asphalt, concrete, and buildings is causing the water cycle of the planet to carry more water into the atmosphere at an ever-increasing rate.

Second, humankind is rapidly removing large quantities of water from underground sources, drying out the subsoils of the continents that have heretofore been saturated with water. When water is removed from beneath the ground, the soils, sands, and gravels become denser and collapse upon each other, causing what are known as sinkholes (subsidence) on the surface of the land. Once an aquifer collapses, it can never again hold as much water as it once did. This point is well made in Sandra Postel's 1996 Worldwatch Paper 132, *Dividing the Waters: Food Security, Ecosystem Health, and the New Politics of Scarcity.* Ms. Postel writes: "In some cases, groundwater depletion permanently reduces the earth's capacity to store water. The extraction of water may cause an aquifer's geologic materials to compact, eliminating the pores and spaces that held the water. The loss of storage capacity is irreversible, and it carries a high cost. In California, for example, compaction of overdrafted aquifers in the Central Valley has resulted in a loss of nearly 25 billion cubic meters of storage capacity—equal to more than 40 percent of the combined storage capacity of all human-made surface waters statewide."

Third, the increased density and weight of collapsed continental subsoils combined with the additional water weight held by dams is increasing the pressure of the continents on the soft molten core of the Earth. This pressure may be resulting in an increase of earthquakes and volcanic eruptions as the Earth tries to stabilize these human-induced shifts of water weight. As the continents carry more weight due to the damming of rivers and removal of groundwater, *the ever heavier continents may sink and actually push the levels of the ocean floor higher*—thus contributing to rising sea levels.

There are two other variables that also come into play with the damming of rivers. Prior to the building of dams, the rivers of the world flowed toward the ocean along courses that had evolved over billions of years. In a natural fashion, the rivers carved their way through rock, sand, and soils to a level below the surrounding lands. Such carving of valleys into the landscape is testimony of the energy and power contained in water. By eroding the rocks and soils, the world's rivers naturally occupy a place where gravity has less influence on the water than when it flowed across the land ages ago. When a dam stops the flow of water, the energy that was once contained in the river goes elsewhere. As the water level behind a dam gets higher and higher, the pull of gravity on the large mass of water gets stronger and stronger. In this way the energy of water becomes concentrated behind the dam over a small area of the continent instead of flowing over a large area at a lower level.

Besides the pull of the Earth's gravity on the water behind a dam, there is also the increased influence and pull of the Moon on the contained water. The effect of the Moon on large bodies of water on

Earth is no secret. This effect is further increased when other planets are aligned with the Moon. Such forces influence captured water behind dams and increase the stress on our world's continents and weather patterns.

In spite of the foreboding appearance of the above human activities, there are some rays of light shining upon humankind's awakening management of water. In the United States, the courts have recently upheld a decision against building the 615-foot-high Two Forks Dam in Colorado. Besides the outcry of many conservation groups, the United States Environmental Protection Agency (EPA) was the key player in blocking the Two Forks Dam proposal. The EPA cited the provisions of the Clean Water Act for protecting the river's "natural" recreation areas and existing fisheries and wildlife values. According to the September 1996 issue of *The Aquifer Journal of the Groundwater Foundation*, the Two Forks Dam would have provided enough water for about 400,000 additional residents and taken care of Denver's water needs for about thirty years into the future. As a result of EPA's stopping this dam, Denver has been forced to initiate water conservation efforts. To date, the city has spent $37 million to place water meters on 87,000 homes, and offers an $80 dollar rebate for the installation of low-volume toilets. Denver has also put together a public campaign to reduce water used for landscape irrigation, which accounts for half of all local water consumption.

Another ray of hope is the Sierra Club's recent proposal to lower the water level in Utah's Lake Powell, located upstream behind the Glen Canyon Dam on the Colorado River in Arizona. It is the position of the Sierra Club, as well as many other environmental interests, that there is more to be gained by returning Glen Canyon to its natural state. They also argue that returning the seasonal water flows to the Colorado River will be healthy for the ecosystems above and below the dam. David Brower, a vocal opponent of construction of the Glen Canyon Dam in the early 1960s, said that the Sierra Club's board of directors voted to make this recommendation after reviewing information from the Bureau of Reclamation that showed Lake Powell is losing about 1.5 million acre feet of water a year to evaporation, leaks, and underground seepage.

Certainly this is good news. Further good news comes from the Bureau of Reclamation's public opinion poll conducted in the late 1990s as part of an environmental impact study of the Glen Canyon Dam. The poll included users of the dam's power output as well as a sampling of taxpayers from across America. According to David Wegner, a hydrologist formerly with the Bureau of Reclamation, "The results showed over 70 percent of respondents were willing to either pay more for energy or pay more in taxes to preserve and maintain natural ecosystems like the Grand Canyon and the Colorado River."

The American Rivers group, an organization that researches and educates about America's rivers, is doing a commendable job of trying to restore and maintain natural river ecosystems. Recently, Rebecca Wodder, president of American Rivers, helped bring attention to river damage caused by dams and faulty energy policies. Peter L. Kelley, of Strategic Communications for American Rivers, provided the following statements by Ms. Wodder and board member Dr. Stephen Ambrose, presented at the Most Endangered Rivers conference in Washington, D.C., on April 11, 2001. Ms. Wodder said:

> For sixteen years American Rivers has listed America's Most Endangered Rivers.... They need our help and they need it this year.... On this occasion we also highlight one emerging threat that puts many rivers, all across the country, in danger. This year that threat is clear: it's 19th-century energy policies. The impacts of outdated ways of developing and using energy are often felt first—and worst— on our rivers.... Six of this year's Most Endangered Rivers illustrate various threats from shortsighted and ill-conceived energy development.

Ms. Wodder then presented information about how the Hudson River is endangered by PCBs; how the Powder River in Wyoming is endangered by thousands of proposed natural gas wells that will dump saltwater; how the Paine Run River in Virginia is, like 1300 other streams in the Mid-Atlantic, succumbing to acid rain from old coal-burning plants; how the Canning River in Alaska is threatened by oil and gas exploration; how the Eel River in California is being dewatered by two dams for hydropower and irrigation, which has reduced by 97 percent the river's endangered salmon and steelhead. In announcing number one on the endangered rivers list, Ms. Wodder stated:

> This year the number one Most Endangered River in America is also our longest river, and one of the most legendary—the Missouri, which crosses seven states in 2,500 miles, and which

carried Lewis and Clark most of the way on their famous ex-
pedition, almost 200 years ago. This is a critical year for the
Missouri.

Following Rebecca Wodder's presentation, writer Dr. Stephen Ambrose stated:

> This is a critical year for the Missouri River. American Rivers
> believes we can and should restore the river to health by restor-
> ing natural flows, wildlife habitat, and community riverfronts.
> The Lewis and Clark Bicentennial is the perfect time for this
> to happen. Twenty-five million tourists are expected, and it
> would be far better for the economy and the environment if
> they were attracted to restored segments along the length of
> the Missouri.... The key to restoring a lot of river miles is re-
> operating the dams on the river to mimic the river's historic,
> natural flows. Allowing for a "spring rise" in water levels, and
> lower summer flows, is a win-win-win for people, wildlife and
> the economies of the seven states.

Dr. Ambrose feels so strongly about restoring the natural flows of
the Missouri River that he is pledging over $1 million of his book
royalties to American Rivers to help with the effort.

Dimming the efforts of Dr. Ambrose, American Rivers, and other
splashes of hope is the recent news that China has entered into an
agreement with the Tennessee Valley Authority (TVA), the largest
producer of electricity in the United States. The TVA is responsible
for building this country's largest system of dams. It will be helping
China modernize hydroelectric plants and may also be involved with
the planning of up to twelve dams for the remote Han River system.
Besides providing electricity for rural development, these dams along
the Han River will also bring water to the water-starved Beijing area.

Beyond the Beijing area, the demand for water in China has reached
historic proportions. It was recently estimated that about three hundred cities in China are now suffering from freshwater shortages,
in spite of the fact that more than 80,000 dams have been built in
China since 1949. According to Dai Qing, a Chinese activist and
author of the book *Yangtze! Yangtze!*, out of these 80,000 dams,
3200 had burst by 1981. For publishing this book, Dai Qing was
jailed for ten months, including six months in solitary confinement.
Yangtze! Yangtze! is about China's Three Gorges Dam project along

the Yangtze River, and includes views of forty top Chinese scientists who object to the dam. If completed, this dam will be the largest ever built, 610 feet high with a span of 1.3 miles; it will generate 18,200 megawatts of electricity, the equivalent of about eighteen nuclear power plants. The lake behind the dam will be an estimated 400 miles long and almost 600 feet deep. At this time, dam construction and the relocation of over two million people is well under way.

Of all the countries in the world, China probably has a unique history in mega-dam construction. Some 2200 years ago the Chinese skillfully built a multipurpose system to control the Min River that rises on the high plateau of Tibet. By building a series of dikes and dams where the main river enters the broad plain from the mountain canyon, the farmers divided the flow into many sections so they could irrigate one-half million acres. The structures these ancient Chinese used were made of bamboo frames weighted down with rocks. Besides providing irrigation and drinking water, this early dam system reduced the heavy toll of life and property losses from spring and summer floods. Perhaps it is this early history of dam building in China that also propels the Three Gorges Dam.

While China blindly continues with this highly destructive project, the seeds of a worldwide grassroots movement to stop such dams appear to be taking root and growing. This worldwide effort was kicked off in Curitibu, Brazil, in March 1997 when over one hundred people from twenty countries representing the Americas, Europe, Asia, and Africa attended the International Conference of Dam-Affected People, sponsored by the Brazilian Movement of People Affected by Dams (MAB). The focus of the conference was to promote political and legal action for damages caused by dams—including loss of farmland, homes, wildlife, and fisheries. MAB's hope is to prevent more dams from being built while also setting the stage to dismantle existing dams. According to MAB, it is now estimated that 30 to 60 million people have been displaced by dams throughout the world.

Certainly an international agreement for managing our Earth's water resources is needed. As humankind is beginning to learn, the damming of large river systems anywhere on Earth will inevitably have some impact on our weather as well as on the health of our rivers and oceans.

In answer to the increasing demand for water by industry, farming, ecosystems, and public water supply interests—we have technology attempting to fix the problem. A few examples of these technological innovations are the removal of salt from ocean water (desalination); the harvesting and towing of icebergs; seeding of clouds to induce rainfall; and the erection of immense plastic screens to capture water droplets from fog in Chile. Each of these technological answers to obtain and control water will require various degrees of Earth's limited resources and energy. As time goes by, these technological answers will in themselves result in an increasing alteration of Earth's water cycle.

To repeat, it is the energy present in water that truly creates and supports our living world on an ongoing basis. If the living world on the planet continues to be replaced with the nonliving, the powerful life-giving energies of water will eventually be unleashed in a detrimental way across the surface of the planet. It is in this way that we see how deforestation and dam building endanger our rivers, as well as the life-giving water and energy cycles of our entire planet.

TWELVE

Water Wars

Man alone is the architect of his destiny. The greatest revolution in our generation is that human beings, by changing the inner attitudes of their minds, can change the outer aspects of their lives.　　　　　　　　　　　　　—WILLIAM JAMES

VARIOUS WATER WARS are now being waged across the face of our Earth. Some of these wars are obvious while others are silent. However, no matter who wins these wars, the outcome will eventually impact every living thing born or to be born on our planet.

One war is taking an estimated 15 million casualties each year. This is the war of chemical contamination and waterborne disease.

The second war is the war of scarcity. This war is fought in the courts, backroom offices of politicians, and—sometimes—in the battlefield.

The third war is the war of entrepreneurial control—the monopolistic purchase of springs and the water rights to surface and subsurface waters.

These wars will not go away. In fact, they will only get worse. Each day they continue to spread.

Who will win these wars?

The way I see it, water wars can have only two outcomes—either we all win or we all lose. Or, as the National Geographic Society's Gilbert M. Grosvenor expressed in 1998, "Civilization as we know it will either survive or fail depending on our ability to solve the problem of water within ten years." According to Mr. Grosvenor's clock, we have about eight years within which to solve the world's water problems.

The war over water reminds me of a video I saw once that takes place at a watering hole in Africa. During the rainy season, the river flowed and there was plenty of water for the fish, hippos, crocodiles, lions, baboons, birds, gazelles, and many other animals. Then a drought came; the river dried up, and only one large watering hole remained. Slowly but surely, with each relentlessly hot day, water evaporated and the watering hole became smaller. As the horrible life-and-death scene played itself out, some animals left the area in search of water; others died of thirst and were eaten; and others were just eaten alive in their weakened state. Cannibalism became rampant. Eventually, it came down to just a bunch of crocodiles struggling in the remaining mudhole. If a crocodile died, it was quickly eaten for its food and blood water. Toward the end, it came down to one large crocodile and a few smaller crocodiles. Seeing their future, the few remaining smaller crocodiles wandered off into the cool shade of nearby scrub brush, or dug deep holes in the side of the riverbank and buried themselves. Alone, in the middle of the shrinking mudhole, the big crocodile buried himself as best he could under the remaining wet mud. When all the mud dried up, the big crocodile died. In the end, there was nothing left but the scattered skeletons of a lot of different life forms.

When the rains returned, so did many life forms. A few of the smaller crocodiles that buried themselves in the side of the dry riverbank had survived.

This story to me is indicative of our present situation at this time in history. The river of freshwater is flowing. Even though there is some scarcity in the world, there is still plenty of water to keep a lot of people feeling complacent and secure. With hardly a thought, water is wasted on trivial things. Inevitably, either due to overuse, natural catastrophe, or a shift in climate, the amount of freshwater available to humans as well as all other life forms will begin to shrink. As the global watering hole we all drink from shrinks in size, those animals with the biggest teeth (armaments) will control who lives and who dies. In the end, even the most powerful animals will succumb to infighting and cannibalism.

Hopefully, with our evolving intelligence and growing water awareness, we will save our watering hole from being contaminated and wasted. Hopefully, we can take action today to save us from fighting over a dirty little puddle of water tomorrow.

The William James quotation at the beginning of this chapter, which says that human beings, "by changing the inner attitudes of their minds, can change the outer aspects of their lives," applies to change in our individual lives as well as in the life of humanity as a whole. Basically, all change begins with a thought within. In time, a thought has the power to change the life of a person as well as the lives of all people on Earth.

In my opinion, if the world of humankind continues treating water as it does now, the future appears as nothing other than war and famine.

Yes, we have the tools and the knowledge to work with the entity of water so other life forms may continue to exist.

Yes, humans need many other life forms to help us survive our passage in this earthly environment.

Yes, humankind can participate in the thought of creating a better inner world and outer world for future generations of life on Earth.

One of the best publications in the world for current information on international water news is the monthly *U.S. Water News*, copublished in Halstead, Kansas, by U.S. Water News, Inc., and the Freshwater Foundation. In an April 1996 editorial, Thomas C. Bell, president and publisher of *U.S. Water News*, wrote:

> We are often very nonchalant about our water supplies, content if water consistently flows from our tap, showerhead, or sprinkler as we use and abuse our most precious resource. However, the global view of water supplies can be very different. Just as range wars were once fought over water in our country a century ago, we will see increasing hostilities between countries fighting over access to water resources as we close this millennium and begin the next one. Water resource managers will be in a position to foster international peace as tension mounts over these limited water resources.
>
> Because the worldwide growth in demand for water is doubling every 21 years, the output from water supplies will be unable to keep up with the demand. As always, because freshwater is not equally distributed across the face of our planet, some areas enjoy abundant supplies while others will face grueling and deadly water shortages.
>
> This year, chronic water shortages will affect about 80 countries, or 40 percent of the Earth's population. According to the World Bank, a billion people will not have access to clean drinking water. For those of us who have grown numb to the constant barrage of large numbers in our lives, that's a thousand million people without clean water. That's a population equivalent to 1000 cities the size of San Diego.

Unsafe water already causes 8 out of 10 diseases in developing countries of the world. It is estimated that this year more than 10 million people will die as a result of unsafe water supplies. Continued population growth will only make the problem worse, with a projected 90 million more babies born in 1996. That's equivalent to adding the population of Mexico to the world in one year.

Freshwater will become the natural resource most likely to cause wars in the 21st century, according to the World Bank. The bank has warned that the river basins of the Jordan, Tigris, and Euphrates will become the areas most likely to erupt into war over water.

A number of observers say water rights may well determine the outcome of peace negotiations between Israel and the Palestinians. Although Israel has formerly recognized Palestinian water rights in the West Bank, it is the extent of those rights that is bitterly contested. The issue is so difficult to resolve that it has been postponed to the very last stages of negotiations to begin in May.

Some observers say water is even more crucial in the peace process than questions concerning the city of Jerusalem. It is hard to believe, but the feeling is that people can live without Jerusalem but they cannot live without water. The issue is the West Bank aquifer, the only source of water for much of the region. It is such a critical issue that most observers say it is the hottest spot in the world today for conflict over water.

But it is not the only hotspot. There are many trouble spots throughout the Middle East where rapid growth in population, agriculture, and industry are occurring amid limited water supplies.

Egypt depends on the Nile River for nearly all its freshwater supplies. But it must share the huge river with nine countries that all lie upstream and thus control the quantity of water reaching Egypt. Jordan, which shares the Jordan River basin with Israel and Syria, claims Syria is utilizing more than its share of water from the Yarmuk River, a Jordan tributary that lies between the two countries. And tension is building in the Tigris and Euphrates river basin where Turkey is constructing dams that threaten downstream water supplies in Syria and Iraq.

Outside the Middle East, the confrontation over water is widespread. There is conflict over the Ganges River basin shared by India and Bangladesh, and there is conflict over the Danube River where Slovakia and Hungary are planning to build a hydroelectric dam. And conflict lies, too, between our own country and Mexico over the trickle of water that is flowing across the border into Mexico from the highly over-utilized Colorado River.

It would be an understatement to say the next quarter century will be extremely interesting from a water resource management standpoint. Water supply professionals will be pressed to find workable solutions to water supply problems around the world. Not many would have imagined that a water resource engineer or manager might one day hold the key to peace by developing, planning, solving, and creating a water supply plan that would unite countries, prevent war, and bring peace to war-weary areas. It is a role not commonly foreseen by water resource professionals, but one they will surely fill in the not-too-distant future.

The closing paragraph in Mr. Bell's editorial indicates how our humble water engineers and water managers will be playing a key role in the future of humanity. This makes it clear that people with knowledge of water will be invaluable to our future survival. In this way, those who spend time learning about water will become an asset to their families, their communities, their countries, and to all life on the planet.

In an attempt to prevent international conflicts over water, the United Nations General Assembly adopted the Convention on Non-Navigational Uses of International Watercourses in May 1997. However, the language in this agreement is too vague and open to clearly define how countries are supposed to work together when it comes to sharing river water. Language such as "equitable and reasonable use" and the responsibility not to cause "significant harm" to neighboring countries that share the same river leaves much to be desired. This ambiguous language is usually something we find in contract law. Of course, it was a group of international lawyers that drafted this language.

On a positive note, every member country of the General Assembly voted in favor of this agreement, except for China, Turkey, and Burundi. What makes the agreement noteworthy is that its articles were based on over twenty years of research by the U.N.'s International Law Commission.

Regardless of the outcome of this initial international water agreement, it is my opinion that the United Nations will serve as an important vehicle for helping us find our watercourse way. If we fail in this effort and civilization collapses—we will find ourselves depending on the local knowledge of those who know water.

Ten Thoughts on Water Conflict

1. This special 13th edition of the *National Geographic* is devoted exclusively to the subject of freshwater—our use and abuse of it, our potential supply, and our prospects for the future. The edition is only the second of its kind in the Society's 105-year history.

    Our first report focused on energy and its major sources—oil, coal, natural gas—as well as various substitute sources. But there is, of course, no substitute for water; it has already begun to replace oil as a major cause of confrontation in the Middle East. The confrontations can only grow and widen. (William Graves, Editor, *National Geographic* Vol. 184, No. 5A, 1993).

2. Eastern European governments must face the prospect of a public health catastrophe or must invest in expensive pollution control systems they cannot afford. But these nations are already strapped with large foreign debts, and do not have the money to overhaul factories, use cleaner and more expensive high grade fuel, or clean up rivers. (Ronald S. Toth, "Eastern Europe's Dying Landscape," *Planet Earth Beyond Repair?* Worldwide Church of God, 1990).

3. As populations grow, the demand for freshwater of any kind—clean or not—increases. For example, Egypt's foreign minister has warned, "The next war in our region will be over the waters of the Nile." (Clayton Steep, "Troubled Waters," *Planet Earth Beyond Repair?* Worldwide Church of God, 1990).

4. Nations like Israel and Jordan are swiftly sliding into that zone where they are using all the water resources available to them. They have only 15 to 20 years left before their agriculture, and ultimately their food security, is threatened. (Joyce Starr, Global Water Summit Initiative, Washington, D.C., 1993).

5. Everything emerged from the water. Water, therefore, is the raw material of every culture or the basis of every bodily and spiritual development. The discovery of the secrets of water makes nonsense of every kind of speculation leading to war, hate, envy, intolerance and discord. It would mean the end of monopoly, the end of all forms of domination and the recognition of individualism in its most complete form.

   By way of naturally occurring oxidation (cold combustion), machine power can be generated, and substances produced in great variety, which in turn can stimulate growth, merely from the air and water.

   It is clear how man can become the master as well as the servant of all creation. Yet this possibility is held on a knife edge, and one mistake could plunge him into the abyss. The man who understands creative transformation is like a god. The one who manipulates this for his own ends is a servant of the devil, who can destroy the world. (Viktor Schauberger, quoted in Olof Alexandersson, *Living Water*, pp. 114–15).

6. In many southern European countries and in England the time is approaching when the water supply for agriculture and industry, as well as the population, will not be able to meet the demand. This has been the case in Israel for some time. Tourism in the dry summer season has aggravated the water shortage in Southern Europe. Because of this the so-called "water barrier," the point at which supply and demand are balanced, will become an important factor in future economies. This critical point will be exceeded in many of these countries by the beginning of the next century. It will be necessary to find solutions by recycling waste water and introducing far-reaching measures to save water, and ultimately the only answer will be the energy intensive desalination of seawater. This results in an entirely artificial heart function [of the natural organism of Europe], and it would not take much for a serious disaster to occur. (Kees Zoeteman, *Gaiasophy: The Wisdom of the Living Earth*, pp. 288–89).

7. Recent cost-cutting successes in seawater desalination technology may help avert future wars over limited water resources in the Middle East and Africa, a conference in Cairo on the politics of water was told yesterday. Egypt's deputy prime minister, Yusif Wali, said at a conference on "Grains, Water and Politics"

that the cost of desalination had gone down to less than a half-dollar per cubic meter. He said that this was far cheaper than the alternative of exporting water from one state to another—a reference to such proposals as those touted by Turkey several years ago for a "Peace Pipeline" to shift Turkish river water to the Gulf States and Israel. (*Deutsche Presse* Agnetur, March 31, 1996).

8. Dwindling water supplies are adding to tension in many regions of the world and the effect will increase in coming years, a Washington-based environmental group said yesterday. By 2025, 40 percent of the world's people will be living in countries experiencing chronic water shortages or water stress, the World-watch Institute said in a report. The report said tensions over water already are common in river basins of the Middle East, citing the Jordan, Nile and Tigris-Euphrates rivers. (Associated Press, September 15, 1996).

9. Water shortages are worsening rapidly in many regions, as population growth and rising water demands stretch supplies to their limits. Tensions over water scarcity could reach a fever pitch this decade not only in the Middle East, but in Central Asia, where five countries newly independent from the former Soviet Union face an ecosystem and an economy suffering from lack of water. As Soviet Republics, they had hoped that Moscow would help by diverting some of Siberia's water wealth to their parched lands and shrinking Aral Sea. With that hope gone, and ethnic and political rivalries running strong, confrontations over control of water seem inevitable.

   The immediate challenge for the international community is to recognize water scarcity as an increasing powerful force of political and social instability, and, accordingly, to raise it to a higher place on the crowded policy agenda. The Middle East and Central Asia are obvious hotspots, but where else might the destabilizing influence of water scarcity raise its head? There is China, which is home to 22 percent of the world's people but to only 8 percent of its freshwater—yet has a population growing by fifteen million a year. And there are India and Bangladesh, both poor, agrarian countries that cannot agree on how to divide the waters of the Ganges River. (Sandra Postel, *The Politics of Water*, Worldwatch Institute, July/August 1993).

10. At international meetings about resources we have frequently heard the statement that even in the 1990s some countries or regions will have to stop their growth or go to war, or both, because of shortages of water....

Global water demand has been growing faster than the limit is being raised by dam building. And as the most favorable sites are taken, and as citizen opposition to dams increases, dam building will slow.

Globally water is in great excess, but because of operational limits and pollution, it can in fact support at most one more doubling of demand, which will occur in 20 to 30 years. Even if it were possible to stop all pollution, trap every drop of flood, move either the water to the people or the people to the water, even if it were possible and desirable to capture the planet's full 40,000 cubic kilometers of annual runoff for human use, there would only be enough water for only 3 to 4 more doublings—a mere 100 years away if current growth rates continue.

You don't have to wait for a global water shortage to see what happens when a society overshoots its water limit. You can look at the parts of the world that have already done it. (Donella H. Meadows, Dennis L. Meadows, and Jorgen Randers, *Beyond the Limits*).

The above only serve as a warning. For the course of humanity to join with the living course of water, much work remains.

Hopefully we will succeed. If not, we may eventually find ourselves in a shrinking watering hole fighting over the last remaining sips of water.

Fear not, however, for no matter the outcome, the rains will come again and life will spring forth. However, whether or not we as a civilization survive to enjoy the spring rain remains to be seen.

Part IV

HEALING

The yin-yang symbol appears as two water drops swirling around each other, representing the positive and negative energies found in water's creative vortex energy.

THIRTEEN

Healing Heart

IN 1984, at the age of thirty-four, I died from a heart attack. I was swimming in the ocean off Martha's Vineyard and felt myself getting nauseous and dizzy. Fortunately, I was able to swim for shore. By the time I reached the beach, I had only enough strength to crawl out of the water. Steadying myself against a large rock, I tried standing, but fainted. Upon awakening, I crawled to my blanket with short breaths and stabbing chest pains. I was alone with no one in sight to help. After reaching my blanket, the pain and choking spasms of the heart attack struck full force. At that point I left my body and floated through a soft, soothing, milky white substance. To be honest, it felt great to be free of the burden of being trapped inside a body.

In hindsight, the scariest part of my dying experience was the extreme pain I endured just prior to leaving my body. My chest felt like it was going to explode, and gasping for each breath was frightening. Besides the pain, there was the split-second thought of "I'm dying!" The astounding implications of this thought filled my mind with fear beyond words.

So, there I was floating through this milky white, ethereal, airlike substance thinking about how great it felt to be free of physical pain. To no longer worry about food or clothing. To no longer think about caring for and maintaining my body. To no longer think of material possessions or worry about a house for my body to live in or a car to drive it around. Like the genie in Aladdin's lamp, I was suddenly set free of this material realm and all its limitations.

After floating about for a time, I found myself feeling very comfortable and joyful. Then I became aware of the presence of other spirits. The energy of some spirits felt loving, while others felt like they were just watching from a distance. It was at about this time that I sensed a telepathic communication of sorts. A soft voice was asking me, "Do you want to return?" For some reason, my immediate inner voice's response was "Yes." Then my mind asked, "What made my inner voice say yes? It feels great being here out of my body. I don't want to return!" However, for some fateful reason, that initial response set things in motion.

I then heard the soft voice return as it instructed me, "Concentrate on listening for the sound of waves crashing on the beach." So, I concentrated. Before long, I could hear the faint sound of waves crashing. "Keep listening," said the soft voice. The sound of the waves slowly became louder. "Now feel the pain," said the voice. At first there was no pain. But then, I began to feel some pain, as though I was sensing the inside of my body again. This frightened me. But the soothing voice said, "Don't be afraid, the pain is good, it will awaken your body." Soon, the pain became intense. It felt like thousands of needles were stabbing my arms and legs. "Keep feeling the pain. That's it, feel the pain," said the voice as it faded away.

Suddenly, I was back in this world feeling excruciating pain shooting through my legs and arms. Then I became aware of chest pain and my body's efforts to gasp for air. As luck would have it, some beach strollers found me curled up on my blanket and called for emergency help.

For the next eight years I was to go through a barrage of tests dealing with my heart problem. At first, the doctors were bewildered because inspection of my arteries gave no indication of blockage. Also, my cholesterol and other blood chemistry gave no indication of why I would suffer such an attack. Eventually, the explanation was that my heart malfunctioned because of a transient virus that had caused inflammation of the sac surrounding it. As a result, my heart had suffered permanent damage that was now causing me to suffer a condition called *cardiomyopathy*. Which means that my heart is slowly dying. Because of this, I was experiencing life-threatening events called ventricular tachycardia (VT). During these events, my heart rate would leap up to 250 beats per minute and I would rush off to the nearest emergency room. If the injection of high doses of drugs failed to correct the rapid heart rhythm, the emergency room doctors would cardio convert me with electricity. During that phase of my life, I experienced cardio conversion on three occasions. Each time, up to two hundred joules of electricity were shot through my heart with the hope that when it started beating again, it would return to a normal rhythm.

During those eight years of suffering heart palpitations and angina, I was under heavy prescription medications called quinidine and atenolol. At different times, I met and spoke with top cardiologists across the country. One of the head cardiologists at Beth Israel Deaconess said that I would eventually need a heart transplant. Another doctor wanted to try an experimental procedure whereby he would crack open my chest and cut away part of my damaged heart.

After almost eight years, I suffered a severe attack in 1991. It was then recommended that I undergo an electrical physiological study (EPS). This study indicated that cells in my lower heart were creating electrical currents that induced rapid heartbeats. In another test a long wire with a miniature pair of pliers was fished down into my heart through the jugular vein in my neck. The pliers grabbed a sample of my heart tissue for microscopic cellular study.

When all was said and done, the cardiologists at Beth Israel Deaconess Hospital in Boston recommended an experimental procedure called an oblation. This procedure involved putting five catheters into my heart at the same time. These long, wirelike devices would be snaked into my heart through the arteries in my legs and the jugular vein in my neck. One of the catheters would have a round device that emitted radio waves that could burn and destroy cells. The other catheters would be used to induce a rapid heartbeat while also trying to locate the cells emitting the problem electrical current.

Before the operation, I was given the option of being awake or put to sleep under general anesthesia. I chose to be awake. I remember clearly the first cut administered to my neck. An artery was cut that sent blood squirting three feet into the air with each heartbeat. In a way, it reminded me of water from a squirt gun.

The invasive operation took over five hours. During that time, I came close to losing consciousness several times because of the electrically induced rapid heartbeat. Finally, after fourteen burns with the radio-wave device, I asked the operating cardiologist, "How many burns does it take before my heart suffers irreversible damage?" The doctor's answer: "We don't know." That's when I told him to stop burning the inside of my heart. At first, the doctor was reluctant to stop. But, I asserted myself and demanded they stop at once.

From that day on, I decided to take responsibility for healing my heart.

Today, ten years later, I no longer take any medications and am completely free of heart problems. How did I heal myself from a life-threatening heart condition? Through hydrotherapy and a self-researched nutrition and healing regime.

Over the past ten years I have learned that each us is truly a unique life form. As such, the ancient adage of *know thyself* applies.

The more I researched and experimented with various water-healing methods, the more I learned about myself. This learning touched my body, mind, and soul on many levels. For instance, while experimenting with various hot and cold hydrotherapy techniques, I tried using a combination of healing agents. One of these combinations was to fill a bathtub with very warm water while I stirred in various herbs and mineral salts, turned on my favorite music, and lit some incense. Just before entering the water, I would also light a nearby candle and then add about ten drops of lavender oil to the water. I would then immerse myself into the water for twenty to thirty minutes.

As time went by, I learned to embellish the tub-soak technique by chanting the word *Om* over and over again for various lengths of time. The addition of the chanting elevated the tub soak to a new level. The use of sound in the enhanced tub water seemed to vibrate every cell in my body. Besides feeling better physically, I also got a new feeling of psychological well-being. It was as if my entire being was being elevated to a higher vibration level of existence.

It wasn't until much later that I learned how the use of the *Om* chant creates a circular healing tone. This circular tone can help energize the cells of the body and return a person to homeostasis, or healthy balance. I was also to learn that each of us has vocal cords that are pitched in tone to help ourselves heal—therefore the importance of using one's own voice as part of any healing effort.

Another hydrotherapy technique I employed was to take hot and cold showers. I would take a hot shower for about six minutes with the water hitting mostly on my chest and back, and then turn the water to its coldest setting for about one to three minutes (depending on my comfort level). I would then alternate back and forth with this hot and cold shower treatment—always ending with cold water.

Besides the above, I began to pay closer attention to the amount of water I drank each day. I was now drinking about eight glasses of water a day, and sometimes more, depending on the temperature and the amount of my physical work, play, or exercise.

These experiments went on for years. Instead of coming home from work and eating dinner, reading newspapers, watching television, and going to bed, I focused on my physical and spiritual development. And, it worked. Slowly but surely I began to feel better about my use of time and how my health was improving.

Along the way, I also blended in the sound of running water from a small water fountain. After about three years of working to heal my heart, I found myself listening to more music. I also began exploring the uses of meditation, prayer, yoga, stretching, color, light, homeopathy, herbs, vitamins, minerals, and food. If an opportunity presented itself while I was walking near a stream or the ocean, I would take off my shoes, roll up my pants, and rejoice in walking ankle deep in the cool water. The same went for water events such as dew, frost, fog, or rain. Sometimes I would find myself walking barefoot in grass covered with drops of cool sparkling dew or a white blanket of ice-cold frost. Other times I would take off my clothes and go outside to stand or run around the yard in the fog or rain.

A big psychological part of my cardiac cure was to take some calculated risks. I guess the biggest turning point came when I received a telephone call from a college friend, Michael King. Michael invited me to join him and some friends on a rafting trip down the Colorado River. After two years of self-healing, I was beginning to regain some confidence and felt I was strong enough to take the trip. Besides the adventure, I also felt there would be some healing derived from the river's water energy.

The river trip entailed rafting 200 miles of river, running thirty rapids, and camping out for about ten days. Besides getting reacquainted with Michael, I in fact did sense some healing taking place from my daily immersions in the cold river water. When I returned home to Martha's Vineyard, I truly felt stronger than before.

In time I learned that there was much more to healing than the mere physical use of water. I learned that we must be patient while on the journey of healing—no matter what the ailment or injury. I also learned and continue to learn how water is a mysterious and beautiful agent for healing and caring for all levels of one's being. But most of all, I learned that water is a vital agent for learning how to love yourself, your family, friends, and this wonderful, life-filled creation.

Perhaps this is why so many people find themselves being seduced and becoming romantically inclined while in a setting near water. Could it be that the water in our bodies responds in kind to the loving energy of healthy water? If this is true, then this may be why so many people seek out clean water for drinking, bathing, healing, and the sharing of love.

Today I take long hikes in remote regions without fear, run, swim, bicycle, and travel. I am also free of taking synthetic medicines. By the way, the last time I visited my cardiologist, he was somewhat bewildered by my recovery.

FOURTEEN

Our Human Bodies and Water

*Water is the blood of the Earth, and flows through its muscles
and veins.*   —KUAN-TSU

*We have water's universal nature to thank for the fact that we
can develop our bodily form in the fluid of the maternal organism; that water can serve us as the life element after we are born;
and that we are able to think because our brains are afloat on
water's buoyancy.*   —THEODOR SCHWENK

Water Bodies

IT WAS JUST one hundred years ago that the French scientist René
Quinton established the chemical similarities between seawater and
blood plasma. This startling revelation opened the minds of many
people to the possible origins of humankind and other so-called
"higher" life forms. Science and medicine tell us that about 90 percent
of blood plasma is water, and that the water in our blood trans-
ports the nutrition-loaded plasma throughout our bodies. The brain
is about 85 percent water, and water constantly washes our eyes
through tiny ducts about twenty-five times a minute. This constant
washing of the eyes allows you to read this book, to see the world
we live in, and to keep your eyeballs free of dust, pollen, and other
airborne debris.

Since human blood plasma is derived from plant sources outside
our bodies, the chemicals used on plants eventually find their way
into our blood. We are seeing more and more evidence of a direct
link between the chemistry of cell water within our bodies and that
of the waters of our planet. As a result, we now know that the health
of the planet's waters we drink will help determine the health of our
bodies.

185

In his book *Water: The Life Sustaining Resource,* Robert Gardner has six paragraphs that succinctly express what "body water" is:

At birth your body is about 78 percent water. In the embryo stage, your body water accounted for all but 3 percent of your weight. By the time you reach adulthood, your body water will constitute only 60 percent of your weight, although this varies from one individual to another through a range of 52 percent to 70 percent. With aging, body water slowly decreases from age thirty to eighty by about 18 percent. The metabolic rate declines at the same rate; hence, the ratio of oxygen intake to body water remains constant.

About 60 percent of your body water lies within living cells; another 25 percent is found between cells; the blood plasma holds 8 percent; and 5 percent is either transcellular water in the cavities of hollow organs such as your eyes, or a lubricant for your knee, hip, elbow, and shoulder joints.

Blood is approximately 90 percent water; kidney tissue is 8 percent water; our muscles are 75 percent water; the liver is 66 percent water; and even "dry" bone is 33 percent water.

Normally we maintain an equilibrium between the water we ingest and the water we excrete each day. The average person drinks 1,650 milliliters each day and gets 750 milliliters from food. Oxidation of food releases about 350 milliliters. Each pound of starch oxidized in the body releases about 0.56 pound of water as well as the energy stored in it....

Our total water output is about 2,750 milliliters. We excrete about 1,700 milliliters in urine, 150 milliliters in feces, and 400 milliliters in exhaled breath. An additional 500 milliliters evaporates from the four million sweat glands in our skin.

We each drink about 6,600 gallons of water in a lifetime and about five times our body weight each year. A loss of one percent of our body weight makes us thirsty. The intense thirst following a 5 percent loss of body water is nearly unbearable. By the time 7 percent has been removed, circulatory failure may ensue. (pp. 51–52).

After reading the above, it is easy to see the important role water plays in our bodies as it flows through some 60,000 miles of arteries and veins. From our inception as a fertilized egg to the time of our death, water is constantly flowing through our bodies; much of it is filtered and recirculated. According to Gardner, our kidneys clean about 2000 quarts of fluid each day while producing about two quarts (1800 milliliters) of urine that contains salt, nitrogen-rich urea, and other waste products from our body's cells.

How can a human body that is as much as 75 percent water appear to be so solid and have the shape and motion that it does? In his book *Quantum Healing*, Deepak Chopra writes:

> All of us are much more like a river than anything frozen in time or space.
>
> If you could see your body as it really is, you would never see it the same way twice. Ninety-eight percent of the atoms in your body were not there a year ago. The skeleton that seems so solid was not there three months ago. The configuration of the bone cells remains somewhat constant, but atoms of all kinds pass freely back and forth through the cell walls, and by that means you acquire a new skeleton every three months.
>
> The skin is new every month. You have a new stomach lining every four days, with the actual surface cells that contact food being renewed every five minutes. The cells in the liver turn over very slowly, but new atoms still flow through them, like water in a river course, making a new liver every six weeks.

When we look at ourselves in the mirror, we think we are looking at a body that is solid and slowly changing as it ages. In reality, we are looking at a body that is constantly renewing itself from second to second as water constantly flows through our physical being. The fact that we can appear to be so solid when our bodies are so fluid is one of the miracles of water. The human body is such a miracle that it leaves the world's preeminent scientists pondering in wonder as they create one theory after another to try to solve its mysteries.

Water for Brains

Since the brain is about 85 percent water, can there be any question about the importance of water to our mental health?

The very act of thinking is made possible only because our brains are floating in water. Thus freed from the pull of gravity, our brains are free to think and to dream. Usually, the reason a boxer gets knocked out or someone becomes unconscious from a fall is due to the forcing of the brain out of its floatation. When the brain hits against the cranium's interior, it causes a short circuit to the nervous system, resulting in the loss of consciousness.

The process through which the brain has a thought and sends a message to initiate motion of the body has been a subject of great study. Body movement, sexual orgasm, talking, laughing, choosing what to look at and listen to—these are functions of the physical body that result from brain messages.

How does the brain send messages to make our bodies function and have motion?

A technical explanation of how the brain cells send messages, or signals, throughout the body can be found in Dr. Fereydoon Batmanghelidj's *The Body's Many Cries for Water.* In this revealing book about water and health, Batmanghelidj writes: "The products manufactured in the brain cells are transported to their destination in the nerve endings for use in the transmission of messages on 'waterways.' There seem to exist small waterways or microstreams along the length of nerves that 'float' the packaged materials along 'guidelines,' called microtubules."

I found the above quote from Dr. Batmanghelidj's book to be intriguing. So I telephoned him and had a discussion about his water writings, with a special focus on the above quote. Dr. Batmanghelidj gave me verbal and written permission to rephrase the above quote in my suggested words as follows: "Apparently, the density of the nerve cells is such that they do not allow for *instantaneous* transmission of information from our brains to other parts of the body. In other words, when the brain creates a thought it sends an electrical signal via the nerve endings to the *waterways* that flow throughout the entire body and connect to every cell in the body. The thought (in the form of an electrical impulse) travels instantaneously (electricity travels instantaneously in body water) throughout the body along these waterways. In this way, thoughts from the brain are carried throughout the body's ocean of water, which in turn gives the body motion."

Because of the linking of the brain to the movement of the body via water, it is important to understand this relationship between body water and thought. It is also important to understand that the electrical impulses that carry thoughts are created from the flow of water around and through the membrane walls of brain cells. The fact that water is instrumental in creating electricity within our bodies and that electricity is the basis for thought tells a story unto itself.

In Eastern Zen teachings, the mind is often referred to as a body of water that reflects the reality of its environment, with any change in the outside world being reflected in the water of our minds. When this aspect of Zen is compared to Western psychology and medicine, we find a similar belief. According to the Western school of thought, each time the mind learns new information or has a new experience of the external environment—it undergoes change. In this way, we see how the East and the West express similar belief systems when it comes to the mind and the external world.

The fact that the brain is composed mostly of water in perpetual motion, and that this motion generates electricity to help generate thoughts and nerve impulses, gives credence to water's link with human intelligence, emotions, and body movement.

Echoing this position to a certain degree is Professor Rolf Faste of Stanford University. Besides teaching at the College of Engineering at Stanford, Faste travels the world giving seminars on creative thinking to academic and corporate gatherings. In a telephone conversation, Faste told me, "Within fifteen seconds of taking a drink of water, most people will be thinking better and have a more positive attitude. This happens because water is vital for the optimum function of our neural systems. The hemoglobin molecules in our blood will absorb up to four times more oxygen in the presence of adequate water."

When asked how he knows this, Faste was quick to refer to articles in *Science News* (March 30, 1991), the recent book *Smart Moves* by neurophysiologist Carla Hanniford, and cutting-edge research at the Educational Kinesiology Foundation in Ventura, California.

"We start thinking better the second water passes over our tongues," said Faste. "Some of the water we drink is immediately absorbed sublingually and sends a message to the hypothalamus. The hypothalamus in turn sends a message to the brain and other organs that new water is on the way. This allows for more water to be available to the brain and enables the brain's neurons to fire more actively and efficiently."

Faste says that over the years he has convinced many academics, inventors, engineers, scientists, and others who attend his "Brain Gym" seminars that "when working on a problem, drinking water is one of the best things you can do to help your brain find a solution as quickly as possible."

When there is very little water available to the body and survival becomes an issue, the brain will hoard as much water as it can while still allowing the body to have some water to function. The brain needs more water than any other organ and will actually "starve" other organs and body areas for water in order to maintain its own water. If the brain becomes starved for water, it can no longer function properly, and the survival of the entire body will soon be placed in peril.

If a person has been without water for a time, and suddenly some water becomes available, the first gulps of water are immediately sent to the brain. Have you ever been thirsty and exhausted and taken a drink of water? What happens to your thinking and mental attitude immediately after drinking water under these conditions? If you pay close attention, you will notice an immediate improvement in your mental and emotional well-being. All of a sudden you find yourself "refreshed" and "alert" and more conscious of your surroundings. It is almost as if you have been rejuvenated—which in fact you have been. Such is the miraculous nature of water.

How the feeling of thirst is manifested in the body is described by Deepak Chopra in *Quantum Healing:*

> The feeling of being thirsty is stimulated by the hypothalamus, a piece of the brain about the size of a finger joint, which in turn is connected by both nerves and chemical messengers to the kidneys. The kidneys constantly monitor the body's needs for water by "listening in" to signals from the blood. The signals are chemical, as with the neuro-peptides, but in this case the molecules involved are salts, proteins and blood sugar, as well as specific messengers. The blood in turn is picking up these signals from every cell in the body, each of which is constantly monitoring its own need for water. In other words, when you want a drink of water, you are not just obeying an impulse from your brain—you are listening to a request from every cell in your body.
>
> If you drink one small glass of water, you will replace 1/400 of your total bodily fluid, yet that will satisfy the precise needs of 50 trillion different cells. Such exact monitoring is often attributed to the kidneys alone, but as we have just seen, the kidneys never make decisions alone; they work in constant consultation with the quantum mechanical body—the whole field of intelligence. The evenness of intelligence is not apparent from the physical

makeup of cells; it coexists with the body's extreme specialization. The neuron, which is outfitted on its cell wall with a million sodium-potassium pumps, is not at all like a heart cell or stomach cell. Yet, the integrity of the message "time for some water" is constant everywhere.

Body Temperature

Water is the great regulator of body temperature. Our human body cannot survive major fluctuations of its internal temperature. The normal internal temperature of the human body is 98.6 degrees Fahrenheit. A 5-degree Fahrenheit change in temperature either way may be fatal for most people. Our body's primary method of cooling is by sweating through pores of the skin. Under strenuous conditions on a hot day we can lose close to a quart of water each hour. This is our body's way of keeping itself from overheating.

A curious thing about the temperature of the human body is that 98.6 degrees is also the temperature at which water can most readily absorb heat. This is why the blood of the body so easily absorbs heat during exercise and on hot days. The blood within us, which is mostly water, carries heat away from the internal core of our bodies to the skin's surface where there are over four million sweat glands. The hot water that is carried to the skin's surface evaporates through our dilated pores as sweat, which in turn cools the skin and helps prevent us from overheating.

The body's heat-regulatory system becomes even more curious when we realize that the body's temperature of 98.6 degrees occupies almost the exact position of the Golden Mean between the freezing and boiling points of water.

The Body's Connection to the Planet's Water

The ancient Greeks believed that there was a watery substance called *physis* that flowed throughout all life and connected the inner body with the outer world. This thought has evolved to where we now use the word "physiology" to refer to our inner world and the word "physics" to refer to our outer world.

Physiologically speaking, we use our minds and bodies to try to relate to the physical world around us. We survive by ingesting water and forms of life created, grown, and sustained by water outside our bodies. In this way, the water inside our bodies is connected to the water outside. Also, in this way, pollutants that are placed in water outside our bodies inevitably end up inside our bodies.

The relationship between our body water and the ocean has long been understood. Human sweat and tears are salty—just like the ocean. The blood and liquid inside the human body are also like the ocean and equally rich in trace elements such as gold and magnesium. If life did begin in the sea, then we are alive only because we carry our own sea within us. For that matter, all living things on land are living in a sea of rarefied water called water vapor. Without water in the form of water vapor in the air, there would be no naturally reoccurring oxygen for us to breathe.

The relationship between air and water is demonstrated further by the fact that sound travels four times faster through seawater than through air. This ratio of 1:4 between air and seawater also manifests itself in the human body. On the average, for every breath of air we take into our lungs, our heart beats four times as it pumps our seawater-like blood throughout our bodies.

Pregnancy and Growth of a Newborn

When a woman becomes pregnant, she may experience what is called "morning sickness." Such sickness is a condition of nausea that is usually caused by the new demands on the body for water as the womb and fetus develop. This demand is created by the fact that the fluid for the womb and the fetus itself are composed of over 90 percent water.

The high content of water as a home for the growing fetus is very important, especially when we consider that almost all chemical reactions take place in the presence of water. As the fetus develops and goes through rapid cell multiplication and diversification (embryogenesis), there are numerous chemical reactions taking place that remain a mystery. All we know is that the mystery of creation proceeds in the protective and nurturing presence of water.

Embryogenesis naturally requires considerable quantities of water. If a sufficient quantity is lacking, the cells of the developing baby as well as the cells of the mother send messages to the mother's brain that more water is needed. These messages often are expressed in feelings of nausea and dizziness, the same symptoms that appear when the body becomes dehydrated. For this reason, a pregnant woman should drink more water than usual in order to keep from becoming dehydrated as her body sacrifices its water to care for the fetus. She should also be extra conscious of trying to drink an adequate supply of the highest quality water available. This advice is recommended by many doctors as well as in the best-selling book *What to Expect When You're Expecting* by Arlene Eisenberg, which says, "If you've always been one of those people who goes through the day with barely a sip of anything, now is the time to change that habit."

Under healthy conditions, each cell of the developing fetus is bathed in nutrient-loaded fluid. The nutrients pass into the cells and wastes are returned into the surrounding fluid. For any cell to remain healthy it must be constantly fed nutrients and have its wastes quickly removed so it does not reabsorb them.

For this reason, it is vital that the nurturing mother do her best to secure the healthiest diet of nutrient-loaded foods and pure water. This will help to ensure the health of her growing baby and herself, make the pregnancy experience more enjoyable and less stressful, and allow for an easy delivery.

Once out of the womb, babies grow so rapidly that they take in more than their body weight in water in one week's time. This is because babies have a high metabolism (from the Greek *metabolē*, meaning "change"). As a baby's body grows, it experiences rapid change. Water in the mother's milk is a baby's most important agent for growth and change. Water carries the nourishment into the baby's body and works with chemicals in the stomach to convert the food to a form usable by the rapidly dividing and differentiating body cells. Water also carries the converted food to the baby's body cells to help them multiply, while also washing away wastes so the cells may live in a clean and healthy environment.

The energy of creating another human being and bringing it into this world of life is a very spiritual event. Just as water flows from the Earth to nourish life, so too does water flow from the breast of a woman to nourish the life of her newborn. It is no secret that the milk of a mother contains special properties for the health and well-being of her offspring. It is a known fact that a mother's milk is almost magical in the wholesome, life-giving nutrients that it delivers to the growing baby. In like form, so does the water that flows from the breast of Earth contain special nutrients and energy for the growth of the life.

Body Health and Clean Water

The constant flow of water through our bodies refreshes and recreates them as it removes toxins and wastes. This is why it is crucial that we do our best to drink the cleanest water obtainable. If the water we drink is polluted, it will not do its job of cleaning out our bodies and will only burden them with unnecessary wastes.

The flow of unpolluted water through our bodies cleans every cell, removes toxins and wastes, lubricates our bone joints to protect them from injury and reduce arthritic pain, keeps our skin clean and healthy looking, prevents constipation and urinary tract infections, helps reduce hair loss by maintaining cleaner follicles and enhancing blood circulation to the scalp, prevents the occurrence of gout by flushing uric acid from the body, protects us from kidney stones, minimizes jet lag by preventing the dehydration caused by pressurized cabins, helps to balance the pressure in and out of our body cells, makes us more energetic and alert, and helps us to have a more positive outlook on life.

Water also aids our health by: keeping our bodies clean through washing; keeping wounds free of infection (only freshwater should be used, never seawater); helping to reduce pain and promote healing when used as a hot water bath or compress, or when applied cold as ice; and preventing dry skin and nasal passage damage and destroying airborne bacteria and viruses when used to humidify our homes in dry climes or during the winter heating season.

It is extremely vital that the circulation through the body's veins, arteries, and lymph system be unobstructed. When there is tension inside the body due to stress or the blockage of blood flow because of fatty substances along circulation paths, a decrease in the size of blood-carrying capillaries oftentimes results in the death of cells. If not carried away and removed by the body's lymph system, the dead or injured cells will accumulate and begin killing nearby healthy cells. When such conditions persist, the stage is set for dis-ease (pain) and the onset of premature aging of the body.

To reduce the presence of fat in the blood, it is necessary to have an adequate supply of water constantly flowing through the body. Without proper irrigation by an adequate supply of water, the kidneys reduce their function; the cleaning of the blood is then transferred to the liver. By making the liver work harder to clean the blood, its primary job of metabolizing fat into energy becomes secondary. Thus, more fatty cells end up staying in the body, building up in the blood vessels and making it more difficult for one to lose weight. The Diet and Weight Loss Fitness Home Page on the Internet says, "Your liver is overloaded when your kidneys don't get enough water. The liver can't metabolize fat well when it does the kidneys' work."

Water, Food, and the Body

Water is the most important food element for the health and longevity of our human bodies. It almost seems foolish to see the emphasis and money people place on eating healthy foods while oftentimes overlooking or downplaying the importance of good water.

Spokesperson Felicia Busch, M.P.H., R.D., of the American Dietetic Association and the International Bottled Water Association says, "When people think about nutrition they think about nutrients and food groups. . . . They forget that water is the most important nutrient. Water is more important than any food, any vitamin, mineral or supplement you would get, because you can go for days without all of those things . . . but not without water." Ms. Busch's words echo those of Dr. Olaf Mickelsen of the National Institute of Health, who in 1959 wrote in *Food: Yearbook of the U.S. Department of Agriculture,* "It is well to remember that it is more important to have an adequate intake of water than it is to have enough calories."

The above advice of Ms. Busch and Dr. Mickelsen bring to mind an old survival adage known as the "law of three"—a person is very likely to be facing death when deprived of three minutes of air, three days of water, or thirty days of food.

A person on a reducing diet is advised to place more emphasis on losing fat than on losing water. Albeit the reduction of fat intake or the replacement of fat with muscle takes a longer time to show up on the scales, the quick loss of body water may end up causing undesired health and emotional problems. Since the kidneys readily dispose of any excess water in the body, such weight will be retained for only a few hours. In fact, drinking water helps to curb hunger pains and is therefore a friend in the war on fat.

When it comes to getting the most out of food, water is an important key. The chewing and mixing of food with saliva in our mouths begins the digestion process. Without saliva, which is 99.5 percent water, digestion of our food would be almost impossible. Each day, our bodies use about a quart and a half of saliva for digestion, one to two quarts of gastric juices (which are 90 percent water), and one to two quarts of bile and other enzymatic secretions. Obviously, without water, the chemistry for digesting and moving food through our bodies is virtually impossible. Since an estimated 99 percent of all chemical and other reactions depend on water, it is important that we drink water of quality to derive the most from the chemical breakdown of our food. Drinking water that is polluted with chemicals can cause unknown reactions within the body's chemistry, which in turn may stress our digestive system, rob our bodies of important nutritive values, and create unhealthy chemical compounds within our bodies.

It is also important for those who are on a reducing diet or exercise regime to keep flushing the body with a fresh supply of good water. As the body loses weight or as muscles are strained from exercise, cellular waste products are released into the body. If there is an inadequate water supply to carry the wastes out of the body, the body's first priority will be to retain fluids to prevent dehydration. In doing so, the body will accumulate the wastes created by exercise and dieting. Wastes that remain inside the body can potentially build up to toxic levels and cause disease and emotional instability.

A word to the wise about drinking water during a meal: The best rule to follow is to only sip small amounts of water if necessary to help wash down food. Other than that, I strongly recommend not drinking water or other fluids with meals. Drinking unnecessary amounts of water with meals will dilute the digestive juices of the stomach and interfere with the breaking down of the food. This interference could end up robbing the body of food nutrients while also causing unnecessary expenditure of energy to handle the additional intestinal wastes. According to Dr. Patrick Flanagan in *Elixir of the Ageless*, "The surface tension of water becomes an extremely important factor in the absorption and assimilation of food by the living system. This is the reason it is not good to drink ordinary water when we eat. Our digestive juices have a relatively low surface tension that can readily 'wet' our food. When we drink ordinary water which has a surface tension of 73 dynes/cm it dilutes the digestive juices and prevents adequate wetting of food particles."

However, it is very important to drink an adequate amount of water during other times of the day to make sure there is enough water available for proper digestion as well as for circulation, cleaning of the body's cells, and other functions. Because of water's many benefits to the human body, it is little wonder that many doctors recommend adults should drink at least eight cups of water a day, and even more when exercising.

The body is constantly losing water through excreta, sweat, expired breath, and as vapor from the skin—even when there is no sweating. This means our body water is in constant need of replacement, and it is a good idea to do so abundantly. If this is done, there certainly will be plenty of water available in the form of digestive juices.

Living Water

A living body needs living water.

All the vitamins, minerals, proteins, amino acids, enzymes, carbohydrates, and other nutrients that the human body needs to maintain itself can be found in fruits and vegetables.

The nature of all fruits and vegetables is to have a high content of living water. This living water contains nutrients that are specially processed by plants from soils, the atmosphere, and the cosmos. How the plants of Earth perform this feat of transforming ordinary water into water filled with energy from the universe remains somewhat of a mystery.

However, most of the world's nutritionists, doctors, and scientists are now believers in the age-old wisdom of eating fresh fruits and vegetables. These people, along with many of the world's governments and health agencies, are now recommending a diet of foods with high water content.

Since our bodies are about 70 percent water, it makes sense that 70 percent of the food we eat should be high in water content. This is simply a matter of common sense. People who eat foods with high water content will not need to drink as much water. The living water from the food they eat will perform the function of carrying nutrients to the cells while also cleaning them. In fact, living water is a far superior way of keeping the body hydrated and cleansed so it may carry out its living functions with as little energy expenditure as possible.

The rule of drinking about eight glasses of water a day applies to the lifestyle and eating habits of most modern-day people, who are so far removed from the living world that their diets consist mostly of processed foods containing little or no water. However, with the advent of a new consciousness about food and water, many people are now in the process of changing their habits. No longer are they buying the sales pitches encouraging them to purchase and eat processed foods that have large profit margins for the manufacturers. More and more people today are buying and eating high-water-content fruits and vegetables that contain the living water necessary for a long and healthy life.

This position is further supported by the research of a scientist named Alexander Leaf, as reported in an excellent article in the January 1973 edition of *National Geographic*. In his research on people who lived long lives in different regions of the world, Dr. Leaf discovered that most of these people ate a diet of approximately 70 percent fresh fruit and vegetables.

Information like this gives credibility to the advice about eating fresh fruits and vegetables several times throughout the day. It also suggests the benefits of using the juice of fresh fruits and vegetables for drinking and recipes. But, a note of caution—care should always be taken to try to eat or drink the juices of fresh fruits and vegetables that are not contaminated by herbicides and pesticides. In this way, one can be assured of filling one's body with the highest quality "living water."

Caffeine, Alcohol, and Dehydration

The human brain is extremely sensitive to changes in the body's water level, therefore making dehydration one of the primary sources of headache. Signs of advanced water deficiency include lightheadedness and increased heart rate, especially when we first stand up from a sitting or lying position. The drinking of coffee, tea, and soft drinks containing caffeine serves only to increase the loss of fluids from the body. Drinks such as these do not add water to the body—they take it away.

A good indicator of dehydration is our urine output. When we urinate there should be an ample quantity that is clear to light yellow in color. If we haven't urinated in a while and see that our urine output isn't that great and that the urine is an odorous dark yellow or orange, then we are becoming dehydrated. The exception to this is when we are taking vitamins containing natural or other color additives, which will change the color of the urine.

Urine will usually appear dark after a night of sleep, since the body dehydrates over a period of ten to twelve hours without additional water. Also, while the body is resting, it has an opportunity to clean its cells of waste products gathered throughout the day.

When Paracelsus first separated alcohol from wine in the 1500s, alcohol's power to intoxicate was believed to come from a "water spirit." This is the origin of today's link between the words "spirits" and "alcohol." Thus, when a person became drunk and underwent a personality change, he was considered possessed by the spirits in the alcohol. I can only imagine what people thought about the cause of the headache that often followed. Perhaps the headache was blamed on the spirits leaving the body.

Today we know that the hangover headache results from the cells of the body (especially those of the brain) sacrificing their water to dilute and flush toxic alcohol from the body. The brain, which is about 85 percent water, is a major contributor of water to dilute poisons such as alcohol. Even though the brain makes up one-fiftieth of our body's weight, it receives about 20 percent of the body's blood circulation. Such information as this shows that our bodies are engineered to give the brain top priority at all times under any set of circumstances.

As this writer and many others can attest, the "morning after" headache can be greatly minimized by drinking water before, during, and immediately after the intake of alcohol. Drinking water saves the cells of the brain from having to sacrifice their water to help rid the body of poisonous alcohol. Drinking water before, during, and after the drinking of alcohol also helps reduce the damaging residency time of alcohol inside the body.

According to Stephen Braun in *Buzz: The Science and Lore of Alcohol and Caffeine*, alcohol "is a stimulating, depressing, mood-altering drug that leaves practically no circuit or system of the brain untouched."

Some researchers have suggested that it is best, if one is drinking, to drink alcohol on an empty stomach. In *Fit for Life*, Harvey and Marilyn Diamond say this about the question of wine helping digestion:

Whoever is responsible for that bit of tomfoolery surely sits on the board of one of the major wineries. The body no more needs help to digest food than it needs help to blink its eyes or to breathe. All are automatic responses. Digestion simply takes place when food is in the stomach. If anything, wine retards the digestion of food. In the same way your motor responses are slowed down when under the influence of alcohol, digestion is also slowed down.

Wine is fermented, which causes any food it comes into contact with to spoil. All alcohol places a heavy burden on the kidneys and liver. If you enjoy wine, try to drink it on an empty stomach. It will take less to "loosen you up," and it won't spoil any food. Moderation is the key.

When food and alcohol are ingested at the same time, the alcohol acts like a food preservative and interferes with digestion, which is why I recommend that no more than one glass of wine be taken during a meal. Research proving the negative impact of alcohol on food digestion was conducted by Dr. George Ulett, director of Neuropsychiatric Service and Psychosomatic Research at Deaconess Hospital in St. Louis, and published in the *Psychiatric Journal of the University of Ottawa* (vol. 5, no. 2, June 1980). Other research relating alcohol to poor digestion and blood-sugar problems can be found in Jean Poulos and Donald Stoddard's *The Relationship between Hypoglycemia and Alcoholism*. During their research, Poulos and Stoddard discovered that 100 percent of the alcoholics they studied were hypoglycemic, prediabetic, or diabetic.

In order to minimize digestion problems, I suggest that alcohol be consumed about one hour after eating a full meal. However, with bacterial pollution being what it is at present, drinking a glass of wine with meat, fish, and shellfish is now recommended. It has been found that drinking a glass of wine with such foods helps to destroy any harmful bacteria that may cause discomfort or a life-threatening reaction.

Alcohol's ability to destroy bacteria has also led to the recent discovery that it can be used to cure diarrhea. One glass of wine for women or two for men is now recommended as a remedy for diarrhea. Apparently, the alcohol in the wine quickly destroys the harmful bacteria causing the gastrointestinal malfunction. This recommendation of one glass of wine for women and two for men is not because of the old myth that women are more susceptible to alcohol because they have less body weight, but because the alcohol-destroying enzymes found in the stomach lining of humans work more efficiently in men than in women. The reason for this difference between the stomach linings of men and women has yet to be completely understood.

Whenever I drink alcohol socially, I always order a glass of water. For every sip of alcohol, I take a sip of water. This protects my body while at the same time allowing me to wash my palette in between sips of alcohol. If I am drinking a fine wine, the wine is appreciated anew with each sip after my mouth is refreshed by water. Besides helping me to better enjoy the wine, water helps to protect my body from alcohol damage while also saving me a considerable sum of money.

In *The Good Water Guide* by Maureen and Timothy Green, we learn that Italians "are easily the world's largest imbibers of mineral waters at 125 litres each annually." We also learn from this book that drinking water with alcohol is the usual practice of many Europeans:

> Bread, wine and water are the first things brought to your table in an Italian trattoria or restaurant. Drinking mineral water has nothing to do with abstention, with going on a diet, with driving. In Italy there are no breathalyser tests for motorists, no licensing laws, and no prohibition on alcohol in any way. But Italians naturally drink mineral water together with their wine, and not as an alternative. This is a long established tradition. . . . The ancient Romans started it all with their interest in good mineral water springs, their thermal baths and their preoccupation with the ideal *mens sana in corpore sano* (a healthy mind in a healthy body). And since classical times, Italian waters have been studied and their effects noted.

It is precisely for this reason that researchers are now exploring the relationship of mineral water consumption in Italy to low rates of heart disease. Such research may further enrich recent theories about olive oil and wine.

The assumption that mineral water (also called hard water) is good for the heart was recognized in 1960 by the medical researcher Dr. Henry Schroeder. In an article in the *Journal of the American Medical Association*, Dr. Schroeder explained how his research indicated that areas with hard water had lower heart-related deaths than those with soft water. "Some factor, either present in hard water, or entering in soft water, appears to affect death rates from degenerative cardiovascular disease," said Schroeder. Years later it was discovered that the presence of magnesium in mineral water was vital to the heart. Without magnesium the heart can suffer arrhythmias, premature beats, or even deadly ventricular fibrillation.

An example of this new awareness to magnesium's importance for heart health can be found in Andrew Weil's *Spontaneous Healing*. Weil recommends the following for cardiac arrhythmia prevention: "1000 milligrams of magnesium (citrate, gluconate, or chelate) at bedtime plus another 500 milligrams in the morning, along with equal amounts of calcium (citrate)." He also recommends the same doses of calcium and magnesium for helping to manage high blood pressure.

One way of testing water for hardness is to see if spots develop on washed glassware. This spotting is usually caused by the dried residue of minerals. Another method is to check your ice cubes. White spots in the centers of the cubes indicate minerals: the larger the spots the greater the amount of minerals. Ice cubes from soft water high in sodium are usually cloudy, while clear ice cubes indicate an absence of minerals.

Bottled Water and Water Filters

The awakening of the general public to the value of good water and the good health it provides is now becoming evident in the sales of bottled water. According to *Water Conditioning & Purification* (October 1997), about 255 million gallons of bottled water were consumed in the United States in 1976. This annual U.S. consumption of bottled water increased to a staggering 3 billion gallons in 1996. It is also estimated that there are now over seven hundred different brands of bottled water in the United States.

When drinking certain bottled waters, especially mineral waters, one should be aware that they contain natural bacteria that impart good health. This water is alive with bacteria as well as with nutrients to keep the bacteria living. For this reason, it is advisable to drink most mineral water as soon as possible after breaking the bottle's seal, since other bacteria will soon enter and alter the health-giving properties of the original water.

The significance of spring water that naturally finds its way to the surface of the Earth has been a matter of international dispute over the past few years. For various reasons, the definition of "spring water" has been in dispute amongst water bottling companies, the legal system, and governmental regulatory agencies of the world. It was rightfully claimed by bottlers of water from natural springs that their water contained special properties compared to water that was pumped to the surface by mechanical methods. For several years, the subtle and obvious health-providing differences between water that naturally found its way to the surface and water that was "mined" was a matter of scientific and legal dispute. It was finally settled recently that only bottled water obtained from sources that flowed naturally to the surface could carry the words "spring water" on their label.

Besides spring water, a word of caution also needs to be added here about bottled water and water filters. Not too long ago, researchers at the University of Delaware analyzed thirty-seven brands of bottled water and discovered that twenty-four failed at least one of thirty-one U.S. drinking water standards.

The Food and Drug Administration (FDA) requires bottlers to test their waters, but there are no requirements about reporting results or using certified laboratories, which do keep test records. Therefore, as of this writing, the public has to depend on the bottling companies to regulate themselves with integrity. One tool the consumer does have is to contact the International Bottled Water Association (IBWA) and see if their bottled water company is a member. The IBWA requires testing of its members by the National Sanitation Foundation (NSF), an independent testing facility. Most members of the IBWA indicate their membership or NSF testing on their labels, so it is a good idea to look. To see if a particular brand is a member, the IBWA can be contacted at 113 North Henry Street, Alexandria, Virginia 22314.

During the final edit of this book, I received news from the American Water Works Association that the FDA is taking steps to require water bottling companies to test their water. This would require bottlers to provide the FDA and the public with water test results. A recent report entitled "Feasibility of Appropriate Methods of Informing Customers of the Contents of Bottled Water" was published in the Federal Register on August 25, 2000 (www.accessdata.fda.gov/scripts/oc/ohrms/), recommending that bottled water suppliers provide customers with test results. These required test results may end up being similar to those required of public water suppliers, known as Consumer Confidence Reports (CCRs).

The same caution goes for home water filters. The NSF also does independent testing to verify the performance claims of filter manufacturers. Filters tested by the NSF will have an NSF label listing the contaminants the filter safely removes. For a list of NSF-certified water filter devices, contact the NSF at 3475 Plymouth Road, Ann Arbor, Michigan 48105.

This awareness about bottled water and water filters is another indication of our growing consciousness about water. What can be more intimate to our everyday existence than the quality of water we allow to enter our bodies? In my opinion, as our relationship with water deepens, it will become the new mantra for maintaining our individual health.

FIFTEEN

A Brief History of Water Healing

Cold water! Let thy praises be sung
By every son of earth;
Yet all the pens of wisest scribes
Can never tell thy worth.
—DAVID HARSHA

IN MY READINGS AND TRAVELS over the past thirty years, I have come across many examples of water playing an important role in the healing of illness and the awakening of minds. One of the most poignant is the story of the role water played in transforming the life of Helen Keller. Without this substance, Helen Keller may have been doomed to a lifetime of silence and darkness.

In her autobiography, *The Story of My Life*, Helen Keller writes that by the time she was six months old she could speak at least four words—"How d'ye," "tea," and "water." Then she was struck by "the illness which closed my eyes and ears and plunged me into the unconsciousness of a new-born baby.... The doctor thought I could not live. Early one morning, however, the fever left me as suddenly and mysteriously as it had come. There was great rejoicing in the family that morning, but no one, not even the doctor, knew that I should never see or hear again."

After the illness struck, Helen lost all memory of the words she had learned except one. "Even after my illness I remembered one of the words I had learned in those early months. It was the word 'water,' and I continued to make some sound for that word after all other speech was lost. I ceased making the sound 'wah-wah' only when I learned to spell the word."

Helen Keller did not learn how to spell, her key to connecting to the world surrounding her, until she was almost seven years old. It is difficult to imagine that for six years after her illness her only glimmer of association with the outside world around her was through the sound derived from the word "water."

At the school to which Helen was eventually sent, Anne Mansfield Sullivan, her teacher, tried in vain for weeks to teach the blind and deaf child how to spell words with her hands. Even though Helen would mimic the teacher's hand motions for such objects as a "doll," "pin," "hat," and "cup" and for a few verbs such as "sit," "stand," and "walk," her mind could not associate the finger motions with the actual names or things they represented. Her parents were about ready to give up. In fact, if the breakthrough of using sign language had not happened in a matter of days, they were going to remove her from the school.

In Helen Keller's own words, published in 1902 in her autobiography, the turning point came on April 5, 1887, when she was almost seven years old:

> One day, while I was playing with my new doll, Miss Sullivan put my big rag doll into my lap also, spelled "d-o-l-l" and tried to make me understand that "d-o-l-l" applied to both. Earlier in the day we had had a tussle over the words "m-u-g" and "w-a-t-e-r." Miss Sullivan had tried to impress it upon me that "m-u-g" is mug and that "w-a-t-e-r" is water, but I persisted in confounding the two. In despair she had dropped the subject for the time, only to renew it at the first opportunity. I became impatient at her repeated attempts and, seizing the new doll, I dashed it upon the floor. I was keenly delighted when I felt the fragments of the broken doll at my feet. Neither sorrow nor regret followed my passionate outburst. I had not loved the doll. In the still, dark world in which I lived there was no strong sentiment or tenderness. I felt my teacher sweep the fragments to one side of the hearth, and I had a sense of satisfaction that the cause of my discomfort was removed. She brought me my hat, and I knew I was going out into the warm sunshine. This thought, if a wordless sensation may be called a thought, made me hop and skip with pleasure.
>
> We walked down the path to the well-house, attracted by the fragrance of the honeysuckle with which it was covered. Someone was drawing water and my teacher placed my hand under the spout. As the cool stream gushed over one hand she spelled into the other the word water, first slowly, then rapidly. I stood

still, my whole attention fixed upon the motions of her fingers. Suddenly I felt a misty consciousness as of something forgotten—a thrill of returning thought; and somehow the mystery language was revealed to me. I knew that "w-a-t-e-r" meant the wonderful cool something that was flowing over my hand. That living word awakened my soul, gave it light, hope, joy, set it free! There were barriers still, it is true, but barriers that could in time be swept away.

I left the well-house eager to learn. Everything had a name, and each name gave birth to a new thought. As we returned to the house every object which I touched seemed to quiver with life. That was because I saw everything with the strange, new sight that had come to me. On entering the door I remembered the doll I had broken. I felt my way to the hearth and picked up the pieces. I tried vainly to put them together. Then my eyes filled with tears; for I realized what I had done, and for the first time I felt repentance and sorrow.

I learned a great many words that day. I do not remember what they all were; but I do know that mother, father, sister, teacher were among them—words that were to make the world blossom for me, "like Aaron's rod, with flowers." It would have been difficult to find a happier child than I was as I lay in my crib at the close of that eventful day and lived over the joys it had brought me, and for the first time longed for a new day to come.

The Healing Gods of Water

That the energy of water has been associated with healing throughout the ages is well documented. There are many stories telling us about miraculous cures associated with water.

Why is this?

Is it just coincidence that people are healed by water?

Is it magic?

Is it the work of the Divine?

Is it psychosomatic?

Certainly, there seem to be many facets to the healing powers of water. Whether it is inhaled as a vapor, swallowed, or applied to the body, water seems to contain a healing quality in its nature. In my opinion, based on my own experience, some of the water healings I have heard or read about over the years are true miracles. Because of this, I feel it is important for people to once again learn how to heal themselves and loved ones with the ancient medicine of water.

The subject of water and health has long occupied the thinking of many philosophers and writers. An example of this can be found in the writings of the Greek biographer-historian Plutarch (A.D. 46?–120?). In *The Writings of Plutarch*, we learn that Plutarch discovered and recorded a Greek manuscript from about the sixth century B.C. This manuscript contained "natural questions" with answers. One of these ancient nature questions with its answer was expressed as follows:

> What is the Reason that Pit-water is less nutritive than either that which ariseth out of Springs or that which falleth down from Heaven?
>
> Is it because it is more cold, and withal hath less air in it? Or because it containeth much salt from the earth mingled therewith?—not it is well known that salt above all other things causeth leanness. Or because standing still, and not exercised with running and stirring, it getteth a certain malignant quality, which is hurtful to both plants and animals, and is the cause that is neither well concocted nor able to feed and nourish any thing? Hence it is that all dead waters of pools are unwholesome, for that they cannot digest and despatch those harmful qualities which they borrow of the evil property of the air or of the earth.

The above question and answer, recorded long before the advent of modern chemistry and its technical ability to test water, shows that early nature philosophers and observers were speculating about what kinds of water were healthy for humans, plants, and animals. How did these early thinkers know that standing water is "less nutritive than either that which ariseth out of Springs or that which falleth down from Heaven"? Obviously, they must have closely observed nature and seen how different forms of life responded to various sources of water.

The accuracy of the answer about why standing water is unhealthy and water that is "exercised with running and stirring" is healthy speaks well of the abilities of the natural scientific thinkers of that time. The last sentence, about dead waters of pools being unable to cleanse harmful qualities, is an extremely accurate statement.

Other thoughts about water from about this time are found in the writings of the Roman scholar Pliny the Elder (A.D. 23–79). In his *Historia Naturalis* Pliny tells us about the miraculous waters of Ferrarelle (in Italy) and those of a town named Spa, near the modern Liège, Belgium, from which the term "spa" has come to represent a place for water healing. How the town of Spa received its name remains a point of conjecture. Some people think the word may represent the acronym for *Sanitas per aquas* (health through water), the words supposedly spoken by the Emperor Nero upon first laying eyes on the impressive fountains of Rome. Others believe "spa" comes from *espa*, the old French word for fountain, or from the Latin *spargere*, which means to sprinkle or moisten. Another perspective is given in a 1977 San Diego State University master's thesis by Robert Quigley, a researcher of spas and a professional spa consultant:

> The word "spa" originated in Belgium in the fourteenth century near the City of Liège. A rich invalid named Collin le Loup learned about a fountain in the woods below Liège. In 1326 he went there to try the iron waters and claimed that they cured him. He founded a health resort at the "spa" (the old Wallon name for fountain) which eventually became known as "Spa." The word "Spa" is not used in Belgium today or, in fact, any but English-speaking countries.... Today the word has a much broader meaning. It is used to describe any club, salon, gym, hotel, or health and rejuvenation facility that happens to have some water either in the authentic form of mineral springs, salt water, a swimming pool, or special baths.

Regardless of its origin, the word "spa" is now recognized worldwide as being synonymous with places providing water therapy, holistic health regimes, and relaxation. Reflecting this renown, the town of Spa in France now enjoys international distribution of its drinking waters and other special water-based health drinks.

More about health through water can be found in *The Encyclopedia of Religion* under "water" (p. 356):

> As vital principle, water allows people to ward off illness and to keep death away. Because water makes the plants of pharmacopoeia grow, or because of the effects of its intrinsic qualities, the Veda associates it with the origin of medicine.... Water is even capable of conferring immortality. Gilgamesh finds the herb

of life, which enables people to escape death, at the bottom of the waters. Several peoples speak of a "water of life" that bestows immortality. Similarly, to give her son Achilles eternal life, Thetis wants to plunge him into the waters of the Styx. The Greeks in general establish a relationship between Okeanos and ambrosia, as Indians do between water and *soma*.

Thus it seems that from the earliest of times humankind developed a special relationship with the healing properties of water. This relationship evolved to the point where water was seen as a life-giver and provider as well as a spiritual being with the ability to heal.

The spring waters of the Italian peninsula were renowned since ancient times for their healing properties. The practice of bathing in and drinking these waters was cultivated and embellished upon by the Romans. Through the Middle Ages to the present day, many of Italy's spring waters have developed a reputation for producing miraculous cures; as a result, about 80 percent of the Italian spring waters today are named after a saint.

The healing properties of water were recognized and highly respected by the ancient Greeks. They frequently built healing shrines near or on top of sources of water, especially springs and running streams, for they believed that spirits dwelt in water, especially in springs, and that the energy of these spirits performed the magic of healing. The Greek god of healing, Asclepius, was believed to use the energy of these water sources. Eventually, the Greeks founded a healing temple on the island of Kos and named it after Asclepius. Various methods of using water in the healing arts were probably taught at this temple. One of the healers trained there was Hippocrates (460?– 370? B.C.), who became known for his exceptional healing powers. In *The Complete Book of Water Therapy* Dian Dincin Buchman writes:

> Hippocrates, whom we consider the "Father of Medicine," is alleged to be a descendant of the legendary Asclepius. Hippocrates used water as a beverage in reducing fever, and for treating many diseases. He also stressed the value of using various types of baths, each with a different temperature, as a therapeutic tool to combat illness.
>
> Later, the ancient Roman physicians Galen and Celsus also advocated specific baths as an integral part of their remedies. A series of cold baths are known to have cured the Roman

Emperor Augustus of a baffling disease that had resisted all other remedies, and thereafter cold baths were much in vogue in Rome.

The physician credited with curing the Emperor Augustus was the hydropathist Antonius Musa, whose feat was commemorated in the poetry of Horace.

When looking at the gods of the Greeks and Romans, it is important to understand that many of them were assimilations of older preexisting gods of conquered peoples. When the Greeks occupied the land of the Canaanites, the Greek god Asclepius slowly replaced the Canaanite god of healing, Eshmun. It was not by accident that the Greeks eventually built their healing shrines for Asclepius on some of the locations formerly occupied by shrines for Eshmun. Besides taking advantage of the historical healing powers of the water sources used by the Canaanites, the Greeks also benefited by allowing the region's people to continue visiting the healing shrines.

This transition from one god to another can be seen in the striking similarities on coins of that period depicting the gods Eshmun and Asclepius. Some coins of the second century A.D. show the Canaanite's Eshmun standing with two serpents, one on each side, while in a similar fashion, coins of a later vintage show the Greek's Asclepius in the company of two serpentlike figures, seemingly holding one in each hand.

This ancient use of one or two serpents to represent the healing arts has carried forth into modern times and remains in use as a symbol of modern medicine. However, the actual creation and meaning of this ancient symbol of healing remains a mystery. We do know that the "caduceus" was carried like a staff by ancient messenger heralds, and that it was fashioned to look like the staff of the god Mercury. In Roman mythology, Mercury is the winged messenger of the gods. He is often depicted wearing winged shoes and a winged hat as he carries a staff with two snakes coiled around it from the bottom up. Just above the heads of the two snakes on the top of the staff is a pair of wings. In similar fashion, we have the Greek god Hermes, who also was a winged messenger of the gods and who also carried a caduceus. In Greek mythology, Hermes is also the god of science.

Taking this a step further, we have the mysterious Hermetic books of Egypt. These ancient Egyptian writings, supposedly written by Hermes Trismegistus (Hermes the Thrice-Greatest), are some of the earliest books exploring magic, alchemy, astrology, the universal order of things, the principles of nature, and the use of various healing arts. Hermes Trismegistus is often considered in some fashion or another to be related to the god Hermes.

There is still much conjecture about what the two serpents of the caduceus represent. Could they represent the ancient "kundalini" or "serpent power" that is believed to intertwine up the spine from the body's sexual center to the brain? Or, could they in fact represent the nerve endings of the adrenal glands that wrap themselves around the spine in the same double-helix shape as our DNA? And what are we to make of the staff that the two snakes entwine themselves around? If the staff represents the spine, then it makes sense to keep your spine in alignment so the vital flow of energies may snake their way back and forth between the brain and body.

Conjecture may also be fueled by ancient references that draw other analogies between the healing and creative powers of water and the two serpentine figures. Could the two snakes represent humankind's ancient beginnings in the area of the Tigris and Euphrates Rivers? Certainly, the analogy of these two parallel rivers snaking their way through the valley until they join to form the Shatt-al-Arab gives pause for thought. A meandering stream or river does look like a snake as it slithers back and forth across the landscape. The same goes for the behavior of water as it "snakes" its way around rocks, gravel, and soils as it flows down, sideways, and up through the earth. This serpentine flow of water allows it to accumulate the properties of the earth it lives in and travels through. Eventually, underground water twists and turns its way upward to the airy surface as it carries life-giving nutrients and special healing properties.

In a similar fashion, as surface water flows down a river or stream it interacts with soils, rocks, living matter, gravity, light, air, sound, and varying temperature changes within and without, as well as with the cosmic forces of Sun, Moon, and, to some extent, other planets. It is the energy that moving water accumulates underground and as it flows back and forth down a curving watercourse that endows it with the energy for sustaining and healing life.

Another ancient god said to be a divine healer was Serapis. The Roman historian Tacitus, who lived in the second century A.D., left behind a considerable body of writing that provides us with information about Serapis, the principal god of Alexandria. According to Tacitus, Serapis obtained his divine ability to heal from the ancient

Egyptian sage and healer named Imhotep. Imhotep apparently practiced his healing arts at a place called Sakkara, which was known as a source of healing waters. In its time, the flowing waters of Sakkara were as famous as the waters of Lourdes are today, and people came there from long distances seeking to be healed. Needless to say, the healing shrine located at Sakkara adopted the name of whatever healing god came to represent the prevailing interests of those in power. In modern times, the location of the healing spring waters of Sakkara has fallen from memory.

From Gods to Humans

Tracking down information about the use of water in healing over the past 5000 years is a journey that flows down many tributaries. However, one message that keeps floating to the surface is that the use of water for healing is something that has oftentimes met with a degree of skepticism.

When asking myself why this is so, the only answer I have come up with is that some people think of water as something that contains no special properties. How humankind has evolved away from seeing the miracle of water and all that it gives to life and to our health is, to me, the true mystery. Although the healers who have been brave enough to promote water for its special properties have often faced various degrees of ridicule and mockery, the facts and truths about water and its power to heal have never left us.

In my explorations of various sources of information on the use of water in healing, the 1871 edition of *Chambers's Encyclopedia* has proven to be a wonderful source. I have discovered other sources scattered like seeds spread across the land by a great wind by exploring the files of different libraries, rummaging through old bookstores and thrift shops, exploring the Internet, and following up leads provided in philosophical discussions with other "seekers of the truth." It has been a rewarding journey.

During this journey I noticed there was a turning point of history when people began to "see" and understand the significance of water. This turning point happened over 2600 years ago when Thales proposed that water was the source of all things. As discussed in Chapter 7, it appears as though Thales was the first human to see water in all its dimensions, godly and worldly. Perhaps it is because of Thales that humankind began to think of water as something other than a spiritual entity. However, I believe he did not mean for humankind to lose sight of the fact that water is also spiritual.

When ill persons find healing through the entity of water, it should be recognized that they are being healed not only by the physical entity of water itself, but by the hidden mysterious creative energy that is present within the water. Because of this, I find it surprising that certain doctors and healers claim credit for healing with water, when in fact they are only serving as the tool through which water may work its miracles. Considerable credit should certainly be given to those people who "learn" from water and help others to use water for healing, for they are serving as the prophets of water. With this said, we continue the history of water healing.

Paracelsus

Following in the steps of Hippocrates over four hundred years later are the Roman medical author Celsus, of the first century A.D., and the Greek anatomist and physician Galen, of the second century A.D. Both Celsus and Galen recorded favorable reports on the use of water for curing disease. They also regarded water's curative powers to be of high value in the treatment of acute health problems, particularly fevers. Carrying on in a fashion similar to his Roman predecessor Pliny the Elder, who wrote thirty-seven books, Galen also left behind an impressive body of work—twenty volumes of medical treatises that average about 1000 pages each.

Throughout the Middle Ages many physicians of renown were writers and advocates of water healing, including Aetius and Paulus Egineta. During the Renaissance Michelangelo (1475–1564) wrote of his own water healing: "I am much better than I have been. Morning and evening I have been drinking the water from a spring about forty miles from Rome (Fuggi), which breaks up my kidney stone. . . . I have had to lay in a supply at home and cannot drink or cook with anything else."

One of the most interesting figures in the history of water healing is Paracelsus (1493–1541), the Swiss physician, chemist, alchemist, and philosopher. The name "Paracelsus" means "superior to Celsus"; his real name was Phillippus Aureolus Theophrastus Bombast von Hohenheim. He is believed to have acquired his ability to heal with water from old European herbalists, from practitioners of ancient healing arts of the East, and from his attentive study of water in nature. He believed that the spirits of elemental water, which he called "undines," were particularly fond of human beings and enjoyed forming close associations with people who invoke them and give them offerings. Perhaps these offerings could be as simple as just believing in their existence.

Paracelsus learned about medicine at an early age from his father, who was a physician and chemist. According to Garrison's *History of Medicine*, Paracelsus received his doctor's degree under Leonicenus at Ferrara in 1515. Soon after, Paracelsus departed to take up the art of wanderlust by traveling through remote regions of Europe, Russia, and the Middle East. Exactly what he learned during his mysterious years of travel is not known, but what is known is that he returned to the world of society and medicine a changed man, overflowing with new ideas about the practice of medicine. One of those was, "In wounds nature is the real healer. All that is necessary is to prevent infection in wound diseases." This saying is now finding many advocates in the current new age of alternative medicine, which has rediscovered that flushing a wound with unpolluted freshwater is most effective in healing and preventing infection. However, it is not advisable to clean a broken-skin wound with seawater, since seawater contains organic matter and microscopic bacteria that will probably further infect the wound.

Paracelsus was also ahead of his time in studying the effects of pollution on health. According to Mishlove's *Roots of Consciousness*, Paracelsus studied bronchial illnesses in mining districts and was one of the first people to recognize the connection between an industrial environment and certain types of disease.

Besides using his knowledge of chemistry and alchemy in the study of water in his laboratory, Paracelsus also used water for healing disease in his patients. Many great people of the time called on him to help cure their sickness. Perhaps one of the most famous was the great scholar and theologian Erasmus.

According to various sources, Paracelsus may have met his end because of his abrasive character and pompous presentation of his new medical theories. Another factor may have been professional jealousy over his fame and success as a healer. According to one source, Paracelsus arrived in Salzburg, Austria, in 1541 at the invitation of the archbishop, and a few months later, on September 29, was thrown to his death from a high window by rival physicians. Contradicting this story is Garrison's *History of Medicine*, which reports his demise resulted from a wound suffered in a tavern brawl in Salzburg.

For his water research, Paracelsus would go about collecting dew on plates of glass under various planetary combinations, supposedly acting on the belief that the water he was collecting might carry within it certain healing energies of different planets. Apparently, he was inspired to such research by his observations of how water and plants responded to the Sun and the Moon and other planetary influences, and how temperature played a vital role in changing the condition of water. These early works of Paracelsus eventually formed the basis of Dr. Edward Bach's floral remedies, which consist of dew collected from flowers.

Today science confirms what Paracelsus figured out long ago—dew is created by plants. The creation of dew occurs after sunset, when plants transpire water vapor through their pores. Evaporation of the water vapor cools the surface of the plants as they rapidly lose the heat they collected from the Sun. Soon, the plants become cooler than the surrounding air, and when this happens, the water vapor transpiring from inside the vegetation condenses into tiny pearl drops of dew on the plant's cool surface. And, since water is made up of tiny crystals that constantly form, dissolve, and collect energy, it is believed that dew may capture the essence of a plant's living energy along with the cosmic influences of the moment.

Water collected from dew at specific times was also believed by some ancient sages to be one of the main ingredients for the making of the "philosophers' stone." Besides being able to transmute baser metals to gold, the philosophers' stone was thought of as a mystical substance that could redeem humankind and the universe, cure all human illness, and maintain life indefinitely. Also known as the "elixir of life," the philosophers' stone reminds us of the world's first philosopher, Thales, and his belief that water was the underlying principle of all things.

This transmutation of water into other elements was reportedly accomplished in 1927 by the metaphysician/artist Walter Russell (1871–1963). As reported in the magazine *Atlantis Rising* (No. 4) in 1996,

> Recently, professional engineers Ron Kovac and Toby Grotz of Colorado, with help from Dr. Tim Binder, repeated Russell's 1927 work, which was verified by Westinghouse Laboratories.

Russell found a novel way to change the ratio of hydrogen to oxygen in water vapor inside a sealed quartz tube, or to change the vapor to completely different elements. Their conclusion agrees with Russell: the geometry of motion in space is important in atomic transmutation.

To me, it is curious how water vapor is the key in this experiment. Could it be possible that when water heals, its transmutative properties actually transform the atoms of living tissue?

Hydrotherapy in the Eighteenth and Nineteenth Centuries

In the 1700s hydrotherapy was a subject of much general interest. In 1723 Nicolo Lanzani, a Neapolitan physician, published a treatise on healing with water. Also in the early 1700s, Sir John Floyer and a doctor named Baynard published a work called *Psychrolousia, or the History of Cold Bathing, Both Ancient and Modern.* Both Floyer and Baynard used water extensively in treating their patients, and this work is filled with interesting learning and practical advice about the use of water in healing.

The water research and writings of Floyer and Baynard in England, along with those of a Dr. Smith at about the same time, eventually led to a wave of water-healing spas across Prussia and Germany that exist to this day. The connection was made through a traveling German doctor named Johann Siegemund Hahn. While touring England in the early 1700s, Hahn learned about the water cures of Floyer, Baynard, and Smith. Whether he actually met or corresponded with any of his English counterparts is unknown. What is known is that Dr. Hahn returned to Prussia and began practicing, experimenting, and writing about the use of water for curing illness. He published some of his findings around 1738 in a book that contained references to the English writings and water therapy research of Floyer, Baynard, and Smith.

However, the practice of using water for healing did not become very widespread in Germany. Perhaps this was because people developed a dependency on the promises and use of formal medicine by "educated doctors." Then, as fate would deliver in 1804, a German doctor named Ertl was browsing through an antique bookstore when, quite by accident, he discovered Dr. Hahn's book from the early 1700s.

Excited by this discovery of how to use water for healing, Dr. Ertl began to study and write about hydrotherapy, eventually publishing a book entitled *Water Cures*. Ertl also took it upon himself in 1831 to reedit and republish Hahn's earlier work. And this 1831 edition was to have a fateful effect on a young German student named Sebastian Kneipp, as we shall see later in this chapter.

In 1778, Franz Mesmer, a German physician, left Vienna for Paris after his experiments into the therapeutic effects of magnetism had been denounced. These experiments were based on theories about magnetism that he originally presented in his doctoral thesis at the University of Vienna. In Paris, where his work remained controversial, Mesmer devoted himself to curing diseases. He designed a wooden tub that could be filled with magnetized water and iron filing, and, supposedly, many cures of various diseases were accomplished using this bath. He did not use hypnotism, although the term "mesmerism" has been attached to that technique.

Back in England, Henry Cavendish, a chemist and physicist, became interested in the late 1700s in experimenting with electricity and water. While sending electric current through a sealed glass tube containing water, he got a surprise—the water disappeared! Many experiments later, he determined that water was made up of two gases. Setting a match to different combinations of these two gases, Cavendish discovered that when he combined two parts of the "inflammable air" with one part of the "vital air," there was an explosion that left a residue of liquid water drops along the walls of the container. Thus it was revealed that the molecular structure of known matter could be split apart and recombined—quite a newsworthy event in those days. The Frenchman Antoine Lavoisier renamed "inflammable air" as hydrogen—"the water producer"—and "vital air" as oxygen. In fact, Lavoisier's tombstone epitaph is "HHO."

Cavendish's discovery that water molecules could be split apart and recombined is noteworthy in another way as well. It was this experiment that eventually put humankind on the path that led to the creation of the atom bomb. On a more peaceful note, the splitting of hydrogen and oxygen with electricity, now called electrolysis, is seen as one of the most promising ways to create a limitless source of energy—hydrogen. It is hoped that this source of nonpolluting fuel-cell technology will help clean the earth of polluted air and water.

As far as the discovery of hydrogen goes, we have Paracelsus doing the groundwork which Cavendish built upon. Then we have Lavoisier, the so-called "father of modern chemistry," further developing Cavendish's research. Lavoisier, by the way, was given the guillotine in 1794 during the Reign of Terror for speaking his mind once too often and being seen as a threat to the new regime because of his scholarly achievements.

Finally, eleven years after Lavoisier's death, we have another profound discovery relating to hydrogen and water. Louis Joseph Gay-Lussac, physicist and chemist, along with Alexander von Humboldt, traveler and naturalist, proved that water is made up of two parts hydrogen and one part oxygen. This breakthrough proved that water was neither elemental (in the ancient use of the term), nor an element in chemistry, but a true compound unto itself. This new designation of water set it apart from air and earth (which are mixtures), and fire, which is a chemical process.

A contemporary of Cavendish, the well-known Dr. James Currie (sometimes spelled Currier), a Scottish physician and biographer of the poet Robert Burns, published a book about hydrotherapy in 1797 entitled *Medical Reports on the Effects of Water, Cold and Warm, as a Remedy in Fever and Febrile Diseases*. This work, based on Currie's research and actual cases, offers practical medical advice, notably, as the title indicates, directions for ways to heal people suffering from fever. Currie believed that the sprinkling and pouring of water on patients in certain specific ways could also cure those suffering from typhoid and smallpox.

Other noted books about water healing published in England at the turn of the nineteenth century were *The Water-Cure in Chronic Disease* by Dr. Gully; *Principles and Practice of the Water-Cure* by Dr. Edward Johnson; and Dr. Lane's treatise *Hydropathy, or Hygienic Medicine*.

English doctors about this time also experimented with different mineral waters. Today people suffering from a broken skin or trauma injury often soak the afflicted part of their body in Epsom salts. Most of them probably don't know that these salts derive their name from the healing mineral springs found in Epsom, England.

Another aspect of dealing with bleeding skin injuries addresses what to do when the bleeding stops and a scab forms. Today's dermatologists tell us in modern technical terms what many ancient healers understood through observation: the scab that forms on the skin impedes the granulation and re-epithelialization necessary for healing. A broken skin wound will heal more quickly and with less scarring if the scab is gently removed by soaking with water, and the area is kept moist thereafter. The area may be kept moist by constant changes of clean moist dressings or by covering the area with an antibacterial herbal ointment.

Besides moist compresses, there is also the use of clay for healing. The crystal properties of clay suspended in water are believed to help heal illness or provide degrees of relief. It is for this reason we find people today using clay-based mud for baths and facials, as well as drinking clay mixtures or taking tablets with clay for digestive problems. For example, the heartburn and indigestion relief product Kaopectate derives its name from the kaolin clay found inside a mountain in the Kiangsi Province of China where it was first obtained. In Chinese, *kao ling* means "high mountain."

During the eighteenth century, mineral springs also began to play a role in maintaining health. As health spas in central Europe, especially Austria, became more popular, people began to realize the healing benefits associated with mineral water. Austria's mountainous environment is blessed with rivers, streams, and natural mineral spring waters of all kinds, which had been used since Roman times. During the reign of the great monarch Maria Theresa (1717–80), Vienna, through which the Danube River flows, became one of the great European centers of medicine and science. During this period, Austria became renowned for the medicinal value of its mineral springs and water-healing spas. As a result, many peculiar stories about water cures and water healers surfaced in that region.

One such story takes place in the countryside near Grafenberg, Austria. It is a story about an uneducated Silesian farmer named Vincent Priessnitz (or Preissnitz, 1799–1851). At that time, Priessnitz gained considerable attention in his rural community for curing himself and his family with water treatments. Apparently, after a heavy hay cart had rolled over on Priessnitz he was told by doctors that he would be crippled for life. Through drinking large quantities of water and applying cold compresses, Priessnitz cured his injured body. This astounded the people in his community and the news quickly spread. Before long, Priessnitz found himself treating and curing diseases among the poor of his neighborhood. As time passed, people began traveling from far and wide to be healed by his water treatments. Based on his observations of water in the natural environment,

Priessnitz developed a holistic program for curing illness. He introduced the wet compress, the douche bath, a variety of partial baths, the use of sweating, the wet-sheet body wrap, and the copious drinking of pure water. In addition to using water in all these forms, he also used exercise, diet, fresh air, proper breathing, and relaxation in the cure of various diseases.

Eventually, due to Priessnitz's spreading fame and success as a healer, a group of jealous physicians took him to court. After the testimony of many people was heard, Priessnitz won his case. A big help to his case was the visit of Baron Turkeim, the leading physician of the Austrian empire. After observing Priessnitz's water therapy methods, Turkeim reported to the emperor that the methods truly worked. This allowed Priessnitz to work under the protection of the Crown for the remainder of his life.

Of all of Priessnitz's water-healing discoveries, his wet-sheet cure is the one that is best documented. Supposedly, the wet-sheet method was used to combat almost every form of acute disease. *Chambers's Encyclopedia*, published in 1871, just two decades after Priessnitz's death, provides us with the following description of the wet-sheet application:

> Over the mattress of a bed or sofa is extended a stout blanket, and on this is spread a linen sheet, well wrung out of cold water, so that it is only damp. On this the patient is laid, and immediately enveloped tightly with a heavy weight of blankets upon him tucked in so closely as to completely exclude all air. The body's natural heat, acting on the damp linen, generates vapour almost immediately, and the patient forthwith finds himself, not in a cold, but in a comfortably warm vapour bath—in a novel but no means unpleasant form of body poultice. The effects of this process on the economy seem to be plain enough. It is clear, in the first place, that the pores of the skin, so numerous and performing so important a function, must thereby be thoroughly cleansed, and the blood itself depurated; with the equalisation of temperature over the entire surface of the body, will follow a corresponding equalisation in the distribution of blood throughout the system, thereby relieving internal congestions wherever occurring; and lastly, from the soothing effects of the nervous system, and the allaying of all irritation, must result not only in the alleviation of pain, but the lowering of the heart's action,

and with it of the circulation of the blood, of such incalculable importance in the treatment of many forms of disease, and especially of fevers. Such is the wet sheet.

Unfortunately, after Priessnitz died there were few if any written records left behind to explain his remarkable healings. Except for the description of the wet-sheet method documented above by an outside source and a few others, Priessnitz left us little indication of how he developed his water cures. This may be because he was uneducated and therefore lacked the ability to leave a written record. Or, as is highly likely, Priessnitz may have served as the "source" through which knowledge about water flowed naturally. It follows, therefore, that only someone endowed with Priessnitz's water sensitivity would have been able to continue curing people using his methods. Priessnitz probably was able to "see" what each individual patient needed in the way of a cure.

It may have been Priessnitz's renown that influenced the research of Austria's Dr. William Winternitz. In 1880, Dr. Winternitz made the amazing discovery that water actually reacts with the nerve endings in the skin. When hot or cold water is applied to the skin, the nerves on the skin generate what he called reflex "arcs." These arcs, according to Winternitz, serve as connectors between the skin and various body organs, glands, and muscles. In a fashion, Winternitz's scientific discovery corroborates the theories behind the ancient practices of hydrotherapy and acupuncture.

Sebastian Kneipp, "The German Water Doctor"

In the fall of 1849, a young German named Sebastian Kneipp was studying to become a Catholic priest. However, after falling ill and coughing up blood, he was diagnosed with terminal tuberculosis. Told that he had about one month to live, Kneipp found his way to the small country town of Dillingen in southern Germany.

Somewhere in his reading, Kneipp had found in the Munich University library a copy of Dr. Ertl's above-mentioned 1831 edition of the book on hydrotherapy written by Johann Siegemund Hahn over one hundred years earlier. Since Kneipp figured he had little time to live, he was inspired by this book to initiate his own water cure. During the cold winter months of 1849–50, he could be seen running through the narrow streets of Dillingen to the banks of the Danube

River. Upon reaching the river, Kneipp would remove his clothing, plunge into the frigid waters for a brief swim, climb out of the river, put his clothes back on, and then run home.

By the spring of 1850, Kneipp was still alive and healthier than ever. In his mind, it was the water cure that saved his life. He went on to complete his studies, became a Catholic priest, and in 1855 took up residence at the Dominican monastery in Worishofen. There he experimented further with his water cure methods, trying such methods as walking barefoot in dewy grass and in snow. He also worked on developing a system of water-cure procedures and water exercises that was in harmony with his spiritual work. His research on nutrition and the use of herbs and medicinal plants for aromatherapy and in bathing water, teas, and compresses was very advanced for his time.

Besides the alternating cold and warm water baths, Kneipp is credited with inventing the herbal wrap—which is widely used in many spas and beauty parlors throughout the world today. As a result of these efforts, many people today recognize Sebastian Kneipp to be the great-grandfather of natural holistic medicine. Kneipp clearly saw that recognizing the interrelationships of mind, body, and soul was integral not only to curing illness, but to preventing it as well.

Kneipp was also far ahead of his time in promoting the eating of organic foods. He advised his patients to eat as much of their food as possible in its "natural state."

As word spread about this humble priest and his miraculous water cure methods, Kneipp became an international sensation. People around the world were soon calling him the "water doctor." By 1890, the small country town of Worishofen became a center for water-cure therapy, attracting over 35,000 visitors a year. Due to the ever growing number of people seeking his water cures, Kneipp eventually enlisted the assistance of a group of monks to work under his direction. In a fashion, it can be said that Worishofen became the predecessor of the modern-day spa. It was also at about this time that the *Washington Post* newspaper in the United States declared Sebastian Kneipp to be one of the three most famous men in the world.

As more and more people came to Kneipp for his water cures and advice, he began writing books about his theories. Two of his books, *Meine Wasserkur* ("My Water Cure"), published in 1886, and *So sollt ihr leben* ("How You Should Live"), published in 1889, became bestsellers. Kneipp further enhanced his reputation when he used a water cure to heal Archduke Francis Joseph of Austria from Bright's disease in 1892. Even the Catholic leaders, who were once critical of Kneipp, became convinced of his water cures. So much so that in the early 1890s, Kneipp became a "Secret Papal Camerlingo," and in 1894 traveled to the Vatican to treat Pope Leo XIII.

When Kneipp died at the age of 77 in 1897, his work did not die with him. Three years before his death, the Association of Kneipp Doctors was founded to carry on his work. Over the past one hundred years an association of Kneipp clubs has sprung up in Germany; called the *Kneippvereine*, today they have over 100,000 members. The same phenomenon has occurred with Kneipp's idea of a water spa—today there are over forty water spas throughout Germany based on the concept of his original spa in Worishofen. These Kneipp spas collectively receive hundreds of thousands of visitors a year from all over the world.

In spite of the worldwide exposure of Kneipp's use of water for healing, a 1929 book entitled *History of Medicine,* by Fielding H. Garrison, showed how much humankind had yet to evolve. Apparently, people at that time were just learning about the ability of water to kill germs and prevent infection. Garrison's book tells how near the end of the nineteenth century the renowned Oliver Wendell Holmes (1809–1894), was among the first in America to propose the washing of hands for sanitary purposes. Dr. Holmes based his assumptions on commonsense field information he gathered at the time. In hospitals where practicing physicians washed their hands there was a greatly reduced incidence of infection and death following childbirth. Surprisingly, Holmes was attacked by several leading orthodox obstetricians for proposing such a ridiculous idea.

Hydrotherapy in the United States

When European settlers first colonized America, they learned of certain springs and watering places that the Native Americans used for maintaining their health and for healing. And, as in Europe and elsewhere, the conquering people of America usurped the indigenous people's sacred places of water.

Three of the oldest watering places of the United States are Berkeley Springs, West Virginia; Warm Springs, Georgia; and Saratoga Springs, New York. All three of these springs held special meanings to early Native American populations as places of healing waters, and all were usurped by the conquering colonialists, who continued to use them for similar purposes. From the arrival of America's first settlers to the present, the above three springs as well as others across the country have become renowned as health and healing centers.

According to the 1977 San Diego State University master's thesis of spa consultant Robert Quigley:

> Berkeley Springs, West Virginia, is acclaimed to be the oldest developed spa resort in the United States. George Washington stayed there in 1749 and returned for years, often with his family.... Another spring frequented by a president was Warm Springs, Georgia. Franklin D. Roosevelt would go there to soak his crippled legs in the warm waters. Later, Roosevelt gave two-thirds of his personal fortune to establish the "Georgia Warm Springs Foundation," with medical and hotel facilities to help other disabled people.

Up to the late nineteenth century, most people in the United States obtained domestic water from local springs, rivers, shallow wells, and cisterns. As cities evolved, so did their need for fire protection. For this reason, the invention of iron pipe was first used to create waterworks for fire protection. Eventually, the same pressurized iron pipes used for fire protection began to find use for carrying water into homes. In fact, this practice of interconnecting fire protection with public water supply has survived to this day. In Ivan Illich's book *H₂O and the Waters of Forgetfulness*, we learn:

> At the beginning of the Civil War, toilets or bathtubs were considerable luxuries. The water department charged extra for houses sporting them. In 1893 four-fifths of all inhabitants of Baltimore had access to an outdoor privy only; in New York, almost half had indoor privies. In 1866 only one-eighth of Chicago was served by sewers. Water and slops were mostly carried by women. Only after World War I did bathrooms cease to be luxuries. In the four years from 1921 to 1924, they doubled throughout the whole of the United States. A national survey in the late 1920s showed that seventy-one percent of urban and thirty-three percent of rural families had installed bathrooms in their homes. Water now mostly served washing, cleaning, and flushing.

This historic piping of water into American homes for daily family hygiene literally altered the course of surface waters as well as the evolution of hydrotherapy. Such in-home convenience for obtaining water was a major step in allowing people to clean and heal themselves.

An anecdotal story about Henry David Thoreau indicates that hydropathy was an accepted practice in America in the mid-1800s. In 1856, when Thoreau was thirty-nine years old, he traveled with his friend Bronson Alcott to New York City. Thoreau was to survey land for a commune in nearby New Jersey. In New York, Alcott introduced Thoreau to the poet Walt Whitman as well as to the founder of the *New York Tribune*, Horace Greeley. For part of their stay, Alcott and Thoreau took a room at Dr. Russell T. Trall's Water Cure and Hydropathic Medical College.

Beyond his New York hydropathical experience, Thoreau experienced a homegrown version while living at Walden Pond from 1845 to 1847. While living on Walden Pond, Thoreau spent much of his time observing water and writing about the cycles of life. And, just like Thoreau, many people like to locate their homes near water so they may enjoy seeing and hearing this mysterious substance. This affinity for water is a strangely natural human tendency. Dr. Patrick Quillin tells us in *The Wisdom of Amish Folk Medicine*, "The Amish try to build their homes near running water to capture its energy and to reap the benefits of the calming sounds."

Other contributors to the development of hydrotherapy in America were Dr. John Harvey Kellogg and Dr. R. Lincoln Graham. Kellogg opened the Battle Creek Sanitarium in 1876 to promote drugless therapy through diet coupled with hydrotherapy. As an innovator, Kellogg sought to educate lay people in the "Uses of Water in Health and Disease," and in 1900 he published the extensive 1100-page book *Rational Hydrotherapy*. We also have Kellogg to thank for inventing dry breakfast cereal and the sweat cabinet heated by electric light bulbs. Over the years, there have been many high-tech embellishments to this early concept of a sweat or sauna cabinet.

Sharing the hydrotherapy spotlight with the inventive spirit of Kellogg was Dr. R. Lincoln Graham, inventor of the graham cracker. Graham wrote *Water in Disease and in Health*, and was widely recognized for having great success with his water cures.

Also spreading the word on hydrotherapy in America was Dr. Simon Baruch. In 1899 Dr. Baruch published a book entitled *The Principles and Practice of Hydrotherapy*, following it in 1920 with *Epitome of Hydrotherapy*.

According to swimwear historian Len Lencek, the efforts of these early hydropathists eventually led to Americans taking to the waters for swimming and bathing. It was only as recent as the early twentieth century that doctors began prescribing fresh air and bathing in nature's fresh and salt waters as a tonic for good health. Because of this development, we saw the evolution of swimwear so as to allow people to freely recreate in water.

On par with the inventiveness of Kellogg and Graham may be that of a man named Roy Jacuzzi, whose invention has had a major impact on both hydrotherapy and domestic life. After coming up with the idea and putting together his first whirlpool jet tub in 1968, Jacuzzi presented his invention at country fairs. The initial presentation of the Jacuzzi whirlpool concentrated on the therapeutic purposes. However, given the great spiritual awakening of Americans during the 1970s, Jacuzzi's invention was soon discovered to be a great way for people to enjoy sharing the water experience. Today many variations on the theme of the original Jacuzzi can be found throughout the world.

There are currently hundreds of spas throughout the United States ranging from the sublime to ridiculous. Certainly there have been many books touching on the subject over the years, including the highly recommended *Healthy Escapes* by Bernard Burt, and *Healing Waters* by Linda Troeller. In these health-conscious times, the spa concept continues to grow rapidly—so much so, that some entrepreneurs are trying to capitalize on the word "spa" without offering any form of water experience. Hopefully, this error in judgment will not detract from the true meaning, which historically has always been synonymous with water.

The Miraculous Water of Lourdes

Near the Spanish border in the southwest corner of France is a remarkable town by the name of Lourdes. It was there, on February 11, 1858, that a fourteen-year-old girl named Bernadette Soubirous saw Mary the Immaculate, Mother of God, appear to her in a vision. The Virgin Mother guided the girl to a patch of ground and asked her to dig. When Bernadette did so, a previously unknown spring of water gushed forth. The stream began as a mere trickle but eventually became a powerful flow of spring water. Bernadette returned home and told her family and others in the village about the vision and the flowing spring water. Other visions followed, and Bernadette reported that The Lady was asking for a shrine to be built on the spot where the water flowed from the ground.

A number of people believed in Bernadette's visions and communications with The Lady, and built a crude shrine. Then the skeptics came, in the form of civic authorities who denounced Bernadette, confiscated the shrine, and closed off the area. Almost by Divine design, however, there soon followed several miraculous healings of people who ventured to touch the special spring water to their afflicted bodies. Word of these cures rapidly spread throughout the country, and the multitudes soon arrived. Before long, the local bureaucrats and theologians accepted the concept that something extraordinary was occurring. Bernadette was eventually canonized in 1933 at Saint Peter's, and the shrine at Lourdes has become renowned throughout the world.

Sitting in a pocket of the Pyrenees, the bucolic town of Lourdes shimmers in the warm season with the living energy of farm fields, grassy hillsides, gardens, splashes of color from wildflowers, lush green trees filled with singing birds, and, most of all—the sights and sounds of sparkling streams of water. On any given day, one may sit and admire the perfect setting of this small town while hearing the songs of pilgrims floating through the air above the town's many church spires. These pilgrims are from every denomination and walk of life. Upon coming to Lourdes, many of them pray and sing with the hope they may be cured of some illness, deformity, or injury.

Over 4 million people visit the shrine at Lourdes each year. It is a simple shrine, no more than an altar in a rock with an overflowing source of spring water nearby. Yet for all its simplicity, thousands of miraculous cures have been attributed to the healing power of its flowing waters.

As much as this sounds like fantasy, or the things that dreams are made of, there have been many verified miraculous cures at Lourdes. These cures have been "certified" by a group of devoted doctors who investigate, study, and document all reported cures. At one time, over five thousand doctors were gathered together in an international association for the study of the cures at Lourdes. Today there is a permanent Medical Bureau of Lourdes to provide ongoing assistance, care, and documentation of cures for the pilgrims who make their way to Lourdes.

And just what are the human maladies that have been miraculously cured by the waters of Lourdes? A small sampling includes: blindness; tuberculosis; paralysis of the legs; convulsions; an ulcerated deformed leg with deep infection; paralysis and accompanying gangrenous sores from a crushed spine accident; double club feet; advanced "incurable" breast cancer; lip cancer; tuberculous skin disease that had eaten half of a woman's face; severe rheumatism with resulting deformities; cancer of the jaw; varicose ulcer; complete paralysis as a result of polyneuritis of the spinal nerves and cord; varicose veins with ulcerations; tuberculosis of the larynx and both lungs, with accompanying complete loss of voice; epilepsy; incontinence of urine and feces; a voluminous fibroid tumor of the uterus weighing several pounds; intestinal tuberculosis with tuberculous abscesses on back and thighs; spondylitis; abscess of the liver with chronic fistula; a fractured pelvis and two legs with bones that failed to unite in a woman also suffering from a concussion after a serious fall; and a host of other illnesses and injuries far too numerous to list here.

It should be emphasized that though the percentage of people who are cured is small compared to the number of visitors to the shrine, the fact remains that these cures do happen. It has now been over 140 years since these water cures began at Lourdes.

In 1988, Dr. Theodore Mangiapan, the president of the Medical Bureau of Lourdes and the ninth permanent doctor of the Medical Bureau, wrote in the preface to the updated Lourdes book by Ruth Cranston: "The most famous and still most frequently asked question, of course, is, 'Are there still miracles at Lourdes?' And only one answer is possible: 'Yes.' There is not one of us who has not experienced, at least once, an extraordinary and benevolent occurrence that we attributed to God—so we are all '*miraculés*,' in a sense. And there are still many wonderful cures."

As far as the future of hydrotherapy is concerned, it appears we are just beginning to comprehend the amazing range of illnesses that can be cured with water. In Burton Goldberg's book *Alternative Medicine*, we have the following information and quote from Douglas Lewis, N.D., Chairperson of Physical Medicine at the Bastyr College Natural Health Clinic in Seattle, Washington:

"In Europe," says Dr. Lewis, "hydrotherapy is commonly found in health clinics, both as a primary and an adjunctive treatment modality. In the United States, there is also a definite resurgence of interest in hydrotherapy, which I feel is due to the growing dissatisfaction people have with the overuse of medications. People are looking for other alternatives." Dr. Lewis points out that hydrotherapy has numerous clinical applications and provides a number of safe, natural, and effective adjunct treatments for conditions that include digestive problems, female health conditions, chronic fatigue syndrome, cancer, and AIDS. The most important application of hydrotherapy, however, may be in the home, where it can be used as a simple and inexpensive means of both preventing and treating the common cold, flus, and many common health conditions. Because of this, hydrotherapy has great potential to play an important role in medicine in the coming years.

SIXTEEN

Healing Our Earth and Ourselves

Live in each season as it passes; breathe the air; drink the drink, taste the fruit, and resign yourself to the influence of each. Let them be your only diet, drink and botanical medicines. Be blown on by all the winds. Open your pores and bathe in all the tides of nature, in all her streams and oceans, at all seasons.
—HENRY DAVID THOREAU

IN MY MIND, water is a powerful living and thinking entity that is always working to create conditions conducive to life. If the environment is too acid or alkaline, water will try and make it more neutral. For it is when the environment is balanced that life flourishes. The same goes for regulating heat. Water vapor buffers life on Earth from the Sun's intense heat and harmful cosmic rays while at the same time absorbing heat in our oceans and seas. It is the storage of the Sun's energy in water that moderates the planet's temperature to allow life to flourish on land and in our oceans. It is also the movement of water through Earth's atmosphere and its surface that energizes and nourishes life while removing harmful poisons and pollutants.

From science we learn that the water in protoplasm gives rise to life. The higher the water content in protoplasm the more alive and active it is chemically. It is this ever so mysterious protoplasm that provides the foundation of life for the world's food chain. Protoplasm is created by certain microorganisms that have the ability to take nonliving substances and transform them into a living substance. Exactly how this is done remains a mystery. However, we do know that water is the key. And we are learning that the chemical conditions under which protoplasm is created have a direct influence on the health of the food chain and the world of life it supports.

In theory and in fact, it is now established that the modern-day chemical soup created by humankind is impacting the health of all life—from protoplasm on up. It has also been shown that certain

231

human-made chemicals are also influencing the genetic coding for the evolution of life. Since water is the medium in which almost all chemical reactions take place, the source of many of our health problems may be found in the unbalances of Earth's waters.

In a fashion, water embodies the Chinese doctrine of yin and yang. Yin and yang represent opposite forces that maintain a healthy balance. Should the yin and yang become unbalanced, ill health to all life forms usually follows. It is curious how the ancient symbol for yin and yang resembles two water drops flowing into one another within a circle—just like the constant motion of water into and out of darkness and light in the hydrologic cycle. The symbol also represents the infinite spiral of vortex energy, and the serpentine, meandering line between the dark and light yin-yang can speak volumes by itself.

It is water's constant motion that helps it to purify itself and to heal life. When water is contaminated with pollution, it will assimilate and dilute the pollutant in an attempt to minimize the deadly impact on life. If the source of pollution is so powerful that it destroys all life in the water, the water itself will continue to survive. And, slowly but surely over time, the moving water will cleanse itself of the pollutant by breaking it down, destroying it, or harmlessly burying it under sediments. In this way, water untiringly works toward creating an environment where life may once again come forth and flourish.

That water has the wherewithal to do these things is in itself a miracle. Water *knows* how to heal itself. It seems to have innate properties for purifying and healing, which is why good quality water is so useful in maintaining our health, cleansing wounds, and helping the sick to heal.

Acupuncture for Our Bodies and Our Planet

In Appendix I of Olof Alexandersson's book *Living Water*, water researcher Christopher Seebach of the Aquarian Society tells us:

> Vortexian energy, particularly in the case of water, derives from sympathetic harmonies and the avoidance of disharmony, as in the flow of energy patterns that are created by water as it becomes *living water* by moving through the bowels of the earth. . . . 'Dead' water is often the result of humanity interfering with the water's natural flow and energy forces. Water creates and follows energy lines in the earth.

Here, according to Seebach, we learn about how water is transformed into *living water* by flowing harmoniously through the Earth. The statement that "water creates and follows energy lines in the earth" can be related to many religious beliefs and practices associated with water. Throughout the ages, the sites of many churches, places of power, and healing centers were chosen because of their proximity to flowing surface or underground waters. Even the Garden of Eden in Genesis was recorded as a place where "a flow would well up from the ground and water the whole surface of the soil."

In *Living Water*, Seebach mentions that water "creates" and then follows the energy lines in the Earth. These energy lines are sometimes referred to as "ley" lines. Since the earliest of times, various references have been made to these ley lines created by the energy of water. Structures such as Stonehenge, Newgrange, the pyramids, and many other human-made "energy" centers have been and continue to be built upon locations where these ley lines are believed to exert an influence.

According to New Hampshire dowser Marty Cain, as quoted in the 1996 April/May edition of *Earth Star* magazine, these energy points created by water domes were frequently the sites where ancient labyrinths were constructed. Ms. Cain writes, "The water rises up from deep in the Earth, but stops before coming through the crust as a geyser. This water has lots of spiraling energy and pulse. It also attracts cosmic energy from the heavens, so there's a meeting of spiraling vortices. You can't see them, but you sure can feel them."

This same principle was the basis for the energy lines of the human body mapped out by the ancient Chinese. Today these lines and the points where they cross each other on the human body are known as acupuncture meridians and points. The ancient practice of healing through acupuncture has evolved over thousands of years in China. The Chinese understanding of the close relationship between the human body and the body of the Earth is shown in the following quote from Chen Ssu-Hsiao, who died in A.D. 1332:

> In the subterranean regions there are alternate layers of earth and rock and flowing spring waters. These strata rest upon thousands of vapours which are distributed in tens of thousands of branches, veins and threadlike openings.... The body of the earth is like that of a human being. Ordinary people, not being able to see the veins and vessels which are disposed in order

within the body of man, think that it is no more than a lump of solid flesh. Likewise, not being able to see the veins and vessels which are disposed in order under the ground, they think that the earth is just a homogeneous mass.

For thousands of years the diviner-doctors of China knew about the channels of water energy flowing through the planet Earth and through the human body. It was believed by these practitioners that the water flowing through the Earth created a "vital force" to keep the planet alive and healthy. Chinese medical practitioners also discovered these channels of vital energy in the bodies of humans long before there were scientific instruments sensitive enough to prove that such things exist. An acupuncture chart of the human body clearly shows the energy lines, called channels or meridians, networking throughout the body to various acupuncture points. The acupuncturist inserts needles at the appropriate points to restore and balance the flow of the body's water energy in order to help restore a person's health.

David Ash and Peter Hewitt elaborate on acupuncture's understanding of the human body in *The Vortex:*

> In acupuncture, it is considered that there are definite flow lines in the energy body called 'meridians'. Each organ in the physical body is said to be surrounded by a pool of subtle energy. The meridians act like streams, connecting pools of energy deep within the body to the peripheral areas of the skin. An acupuncturist treats the organs through the meridians.
>
> He stimulates or sedates the flow of energy in the meridian according to his diagnosis of the energy state of the organ concerned. He does this by inserting needles into the appropriate meridians at strategic acupuncture points. In this way, acupuncture seeks to harmonize and balance the energy body, encouraging the physical body to heal itself.

The Healing Sounds of Water

Just as the touch of water heals, so too does its sound.

The ocean's rolling surf; the babbling of a bubbling brook; the pitter-patter of raindrops; the rushing windy splash of a cascading waterfall, the sprinkling music of a water fountain—all are water sounds and vibrations that touch our ears and perhaps the essence of our souls.

Evolving modern medicine, Eastern wisdom, and recent research reveal how exposure to sound from certain vibrations and music may have positive lifelong effects on our health, learning, and moods. Shamans, primitive-medicine doctors, musicians, various faith healers, and naturopathic practitioners use music in treating everything from anxiety to zoophobia—including chronic pain, cancer, dyslexia, and mental illness. Just as water flows throughout our bodies on a subcellular level, so too do waves of sound.

Within each of our bodies there are water-filled cells containing microscopic crystals that vibrate in harmony with the energies of the universe and our world. The fact that each of our individual bodies is unique in its manifestation allows for a unique sound or tone to vibrate within every person. Finding the music or sound vibration that resonates in harmony with your body's unique tone will help provide a pathway to health. When you find music that helps you relax or lifts your spirits, you are dealing with music that fits your body type.

Most people know there is a spectrum of sound our ears cannot hear. People who understand animals such as elephants, dolphins, whales, dogs, cats, birds, horses, and many others know these animals share a rich world of sound beyond our limited hearing. The fact that we cannot hear certain sounds does not stop them from penetrating our ears and resonating within our bodies. Besides the undetectable sounds of other living creatures, the air around us is filled with inaudible sound waves from radio and television transmitters, cell phones, distant lightning, satellite communications, and other mechanical and cosmic sources. And, just as there is a rich world of sound in the air, there is another world of sound below the surface of the waters that grace our planet.

Theodor and Wolfram Schwenk's book *Water: The Element of Life* reports the curious fact that the Moon actually causes water bodies on our Earth to vibrate and make sounds:

> But now we must add to this fact that pulsations or vibrations of this kind follow exactly the same laws that govern vibration in wind instruments, flutes for example. These are rhythmic movements lying below our hearing threshold, but nevertheless present and actively setting bodies of water vibrating. Thus, we may speak metaphorically and say that the moon, traveling on its orbit around the earth, "plays" on all the various bodies of water, from east to west, and they all "resound," each in its own

individual resonance and tonal style. Since fairly large bodies of water are involved here, these vibrations last correspondingly long, and are subject to ever renewed stimulation by the moon. Can we not talk of this in musical terms and say that a multiplicity of single instruments has been joined in an orchestra that plays its score loudly or softly day by day, year in, year out?

The realization that bodies of waters on our planet vibrate with sound amazed me. With a small leap of thought we may also realize that each of our unique human bodies, which are about 60 to 80 percent water, also vibrates with its own individual tone. In fact, there is now an evolving science of health that seeks to determine the musical sounds that are best for each of us. Once the proper "tones" for a person's body are determined, certain music may be prescribed for maintaining health and for helping to cure illness.

The use of sound with water is based on ancient wisdom as well as on recent scientific research. In 1973, Dorothy L. Retallack published a work entitled *The Sound of Music and Plants*. In her research, Retallack discovered that the transpiration rate of plants increased when she played Bach, 1920s jazz, or the Indian sitar music of Ravi Shankar. This increase of transpiration is an indication of enhanced photosynthesis activity, which in turn creates cellular growth. Ultimately, such activity provides for a healthier and more productive plant. The one caveat to this research was that certain music, such as "hard rock," accelerated the transpiration rate so high that some plants became ill and died. Based on this, Retallack determined that certain music can be in harmony with the health and growth of living tissue while other music can harm cells.

Similar research corroborating Retallack's 1973 work was recently performed at the University of California in Irvine, where it was discovered that listening to Mozart and other forms of music could boost a person's IQ test rating by up to 10 points. Researchers concluded that "the relationship between music and spatial reasoning was so strong that simply listening to music can make a difference." One of the researching physicists on the project, Gordon Shaw, says, "We suspect that complex music facilitates certain complex neuronal patterns involved in high brain activities like math and chess. By contrast, simple and repetitive music could have the opposite effect."

Based on this type of information, one may reflect on the Cold War days when Russia bombarded the United States Embassy with quiet sound in an effort to create mental upset and ill health. One may also contemplate the impact various forms of music, sound, and noise have on plant, animal and human health, as well as on the evolving structure of our DNA and our brain cells.

From her homestead near Telluride, Colorado, Nicole La Voie told me in a telephone conversation about her method of healing with sound. "I produce computer-generated sound of about 15 to 30 hertz," says La Voie. "These sounds are based on ancient sacred geometry as well as the 52 frequencies of foods for the seven chakras. I have a series of six tapes that help people to stay healthy and to heal." When not traveling the globe to promote her *Return to Harmony* book and tapes, La Voie spends her time at home researching sound and marketing her concept.

In her life's journey, La Voie was transformed while traveling her healing path. At age twenty-five, after having three children, not paying attention to her diet, and being exposed to radiation for six years as an X-ray technician, she developed osteoporosis and lost all her teeth. Hoping to correct her problem, she embarked on a twenty-five-year journey of taking large doses of minerals and other supplements. Eventually her hands and right hip developed agonizing pain from arthritis and other bone problems. At times, she was unable to walk.

Hearing about the use of sound for healing, La Voie began experimenting with sound frequencies that relate to the minerals her body needed. (According to the periodic table, each element corresponds to a specific frequency.) Within five weeks her arthritis and hip pain disappeared, and within a year her osteoporosis was reversed. According to La Voie, "After five years of treating myself with sound, I no longer need supplements, and I feel better today than I did in my twenties." She says that in her sound frequencies she utilizes principles of ancient sacred geometry that has its roots in early Christian and Judaic teachings.

Explanations of ancient sacred geometry in Christian and Judaic teachings can be found in Paul Devereux's *Earth Memory*. Relative to water, Devereux explains various aspects of sacred geometry. For example, if two circles of equal radius overlap such that the circumference of one touches the center of the other, a fishlike shape called the *vesica piscis* (vessel of the fish) is created. "The *vesica piscis* is...relevant to Christian esotericism, and it became the symbol of early Christians in the catacombs, later becoming an essential part of sacred geometry in Christian architecture....The esoteric name for Christ was Jesus the Fish, and the Christian era coincided with the Zodiacal Age of Pisces." The fish-shaped form can then be extrapolated into a hexagon, which "in natural mechanics...manifests in the boiling and mixing actions of liquids."

For these reasons, the relationship of sacred geometry to water also extends to include music and architecture. Ancient stone megalithic structures and the Great Pyramid of Egypt, for instance, are fine examples of the use of sacred geometry.

In this fashion, we learn how sacred geometry, via sound, is used to stimulate and energize the water in our body cells. When the water in our cells vibrates, patterns are created that are said to relate to sacred geometry.

Using Sound in Water for Healing

Can sound in water heal? Without a doubt, the answer is yes.

On a blatant level, modern medicine now uses sound waves to break up certain tumors as well as kidney stones and gallstones. This is accomplished by strapping the patient in a chair and then submerging him or her in a tub of water. The area to be treated is then exposed to high frequency (up to ten million hertz) sound waves. In breaking up kidney stones, for instance, two sound-wave generators are aimed through the water at the stone from two different directions. The crossfire from the two machines then delivers about 1500 sound-wave blasts in bursts of 50 at a time. This use of sound waves has taken the place of invasive surgery and its potential secondary problems of bleeding and infection.

Sound is also used as a diagnostic tool for examining an unborn fetus; for studying the condition and flow of blood through the heart; for detecting testicular and breast cancer; for cleaning teeth; and for many other health-related uses.

On a more subtle level, when sound is used in healing the body, it is the living water within us that responds to the sound and vibrations. As blood flows throughout our bodies it creates mini-whirlpools. These whirlpools, or vortices, stretch the molecules of water and make them sensitive to absorbing the energy of sound. The same phenomenon occurs on a subcellular level as water flows back and forth through the semipermeable membrane of a living cell. The movement of water through the cell's membrane also creates vortices that stretch water molecules, allowing the cell's water to absorb sound energy and, in a sense, become converted.

It is worth repeating here Nobel Prize winner Dr. Alexis Carrel's arresting hypothesis already quoted in Chapter 5: "The cell is immortal. It is merely the fluid in which it floats which degenerates. Renew this fluid at intervals, give the cells what they require for nutrition and, as far as we know, the pulsation of life may go on forever."

The renewal of blood and cellular water is vital to the health and longevity of every life form. However, for the renewal to take place there needs to be an adequate amount of water.

One of the key measures of human health and vitality is the rate of oxygen consumption in the body. Science now recognizes the fact that, regardless of age, our rate of oxygen use is directly related to the ratio of our body weight to water. According to H. G. Deming in *Water: The Fountain of Opportunity,*

> We age because we become dehydrated. An average man, between the ages of 30 and 80, loses about 18 per cent of his body water. This loss is intimately related to a loss of about 12 per cent in body weight. Nearly every organ, from the heart and other muscles to the kidneys and brain, suffers the loss of a considerable number of cells. There is a consequent loss of function, which is very roughly in proportion to the number of cells lost. The filtration rate through the kidneys may decrease 43 per cent, and plasma flow through the kidneys almost as much.
>
> Yet, these are all average figures. There are men of 80 whose rate of oxygen consumption and kidney function are those of a man of 50. One of the most earnest problems of this century is that of determining why a few persons continue to function well into very advanced years. If we could confer this ability to everyone, we all might continue to be taxable at 80, instead of retiring on Social Security and relapsing into Medicare at 65. This hope is surely as worthy of government attention as rocket shots to the moon. (pp. 49–50).

Besides the water in our blood and cells responding to sound, we also find that the cellular composition of any part of our body has its own specific resonance or sound. It is almost as if the arrangement of cells in any organ, gland, or other bodily structure creates its own special musical symphony.

Evidence of the power of sound dates back to the earliest Sanskrit writings and can be found in the cultures of ancient Egypt, China, Greece, Persia, Rome, India, and Tibet. In the first book of Samuel we learn how David used music to heal Saul of depression. In Homer's *Odyssey*, music takes away the pain and heals Ulysses' knee after it is gouged by a wild boar. The sound vibrations created by the ancient chants of Tibetan monks are now being applied as one of several healing vibrations used for healing under water. Another example can be found in early Indian Hindu tradition, where it is taught that six of the body's seven chakras (vortex energy centers) contain all fifty sounds of the Sanskrit language. In theory, the *bija* (sacred "seed") syllables of Sanskrit are said to stimulate and energize the "petal" sounds of each chakra. The intonation of these syllables in a repeated sequence is believed to synchronize and balance the body's chakras.

It was only in the eighteenth century that the sound-wave research of the German physicist Ernst Chladni (1756–1827) first rendered sound into visible forms. Chladni discovered how playing a violin would create unique forms in sand scattered across steel discs. Depending on the note he was playing, Chladni saw that the sand particles would take various fluid-type shapes as they interacted with the vibrating steel disc beneath. The curious thing about some of the photographs depicting the wheel shapes of Chladni's vibrating sand is that the shapes are strikingly similar to the shapes of water drops in photographs taken by Theodor Schwenk. The drop photographs of Schwenk demonstrate how water responds to the cosmic vibration of the Moon and other sources. Schwenk proved that the shape of the drop is determined by the health of the water (polluted waters show disfigured circles), whereas Chladni proved that the circular shape formed by the vibrating sands was determined by the quality of the violin's note.

This book is the first, as far as I know, to associate the relationship of Chladni's work with Schwenk's. Certainly the seminal work of these two great men with sound, cosmic influences, and water needs to be further explored.

Intrigued with Chladni's work, Dr. Hans Jenny (1904–1972) of Zurich spent over ten years researching the relationship of sound waves to matter. Seeing this evolving work with sound as a new science, Jenny coined the word "Cymatics." In his groundbreaking film *Cymatics*, he visually shows us how sand particles respond to the rising pitch of sound in harmony with the "fluid" vibration of music. By this method Jenny proved how invisible sound vibrations literally influence the shape of matter.

To take his research one step further, Jenny used a machine called a "tonoscope." Sounds from human vocal cords were passed through a microphone into the tonoscope, which in turn created a visual shape on a screen. While doing tests with this method, Jenny discovered that a human voice uttering the ancient Hindu syllable "Om" produced the shape of a circle on the screen. According to the renowned mystic Alan Watts, who spells Om as Aum, the use of the Aum sound uses the whole spectrum of sound from the back of the throat to the lips. Watts says the sound of Aum is known in ancient teachings as the sound of God.

Chladni's and Jenny's pioneering work eventually led to the explosion of sound healers in this century. In England, for example, the physician Peter Guy Manners has created a device called the Cymatic applicator to heal muscle and other ailments. Manners, as well as the French biologist-physical therapist Dennis Brousse are doing cutting-edge research into the use of underwater sound for healing.

This and other research has shown us how sound waves may heal our bodies by stimulating our internal waters on a subcellular level. Research has shown that inside the cell of every life form is the protoplasm (or cytoplasm) that surrounds its nucleus. Floating within the protoplasm of the cell are the structures or organelles called mitochondria, which provide energy through cellular respiration. Science tells us that mitochondria naturally resonate at about 25 hertz or cycles per second. Science also tells us that mitochondria are shaped in the form of a violin or guitar.

As sound vibrations touch our ears, brain, the skin (our largest sense organ), and our body's water, the vibrations penetrate into each and every cell within us. The vibrating of mitochondria inside our body cells shakes the watery protoplasm surrounding their nuclei. This shaking creates wave energy with vortices that may help energize the cells and bring them into balance. If the sound waves being absorbed are in harmony with the optimal "tone" that represents a person's cellular structure, he or she will probably experience accelerated healing.

Besides helping to heal, certain sound vibrations may act as a health tonic in preventing illness. This "toning" of the body's water to compatible sound, whether by one's vocal cords, music, or vibrational frequencies, is one of the ancient Eastern secrets of natural healing. According to Tim Wheater, one of the world's most recognized flute players, toning produces a very pure sound that creates a magical set of vibrations around the body. This toning literally influences the chemical balance of the body and the brain.

This use of sound is also one of many ways of stimulating the body's endocrine system. The endocrine system is composed of various glands throughout the body that produce internal watery secretions that enter the bloodstream. The secretions then travel to parts of the body whose functions they physically regulate or control. These functions include respiration, digestion, heart rhythm, blood pressure, mood, sex drive, and others. The endocrine glands include the pituitary, thyroid, parathyroid, hypothalamus, adrenals, thymus, pineal, part of the pancreas, and the gonads. Stimulation of these glands with sound may help us heal as well as help define our mood and behavior.

As mentioned earlier, sound travels through water four times faster than through the air. Because of this, dolphins, whales, and some fish are able to communicate with each other through thousands of miles of water in a very brief period of time.

In a related fashion, the sound produced by dolphins is believed to help heal people. Apparently, the sound wave and brain receiving system of dolphins is credited with being able to "see" inside the body of other living species—including humans. Perhaps by seeing within the human body, dolphins can focus sound waves to help heal ailing organs and cells.

In the seminal book *Dolphins and Their Power to Heal*, Amanda Cochrane and Karena Callen tell us:

> According to the British doctor Peter Guy Manners, who has been investigating the therapeutic use of sound for 20 years, every part of the human anatomy produces a sound or vibration. When there is an illness or dysfunction in an organ or gland, there are measurable changes in its vibratory or resonant characteristics.... He suggests that because energy flow is audible and magnetic in nature, it can be rebalanced by magnetic cymatic or sound energy.... Manners observes that "When

swimming with dolphins, they come alongside, as if investigating, sounding us out. Investigation shows that dolphins do have a therapeutic effect on humans."

The use of sound therapy is now finding its way not only into the rooms and outside lounging areas of spas, but also into their healing water baths. Some spas now offer a dip in a pool or tub that is rigged for sound. As a person swims, floats, gets a hands-on water massage, or sits with Jacuzzi jets swirling water and air bubble energy, sound energy is vibrated through the water. In *Healing Waters*, Linda Troeller expresses her water sound experience this way:

> In a perfectly balanced saline pool I was bathing in underwater music and laser light. The songs of the Orca bubbled around me. I opened my eyes and found the other participants gathered like schools of fish, gliding on the surface, resting and sinking into deep blue, red, and green hues of light. My body yearned to dance with the others. A yellow sun covered my face and a vision of whiteness followed.

As sound vibrations penetrate the body and bounce around the tub or pool, a person will experience a healing and perhaps a more penetrating form of sound therapy. This water-sound-therapy (WST) may be further enhanced with the addition of water-light-therapy (WLT). Presented together they form water-sound-and-light-therapy (WSLT). Once individuals understand the colors, music, or tones that compliment the health and moods of their particular being, they may accordingly customize their WSLT experience. WSLT can be further embellished with aromatherapy by the addition of selected incense, oils, crystals, herbs, mineral salts, or flowers. Such enhancements to the WSLT experience may very well bring one close to enjoying heavenly healing.

Sexual Toning and Healing with Water

When two people fall in love, the water in every cell of their beings resonates in harmony. This is why mutual love has such a tremendous effect on the people involved. Love is so powerful it completely alters the way a person exists from moment to moment. In a fashion, love is a path to transformation. Those of us who have experienced love often realize how we are forever changed.

When two people fall in love, they usually like to consummate their love with sexual intimacy. Since there are many variations on the theme of sex, I would like us to look at the role of water. Water is the one thing that is often taken for granted and rarely thought about during sex. This happens in spite of the fact that water is probably the key element in the sexual experience, and not just because it is the very essence of what makes sex physically possible. On many levels—spiritual, mental, physical, chemical—water serves as the vehicle for orgasm as well as creation. Besides the creative juices provided by the genitalia during lovemaking, the sweat from the skin also has special significance.

In the book *Sexual Secrets* Nik Douglas and Penny Slinger tell us:

> The common tendency to rush off to the bathroom to wash, douche or shower after love-making is condemned in the Eastern love treatises. The perspiration produced on bodies making love contains subtle minerals and vital secretions that are beneficial if absorbed. Yoga texts advise the couple not to bath shower for at least an hour after climaxing. The absorption of love-secretions is of great benefit to the couple. These essences contain many vital elements that are beneficial to both body and mind.

This advice based on ancient yoga texts is similar to that offered by other sources, both ancient and modern. Through research over the years, many scientists and healers have become acutely aware of our skin's ability to release and absorb chemicals.

Skin is a semipermeable membrane that breathes while also releasing watery fluids. The skin-to-skin contact of two lovers actually creates a unique exchange of fluids between the bodies. As the heated fluids from the two bodies interact between the touching skin surfaces, they transform into a new mixture; this new mixture is then reabsorbed if given some time before being washed off.

This exchange of bodily fluids via the skin creates another potential level of intimacy, which is quite different from the shared intimacy via genital contact and kissing. The exchange of body waters through the skin is something that may be appreciated as an added dimension to lovemaking and healing. For example, the simple act of lovers holding each other for a prolonged period of time, such as in the "spooning" position, creates an intimate exchange of energy and fluids that is akin to spiritual intercourse. When two naked lovers hug, embrace, and cuddle, they create a special form of bonding energy. The rubbing of skin surfaces causes the ensuing body moisture to become transformed into an electromagnetic fluid charged with unique chemicals and energies. To shower or bathe immediately after making love will remove this special moisture before the skin has an opportunity to absorb and transfer it.

This communication of skin moisture with our internal body water was discovered not too long ago. We learn about this from Dian Dincin Buchman's book *The Complete Book of Water Therapy: 500 Ways to Use Our Oldest Natural Medicine—Inside and Out:*

> In 1880, Dr. William Winternitz of Austria discovered the startling fact that water acts on the nerve points of the skin. The skin then delivers messages directly to a nearby organ, or indirectly through reflex "arcs."
>
> These arcs connect the skin to muscles, glands, and organs. When water—either hot or cold—is applied to the skin, the reflex arcs stimulate nerve impulses that in turn travel to other parts of the body. This action is similar to the transfer of electricity that occurs when a light switch is turned on, or to the effect on a nerve when acupuncture is applied.

The sharing of body waters via skin contact through lovemaking may also reaffirm the ancient writings that refer to two people "becoming one." The tactile touching of skin to skin with loving intent has also been proven to transmit healing energies to newborns. Babies who receive cuddling and touching are much healthier and grow more rapidly.

Our skin's ability to absorb the chemicals on its surface also has cosmic ramifications. For example, women who suffer from or who wish to prevent osteoporosis are advised not to shower for four to six hours after spending some time in the Sun. This allows time for the skin to transform the Sun's energy into vitamin D and absorb this and other Sun induced skin chemicals into the body. The vitamin D from the sunlight has many benefits, including that of maintaining healthy bones.

Earlier in this book, mention was made that the water in our bodies responds to cosmic influences such as the Sun or Moon. With this in mind, perhaps we can relate to the Sun's energy creating vitamin D on our skin as a form of cosmic intercourse.

The same idea applies to moist herbal compresses and essential oils. From the earliest of times, healers had knowledge of the skin's permeability and cured various ailments by applying compresses and poultices containing moist herbs. This form of traditional medicine is now being mimicked by today's transdermal patch. Today we have transdermal patches for various addiction abatements, for alleviating air and water travel sickness, for medicating heart conditions, for monitoring and treating diabetes, and for manipulating a variety of body functions. Pharmaceutical companies are now or soon will be introducing transdermal patches containing aphrodisiacs, allergy relief medications, herbal and homeopathic remedies, birth control and hormone-influencing chemicals, mental health medications, and many other medications.

In a way, we may view the exchange of herbal energy through the skin as a form of intercourse with plants.

When one thinks of it, our exposure to chemicals via the skin includes such things as perfumes, aftershaves, lotions, soaps, clothing, powders, light, chlorinated water, and airborne chemicals. Because of this, it is a good policy to be careful of what you let get under your skin.

On a closing note, when it comes to love, it need not always involve other people as the object of one's love. Love can and often does include a "Divine relationship." The experience of Divine love is just as real and can produce similar biochemical changes in the body as love of another person.

On the physical level, our sexual health is strongly related to the condition of our pubococcygeal (PC) muscle. This muscle is found between our pubic bone in the front and the tailbone (coccyx) in the back. Like any muscle in the body, the PC muscle requires exercise and a flow of blood in order to stay nourished and healthy. If the PC muscle is not exercised or supplied with fresh blood from time to time, it, and the veins and capillaries serving the tissue, may suffer from blockage. When this happens, the PC muscle may lose its tone and become less likely to perform well when called upon during sex.

When we are young, the tone of our body muscles is usually maintained with a minimal amount of exercise. However, as we age, our muscles require regular conditioning in order to stay in youthful condition. The PC muscle is no exception to this rule.

There are several exercises that can strengthen the PC muscle and other genital-related organs. Perhaps the most well known are the Kegel exercises, developed in the 1940s by a gynecologist named

Arnold Kegel. Kegel originally designed these exercises to help women with bladder problems, but it was eventually discovered that they benefited the entire genital region of both women and men.

Kegel exercises involve three different motions:

1. The slow clenching of the PC muscle as though trying to stop urination. Hold it clenched for a count of three to five and then relax.

2. The rapid clenching of the PC muscle.

3. The pushing out (also known as bearing down) of the PC muscle as though trying to force a bowel movement.

Each of these exercises is done separately and in a series of repetitions. In the beginning, I recommend repeating each exercise ten times. When done five to ten times a day, these exercises will strengthen the PC muscle, the prostate, and related sexual organs. The beauty of these exercises is that you can perform them anywhere at any time—sitting in a chair; in the car; at your desk; lying in bed; standing in line at the grocery. It doesn't matter where—just *do* them several times a day every day.

When the Kegel exercises are used in combination with hydrotherapy, there can be even greater improvement in a person's sex life and genital-related organ health. The use of the Kegel technique is further enhanced when performed in a tub filled with water (hot, warm, or cold), since water and its pressure will further stimulate the PC muscle.

Another secret to using water for enhancing sexual health is accomplished very easily. All one has to do is have cold water come into contact with the genital area—especially with the PC muscle.

How does cold water improve the tone and health of one's sex organs?

When cold water comes into contact with the genitals and the PC muscle, it constricts the area's blood vessels and forces blood away. This action sends a signal to the brain, which in turn sends a signal to the liver to send fresh blood to the genitals to protect the cells from the cold. This is a natural survival response of the body. The supply of fresh blood helps to invigorate and strengthen the genital muscles and organs.

The actual procedure for undertaking a water cure and tonic for the genitals can be accomplished by sitting in a cold running stream, sitting in a tub, running water from a hose, using cold compresses, and/or taking a cold shower.

The key to each of these procedures is to bring the cold water into contact with the genitals, especially the PC muscle, for a time of one to three minutes. Immediately following the cold water exposure, the genitals may then be exposed to warmth. This will ensure that the constricted blood vessels dilate and flush out any constipation that may have gathered in the genital area. Warmth can be brought to the genitals by wrapping the area with a heavy towel or bathrobe, applying a warm to hot compress, exercising, or spraying with warm to hot water from a hose or water outlet in a tub or shower.

In recalling the story about Sebastian Kneipp in the previous chapter—he ran through the streets before removing his clothes and diving into the chilly waters of the Danube. After a brief swim, he again ran home. This was Kneipp's way of warming up his body before and after exposing it to cold water. Later on, when Kneipp opened his healing center, he would have clients chop wood and do other exercises in order to build up body heat prior to water treatments.

If using a tub is the preferred method, the water in the tub should only be high enough, about six to nine inches, to allow complete submergence of the genitals when in the sitting position. When you are sitting in the tub, the arms, hands, legs, and feet should be placed out of the cold water. If two tubs are available, all the better. Fill one with cold and the other with warm to hot water to the proper level, and alternate back and forth between the two. Sit in the cold tub for one to three minutes; then transfer to the warm or hot tub for a minimum of three to nine minutes. Start out this exercise with two or three alternate submergings in each tub, and then increase the number according to your body's strength. On some days you may have a lower tolerance for cold water than others. Listen to what your body tells you—if you feel a chill, avoid the cold-water sitz and just use warm water.

If using the shower method, the showerhead can be pointed so the flowing water hits the abdomen or lower back. Either location will stimulate the blood flow to the organs that give support to the genital system.

Using hot and cold hydrotherapy on a regular basis in combination with the Kegel exercises will work wonders in healing and maintaining the health of the sexual organs, including the prostate, while potentially increasing one's fertility and sexual potency.

The Magic of Healing Dew

The magical creation of dew on vegetation has long been the subject of special consideration. As we saw in the last chapter, Paracelsus believed the dew on vegetation possessed the healing energy of the plants as well as the various planets in the sky. Others believe that the dew on grass may act as a conductor to help transmit the healing energies of magnetic earth and the universe. The famous Bach's floral remedies, for instance, are based on the principle of dew capturing the essence of various flowers. Of course, flowers in themselves are believed to contain considerable amounts of energy, since it is the flower that provides the wellspring for fertilization and creation.

If we were to perceive the presence of dew as small twinkling drops of liquid crystals, our minds might then grasp how each drop captures the energy of the universe and the living world here on Earth. Powerful stuff when one stops to think about it—a drop of dew can be seen as a minuscule hologram of the universe and its energy.

One common technique for healing the body with dew is to kneel in the nude and brush the open fingers and palms of one's hands across dew-laden vegetation. Once this is done, the cool virgin moisture is gently applied over and over again to whatever part of the body needs healing—heart, sexual organs, face, etc. Using dew to moisturize one's face is believed to help in retaining a youthful appearance while also energizing and refreshing the five bodily senses. The sense of seeing, for example, can be strengthened and invigorated by repeatedly applying dew to one's closed eyelids.

Another method for touching the body with dew is to lie down naked on soft dewy grass and roll about. This is especially cosmic when done under one's celestial birth sign or when the light of the Moon is smiling or in full bloom. While rolling about in the grass or moisturizing one's face, it may be sensed that the essence of the vegetation's odor is carried into the nostrils as the dew is transformed to water vapor by the body's warmth. In a fashion, this is a form of cosmic aromatherapy since you are also inhaling the essence that was captured by the dew as it formed and exchanged molecular energy with the vegetation. Taking a barefoot walk in fresh dew is also highly recommended, since it is easy to do and offers many health benefits.

Elaborating on the concept of walking through dew is the Swiss-born Dr. Alfred Vogel, who is world renowned as "the Nature Doctor." Dr. Vogel has been researching, writing about, and practicing herbal medicine for more than sixty-five years. His 1952 book *The Nature Doctor* has been translated into over fifteen languages and has sold more than 2 million copies. In the revised edition published in 1991, Dr. Vogel gives this advice about the healing values of dew:

> If you go for an early morning walk on dewy grass you will soon notice that going barefoot makes you feel really good, generating new strength when you have been feeling tired and worn out. It is like recharging one's batteries, so to speak, recharging your run-down nerves with energy. It seems as if Mother Earth is giving off energy that improves the glandular functions. That is why I consider it rather strange that, although overtired and worn-out, we do not take full advantage of this simple regenerative treatment, which is able to stimulate our endocrine glands to increase their activity.... Take care, however, to walk only on natural ground, for the more unspoilt the ground the greater will be the benefit derived from its magnetic field. Never believe that walking barefoot on asphalt, concrete or any other artificial surface will do the same good. No, it is better to wear your shoes on this kind of surface, because you will not stand to gain anything by it, rather the opposite.

The Nature Doctor is a wonderful book, and the world is most fortunate to have Dr. Vogel as a resource for alternative healing.

Beyond the use of dew for healing, there is also the joy of running and jumping stark naked through thick fog or a rain, sleet, or snow shower. While doing so, you may feel inspired to use your hands for massaging the virginlike water into your skin and hair, or for pounding your chest like a gorilla in the wilds. Along with the playful joy of experiencing various waters from the sky, you may also have the urge to make sounds by singing, shouting, whistling, or humming. Perhaps this urge for making sounds while playing with water will help to remind you of just how closely you are related to other animals that also need water.

As a final thought on dew, I offer these lines from James Whitcomb Riley's "Thoughts fer the Discouraged Farmer" [*sic*]:

> Fer the world is full of roses, and the roses full of dew,
> And the dew is full of heavenly love that drips fer me and you.

Part V

HOPE

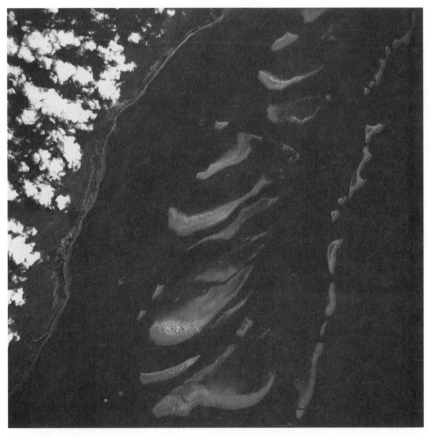

Great Barrier Reef, Queensland, Australia, August 1992. This reef is a complex of hundreds of individual coral reefs that extend along the Queensland coast for approximately 1200 miles (2000 kilometers). This reef complex is the largest and the longest in the world. The reefs in this NASA photo are located along the eastern coast of Cape York Peninsula.

SEVENTEEN

The Power of One

*And, of course, for those of us to whom the water is a special
attraction, this is heaven on earth.* —WALTER CRONKITE

WHEN I FIRST SET UP my water-testing laboratory on Martha's Vineyard, many local folks thought I would never make a living testing
water on the island. I remember that several local folks stopped by
to visit and to take a look at my new water-testing equipment. One
comment I recall was, "Interesting equipment you got here, but with
the good water we have on the Vineyard, I don't think you'll get much
chance to use it."

As the months and years came and went, I found my little lab doing more and more business. New state regulations required day-care
centers to have their water tested; the wastewater treatment plants at
Martha's Vineyard Hospital and the U.S. Coast Guard Station found
they needed certain parameters tested on a weekly, monthly, and quar-
terly basis; town public water supplies needed quality control water
tests; a passable water analysis was required before a home could be
bought; new wells had to be tested; shellfish beds and public swimming areas had to be tested for bacteria pollution. Eventually the
towns began to hire me to compose underground fuel tank bylaws,
write open-space plans, and prepare applications for grants to preserve and protect aquifer recharge zones. As years passed, the people
of Martha's slowly came to realize the importance of having a certified
water-testing laboratory on the island.

One spring day while I was working in my laboratory, I received a
telephone call from Walter Cronkite. To hear his familiar voice over
the telephone was, at first, a bit of a surprise. Like so many people, I
was used to seeing Walter Cronkite on television reporting the news
for CBS or doing a special on Discovery, PBS, or the *Cronkite at
Large* program. As many local people know, Walter Cronkite has deep

family roots on Martha's Vineyard. He is related to the Norton family, which were some of the original white settlers on the island. Cronkite also owns a home overlooking the scenic Edgartown Harbor.

In his telephone call, Walter expressed his concerns about the health of the Edgartown Harbor waters, especially because of the increasing number of boats. "I am a sailor," he said, "and one thing I know for sure, is that some of the boats coming in here have very limited holding capacities for their toilets." After a few telephone conversations and meetings at Walter's home, we developed a strategy for studying what impact, if any, the ever growing seasonal boating community was having on the fragile ecosystem of Edgartown Harbor.

The strategy we devised was quite simple. Every morning and early evening throughout the spring, I would traverse the harbor in my small boat and take water samples at predetermined locations. The test results from these spring water samples would help provide a baseline before the arrival of boats for the summer season.

Each time I was out on the water, the splash and smell of vaporized saltwater off my boat's hull touched my nose and caressed my face. I always had the same feeling: God, it feels great to be out here doing this! "Yes," I thought, "this body of water deserves protection. Thank goodness for people like Walter." I remember one time laughing aloud when the thought struck me about taking the "l" out of Walter's name, and bestowing on him the name Water. "How appropriate, Water protecting water."

The water in Edgartown Harbor tested clean throughout the months of April, May, and June. However, as the July boats began arriving in preparation for the regatta's race week, the harbor's fecal coliform bacteria levels slowly began to rise. On the very first race day of the season, the coliform levels were so high that I had to perform several dilutions just to get a rough estimate of the pollution levels. Each day during race week, the lab results for levels of bacteria were always the same, TNTC (too numerous to count). Anyone taking a swim in Edgartown Harbor during this time certainly ran a high risk of contacting some sort of bacterial or viral infection.

Why did the bacteria levels in Edgartown Harbor suddenly increase during race week? Apparently, the competition to win these sailing races is so keen that the sailboats were emptying their heads (toilets) in order to lighten their load. By lightening the weight of their boats, they gave themselves a better chance at winning the race.

After reporting the final lab results to Walter Cronkite, he decided to present the written report to the town with Robert Hubner, the commodore of the Edgartown Yacht Club. Since the community of Martha's Vineyard is relatively well-connected, it didn't take long before the word leaked out about Walter's forthcoming appearance. On the evening of his presentation, the Edgartown Selectmen's room was filled to overflowing. The audience in the small room sat in silent awe as Walter walked in and gave them the bad news. With a hint of dire alarm in his ever-so-distinguished voice, Walter reported the facts about how the boats were polluting our town's beloved Edgartown Harbor. The Edgartown Selectmen expressed both surprise and gratitude for Walter's concern and information.

Within months, following on the heels of front-page news in the local *Vineyard Gazette*, the town's Selectmen and Board of Health, the Edgartown Yacht Club, and Leonard Greene, owner of Edgartown Marine, devised a plan to put an end to the harbor's boat pollution. The town and Mr. Greene eventually set up a free pump-out facility for boat toilets and passed a bylaw requiring sealed heads with zero discharge of all boat wastes into the harbor's waters.

Thanks to the actions of Walter Cronkite and a responsive community, a local health and water pollution problem was quickly solved. This one example demonstrates what can be done through an awareness of our watery world, and how thinking about and respecting our intimate connection with water can bring about positive change.

Years later, Walter Cronkite and I again crossed paths. Besides running the water-testing laboratory, I was now publisher-editor of *Martha's Vineyard Magazine*, which had an environmental focus. Again, Walter and I talked about water and its special meaning for many of us living on an island. At my request, he agreed to write an article that he entitled "A Vineyard Feeling." In part, this is what he wrote:

This is a place for nature lovers, and for them it offers the real excitement of the forests and moors and cliffs and ponds. Thank goodness there are still some folks to whom flora and fauna are something more than subjects for syndicated television shows, and for them the Vineyard is a paradise.

And, of course, for those of us to whom the water is a special attraction, this is heaven on earth. For me the thrill is in living on Edgartown Harbor, in having *Wyntje*, our 42-foot yawl, anchored just off my dock, bouncing at her mooring, inviting me to get aboard for a spanking afternoon sail out on Nantucket Sound where it is a rare day that the wind doesn't rise by early afternoon with enough gusto to move along the most sluggish old tub.

When I'm not on *Wyntje*, I play unappointed and unofficial assistant to John Edwards, our harbormaster. I make occasional sorties out in *Pequod*, the Whaler, to survey the new arrivals and frequently to greet old friends among the cruising fraternity.

From the water I can marvel again at the beauty of our town at one end of the harbor—dressed in her sparkling white and serviceable, no-nonsense Yankee greys—and the wide expanse of Katama Bay at the other end.

While visiting with Walter, I also had the pleasure of meeting his lovely wife, Betsy, and his charming mother, Helen. What struck me the most was that the concern for the health of the water was something that was shared by Walter's entire family. Besides spending time sailing local waters, Walter also had grandchildren and friends of all ages who would visit and spend considerable time playing on the nearby beach and its harbor waters.

As the Edgartown harbor-water research project came to a close, Walter invited me to his house for cocktails. As we sat on cushioned wicker chairs in his screened porch overlooking the harbor, we discussed how this project would help keep the harbor clean for people long after we are no longer here. That was when Walter shared a bit of wisdom with me. "You know," he said, "my generation, as well as yours, has been spoiled. We have lived through a time in history when natural resources have been relatively cheap and plentiful. But this cannot go on forever. In the future, people are going to have to learn to live with less. Perhaps future generations will redefine the word 'success' to mean something different than acquiring wealth and material possessions. Maybe in the future the word 'success' will be defined as living in harmony with nature."

These prophetic words of Walter Cronkite's have stuck with me over the past ten years. Today, as our world faces a shortage of water, food, energy, housing, and many other things, it appears as though Walter had his finger on the pulse of time and was seeing into future.

As expressed elsewhere in this book, you do not have to be a famous personage to help the world of life by practicing water awareness or by adopting a low-impact lifestyle. All you need to do is care and think about water and all it provides in life. You can share this information with family, friends, and those you work with. Ask about their thoughts on water and have open and relaxed conversations. You may be surprised at what others think about the all-encompassing subject of water.

And, if you want to learn from water itself, go spend some time with water in a natural setting or near a fountain, or take a walk in the rain. By opening all your senses to water, your will soon find yourself a worthy pupil.

EIGHTEEN

The Awakening

Humanity has not only lost touch with the spiritual nature of water, but is now in danger of losing its very physical substance. The drying up of countless springs all over the world is a symptom of this development, and the great efforts that are being made on all sides to compensate for the damage done show how serious the situation is. A prerequisite for an effective practical course of action is the rediscovery in a modern form of the forgotten spiritual nature of those elements whose nature it is to flow. —THEODOR SCHWENK

IN THE 1901 BOOK *Cosmic Consciousness,* Richard Bucke wrote about humans who were being born onto Earth with an "awareness of oneness with all life." According to Bucke, these people would become more numerous with each passing year, and would know Earth in ways others do not. "This new race is in the act of being born from us, and in the near future it will occupy and possess the earth," said Bucke. This statement made one hundred years ago seems to be coming true. In all my readings and travels around the globe, it appears as though people are *awakening to the idea that all life is related through water.*

History teaches that humankind and other life forms are always evolving. Thoughts about the direction of our evolution vary greatly. Some apocalyptic writers see widespread chaos, starvation, and violence as our inevitable end. Others see us being saved by the coming of another spiritual leader. Few see us saving ourselves through an awakening of knowledge gained from water.

In my opinion, as we continue to evolve, we will learn how water was, is, and always will be the source of our awakening and survival. If fate delivers the truth of these words, I have faith many more of us will begin giving time and attention to the care of water.

It is in the caring for water that we have the potential for finding

259

peace within ourselves and for sharing that peace with our families and friends, our communities, and all other people and living things on Earth. And, it can only be in a peaceful atmosphere that humankind can truly attain a lasting change that will lead to health and prosperity.

Even though peace may sound like a trite idea, there are indications that this is the reality humankind is capable of achieving. Worldwide communication systems are now allowing people to talk with each other with minimal governmental censorship. In a subtle way, the opening of communication amongst people of different countries has provided vital support for the peace initiatives proffered by those in power.

A tangible example of this is the recent series of CD-ROM atlases created from information derived from heretofore secret sources in Russia and the United States. These atlases contain information gathered by scientific and military people about Earth's oceans and weather, including Russia's extensive data on the Arctic Ocean. Out of this joint effort has come the creation of the Environmental Working Group, composed of scientists and political leaders from both countries. This group's focus is to better understand our Earth while attempting to integrate various human impacts on the global environment. Gathering and analyzing information about water in its three expressions, liquid, gas, and ice, is a major component of this group's efforts, and is most obvious in the data provided on their CD-ROM atlases.

Helping to lay the foundation for this effort was the Russian leader Mikhail Gorbachev. During his reign in power, Gorbachev led the way in fostering world peace as well as environmental awareness. And, even though no longer in the seat of power, he has continued his environmental effort as president of Green Cross International, a group he was instrumental in founding. In the foreword of *Water: The Drop of Life,* Gorbachev writes:

> Water, like religion and ideology, has the power to move millions of people. Since the very birth of human civilization, people have moved to settle close to it. People move when there is too little of it. People move when there is too much of it. People journey down it. People write, sing and dance about it. People fight over it. . . .
>
> We need it for drinking, for cooking, for washing, for food, for sanitation, for industry, for energy, for transport, for rituals,

for fun, for life. And it is not only we humans who need it; all life everywhere is dependent on water to survive.

But we stand today on the brink of a global water crisis.

Helping the water effort of political leaders, scientists, artists, philosophers, etc., are organizations such as the American Water Works Association (AWWA) and its international affiliates. The AWWA is a long-standing organization with membership that spans a spectrum of professional water managers, educators, students and other people interested in water.

As an adjunct to these water efforts, we have computer programmers gathering useful information. The water programs produced by these programmers help to raise water awareness of people of all ages around the globe. On a level aimed at a broad range of people, a CD-ROM entitled *WATER*, created by Enviro-Media, Inc., in Honolulu, Hawaii, is a wonderful teaching tool for people of all ages and educational levels. Covering topics from basic science about the microscopic composition of water to Earth's hydrologic cycle to water gods, *WATER* is a wonderful adventure. On a similar note, the Water Environment Federation recently released a CD entitled *Aqua Venturer*, which tells about the history of water, its vital importance to all life, and the role it plays in the development of civilization.

Slowly but surely, all facets of human evolution and creativity are centering on the basics of survival for life on Earth. People from all walks of life are once again learning about the true source that empowers this life. I feel that once the people of Earth reawaken to water, they will also awaken to the wonder of witnessing the ongoing creation of other water beings. In so doing, they will clearly see how those who control water also control the destiny of all life forms on Earth. But if the power of water is abused for selfish gain instead of for helping to support life, much destruction and hardship will surely follow.

For instance, as expressed in Peter Swanson's *Water: The Drop of Life,* a companion book to the PBS program, we have a warning about how the world's limited well of water is running dry. In the book's introduction we read:

Every year, chemical contamination and waterborne diseases kill 15 million people. Some of this pollution comes from human waste, some from agricultural waste, and some from industrial waste. Together, they are choking our rivers and contaminating our groundwater. Painfully, we are learning that the penalty for polluting our waters is severe. Every eight seconds...somewhere in the world...a child dies of a water-related disease.

For many years, prize-winning author and environmentalist Isabel Allende has been concerned about these disturbing developments. [According to Allende] *"Water symbolizes everything that is fresh and renewed and transformed in us as human beings. Clean, running water is an incredibly precious thing that not everybody has, very few people have."*

Different voices speak the water message at different times to different ears. Writers, actors, songwriters, politicians, cartoonists, newscasters, scientists, artists, educators, parents, healers, religious leaders, filmmakers, and corporate leaders are all potential contributors and distributors of information about water. So, too, is the common person in the street endowed with the ability to make a difference when it comes to water.

When it comes to writers who have eloquently expressed water thoughts, I think of people with names like Thoreau, Burroughs, Muir, Leopold, Carson, Abbey, Lowell, Schwenk, Hahn, Whitman, Darwin, White, Emerson, Humboldt, Commoner, Nearing, Schauberger, St. Barbe Baker, Watson, Flanagan, Outwater, Briggs, King, Buchman, Davis, Franks, Pettyjohn, Hunt, Watts, Cocannouer, Wild, McPhee, Aristotle, da Vinci, Batmanghelidj, Kneipp, Lao-tsu, Sanford, Gardner, Szekely, Powledge, Masani, Smith, Deming, Milne, Bird, Walton, Morgan, Postel, Symons, Seebach, Wiesenberger, Harr, Chopra, and others too numerous to list. Writers like these help to awaken us to what most of us innately sense to be true about water. For those who seek to expand on their knowledge and appreciation of water, I recommend the bibliography at the end of this book.

However, one does not need to read or write in order to live, understand, and practice the ways of water. Examples of people working in harmony with water can be found everywhere—from remote villages to those of us using water-conservation devices in our homes. No matter who you are, the following message is always reaching out to you: *Water is your source of life; water is the most important element for your health—without clean water, there is a dismal future awaiting you and all other life.*

On another level, the stress of not having good-quality drinking water readily available is potentially unhealthy for the human body and mind. Many "modern" cities have neglected to adequately provide the basic need of water for their people. Public drinking-water fountains are almost nonexistent in many cities. As a result, many urban people do not have easy access to quality drinking water.

"For this and other reasons," says Steven Kay of the International Bottled Water Association, "bottled water sales in the United States increased from 3.1 billion gallons in 1995 to 4.6 billion in 1999. That's about 17 gallons per person in 1999 alone." But those urbanites who opt to buy bottled water usually end up paying a high price to safely quench their thirst. With each passing years, it seems as though bottled water becomes more expensive.

In a fashion, humankind has created urban deserts. In many of today's cities, the basic need for water is oftentimes difficult to fulfill. And, as documented in this book and elsewhere, thirsting for water is one of the most painful experiences for any life form. It is my opinion that the lack of public drinking-water fountains in cities may be a contributing factor to crime. Certainly, there is no doubt that a person without money and with no access to water would give little thought to committing a crime to get money for quenching thirst. While few if any people would give such a scenario much thought because it sounds so ridiculous, the fact is that many people, especially impoverished urbanites, suffer from the emotional stress of dehydration and don't even realize it.

For an extreme example, we read in the May 2001 issue of *U.S. Water News:*

> KARACHI, Pakistan—Police fired tear gas, beat demonstrators with iron-tipped sticks and arrested at least 90 people in the restive port city of Karachi for protesting against an acute water shortage, witnesses said. Protesters shouted slogans against the military rulers.... "Give us water"...shouted the activists.... Pakistan has suffered a severe drought for the past few months because of lack of snow and rain this past winter.

Somehow along the trail of human evolution, our education system stopped teaching children about the care, need, and use of water for health and survival. Soda pop, artificially flavored juice drinks with high sugar content, milk, coffee, tea, and alcohol are what most children are exposed to in the modern home environment. Making matters worse, soft-drink machines are now common in many school halls and cafeterias. This imprinting helps to establish unhealthy habits at an early age. Many of these drinks, although generally assumed to be thirst quenching, are actually dehydrating. Because of this, many urban and suburban children grow up with little understanding of their body's need for water. Hyperactivity and emotional stress are both signals from the body's cells to the brain that something needs to be done to satisfy thirst. Not knowing the source of their bodies' physical stress, children and adults may act out this stress as anger or violence at home, in the streets, or in the workplace.

Fortunately, there are glimmers of hope flowing from political circles.

Recently New York City has initiated a multibillion-dollar program to refurbish 331 newsstands and 3000 bus shelters, and to establish thirty pay toilets. Certainly the implementation of this program will make New York City more people friendly. What this program neglected to include, however, was the installation of public drinking-water fountains. It is hoped that correction of this oversight will be addressed by water-conscious people plugged into the urban political process in New York and Washington.

Another glimmer of hope is the awakened effort of regional political leaders. These leaders often understand how teaching water awareness to children is actually an investment in Earth's future survival.

An example of this can be found in Burbank, California. Pat Rude, of Burbank's Conservation Services, woke up one day with the idea of using art as a way of teaching children about water. Working with Burbank's middle schools—John Muir, David Starr Jordan, and Luther Burbank—Ms. Rude put together an art contest about water. This contest was to take place during the Water Awareness month of May. Students from the three middle schools submitted their individual artistic expressions of water. The student artworks were then evaluated by renowned artist Nan Rae, and each child was given an award. The resulting news stories and the sharing of the art with the children's families helped to raise considerable water awareness.

However, Pat Rude took this one step further. She also created, on a very tight budget, a video relating to the contest. The video was hosted and narrated by famous character actor Ed Lauter, and included an interview with Nan Rae and the "Classical Gas" music of Mason Williams. Nan Rae, Ed Lauter, and Mason Williams are three artists who often use their respective talents to help protect and conserve water.

As a result of this collective effort, Pat Rude produced a unique public-service video about water that touched many lives. Her *Water Is Life* video was played three times a day for six weeks on Burbank's Government Access Channel, and continues to be played from time to time.

On a similar note in Passaic County, New Jersey, we find school children also creating art for the purpose of protecting and conserving water. This spring, eleven pieces of art were chosen from the contributions of many Passaic grade-school students. The selected artwork will be composed into a poster, which, along with other information and games relating to water, will be made available at local libraries, town halls, and many other county facilities. One child drew a lake with a pair of arms wrapped around it and the caption "Protect Our Water"; another drawing warned businesses to stop polluting. Others showed how air pollution eventually contaminates surface and ground waters, and delivered messages about dumping oil and garbage into rivers and streams or leaving the faucet water running when not needed. The effort from this Passaic County Natural Resource Program reached hundreds of adults through their children, the media, and the public display areas.

Besides the creative efforts of regional governments such as Burbank, California, and Passaic County, New Jersey, it is often the organic process of people asking leaders to provide the basics of survival, such as clean water, that produces change. In this fashion, worldwide trends come from the collective mind of the masses. The influence of the will of the people acting at the grassroots level is helpful in protecting water and raising water awareness.

An example of one successful grassroots group is Greenpeace. Using creative methods and riding the wave of broad-based public support, Greenpeace has brought considerable attention to many water issues. A small sampling of these issues includes overfishing our oceans, water pollution, dams, and the clear-cutting of forests. On the issue of cutting down forests, Greenpeace brings attention to the resultant water pollution from eroding runoff, the loss of aquifer recharge, and deadly impacts on wildlife habitat.

The actress Sharon Stone has recently helped Greenpeace by serving as a spokesperson in several heart-wrenching television commercials. These commercials teach us how the web of life is broken when forests are destroyed. In one commercial she tells us how many trees are cut down each year to make paper towels. Because of these commercials, I personally have stopped using paper towels and paper plates and cups in my kitchen. In place of paper towels, I now use sponges and washable dishcloths.

Another grassroots example is the American Oceans Campaign (AOC), which was created in 1987 by its founding president, actor Ted Danson. Since then, AOC has built an impressive record in its effort to stem the rising tide that is degrading our coastal and oceanic waters. "Clean water is the key to our health, economic sustainability, and the world's biodiversity," says AOC Executive Director Barbara Jeanne Polo. When asked to define the purpose of AOC, Ms. Polo answered, "Almost everything we do is focused around water. Some of our projects include saving the coral reefs off the Hawaiian Islands, organizing beach clean-ups, preventing storm water from entering our coastal waters, saving the Stellar sea lion habitat from damaging fishing, helping to educate about water, and lobbying for the passage of coastal marine water pollution monitoring."

Echoing Ms. Polo's position is Ted Danson. As few people know, Mr. Danson has received many awards over the years for his efforts to protect water. On January 21, 2001, Ted Danson wrote the following in Santa Barbara's *News Press:* "Storm water pollution damages essential fish habitat by smothering sea grasses or stream bottoms with mud, litter and other pollutants. It triggers harmful red tides and algae growths. It exposes fish and shellfish (and humans who eat them) to dangerous toxic chemicals. It causes beaches to close.... A 1996 study ... found an increase in risk of illness associated with swimming near storm drain outlets."

Whether the issue is a change in consciousness about protecting a river, providing a public drinking-water source, saving trees and rainforests, or preserving biodiversity, it always comes full circle to the subject of water as the basic element to preserve and protect for our survival.

These trends begin in the hearts and souls of individuals like you and me. The more of us who believe in the idea that we can create a world that lives in harmony with the teachings of water, the greater the possibility that it will happen in reality. Hopefully, the idea of understanding water will touch the right chord, and by doing so, will resonate in a way that will alter the existence of all life on Earth.

At this time in history, I believe there is the beginning of a trend to protect and learn from the waters of our Earth. This idea is flowing through more minds each day.

In fact, there is now an international water prize that has, in my opinion, as much significance as the Nobel Peace Prize. The $150,000 Stockholm Water Prize is awarded annually by the Stockholm Water Foundation. Since 1991, this prize has been given to any institution, organization, company, or individual that has demonstrated unusual achievement in increasing our knowledge about water and protecting its usability for all life. The patron for this prize is King Carl XVI Gustaf of Sweden. To date, this prize has been awarded to institutions, organizations, companies, and individuals. Every year, scientists, environmentalists, the business sector, and the general public submit nominations for the prize. (For more information or to receive a nomination form, one may contact the Stockholm International Water Institute: telephone +46 8 522 139 60; fax +46 8 522 139 61; or e-mail siwi@siwi.org.)

In my opinion, learning from water may prove to be the most powerful idea to touch the minds of humanity since the creation of our species. The following pages offer a few examples of other efforts to awaken our understanding of water.

The Groundwater Foundation

In 1982 Nebraskan Susan Seacrest had her first child fall seriously ill as an infant. At about the same time, there were local newspaper stories about the high rates of lymphoma and leukemia occurring in the Platte Valley near her home. The cause of these cancers was suspected to be contamination of the groundwater aquifer by pesticides and fertilizers.

Fortunately, Seacrest's son, Logan, recovered from his illness, and contaminated groundwater was ruled out as the culprit. However, sensing a potential threat to her family, Susan began doing her own research about the pollution of groundwater by pesticides. While doing so, she wrote a researcher at the University of Nebraska Medical Center. The reply included a challenge for Susan to learn about groundwater pollution and to do what she could to help solve the problem.

It did not take long for Seacrest to learn that Nebraska is the third largest groundwater user in the nation and that the Ogallala aquifer, which stretches from South Dakota to Texas, is North America's largest. Susan also learned the sobering information that due to overpumping, pollution, and wasteful use, the Ogallala aquifer is in danger of going bust in her lifetime.

So, Seacrest, a teacher with a master's degree in education, decided to do something about the situation by establishing the Nebraska Groundwater Foundation to educate people in her state about the importance of groundwater. With disarming charm, she carried forth her purpose like Joan of Arc beckoning troops to battle. Her enthusiasm and seemingly wide-eyed innocence won one convert after another. Perhaps, too, there was the hidden support of groundwater energy channeling its way from the Earth into and through her being.

Seacrest started by enlisting the help of state and local leaders. The Nebraska Association of Resources Districts provided a mailing list, as did the state's Department of Environmental Protection. Eventually, Seacrest found herself working from her kitchen table to organize the first statewide groundwater conference, with then-Governor Bob Kerrey as one of her speakers. In the fall of 1985, over 150 people attended this conference, including most water experts from across Nebraska.

Following this initial success, the Nebraska Groundwater Foundation evolved in an organic fashion. Seacrest, now pregnant with her second child, began to focus on a larger vision for groundwater education. The foundation created its first newsletter and expanded the annual fall symposium into a national event that included a groundwater protection awards program. Then, out of the blue Seacrest got the brilliant idea of creating a children's groundwater festival. With her background in education, she thought it imperative that children become a part of the answer to solving the world's groundwater plight.

In the beginning, of course, money was tight. Seacrest paid many bills out of her own pocket in the start-up years. However, slowly but surely, the purpose of protecting Nebraska's groundwater found support.

Jack Thompson, then president of the Cooper Foundation, provided a $1500 grant for the first Children's Water Festival in 1989. According to Seacrest, "Many people expected a wishful attendance of about 100 children." But she, as well as many skeptics, was surprised when over 1200 children signed up the first week alone. The couple of rooms originally reserved at Central Community College in Grand Island were soon increased to take in the whole building. Eventually, the entire college closed down for the event, and over 2000 children spent a day playing with and learning about water.

By 1991, over 8000 children were signing up for future festivals, which are now limited to about 3000 for each event. By the time this book is published, hundreds of thousands of children from across the United States and other countries will have taken part in water festivals based upon Seacrest's water festival model. To provide support for these other festivals, the Groundwater Foundation has published a booklet to help any interested community or group to get underway.

And, just what is it that happens at a children's groundwater festival? Things like storytelling; exhibits of different student projects relating to groundwater; talks and workshops by various water specialists; water experiments such as the creation of mini-tornadoes; snake petting; demonstrations of how irrigation is used for growing food; the artistic creation of murals dealing with groundwater and wetlands; and, perhaps most importantly, sharing the excitement of children as they learn the value of water to life.

Educators across Nebraska have praised the Nebraska Groundwater Foundation for staging such an innovative children's event. As a result of the children's water festival, Seacrest's local success story began to attract national and international attention. In March 1993, an article on the Ogallala aquifer in *National Geographic* gave the Groundwater Foundation international exposure. Telephone calls and letters poured in from around the globe. In the fall of 1993, Seacrest and her Board of Directors decided to drop "Nebraska" from the Groundwater Foundation's name. In doing so, the Groundwater Foundation redefined its mission from educating people on a statewide level to educating people worldwide.

Seacrest says that she feels she owes much of her success to long hours of hard work, the help of many volunteers, the support of her husband and family, and what she semi-jokingly refers to as "The Moral Force of Groundwater Speech."

The Groundwater Foundation presently works out of a small office located above a bait and tackle shop in South Lincoln, Nebraska. With a small but highly effective staff, the foundation is carrying on its nonpartisan effort to educate the world about managing the groundwater resources of Earth. In the United States alone, the Groundwater Guardian program of the foundation has affiliates in almost every state.

Money, once in short supply, appears to be flowing more easily these days. Like a blossoming child, the Groundwater Foundation grows a little more each year. Besides its outreach programs, the foundation publishes a monthly water education newsletter called *Sprinkles*, which goes to over 5200 experts and laypeople throughout the United States, Canada, Mexico, and overseas.

What will Susan Seacrest, her many friends, volunteers, and the dedicated Groundwater Foundation staff and Board of Directors come up with next? We will soon see. But most probably, it will deal with the protection of groundwater through education. By doing so, it will provide hope for the human race as our children learn to care for the Earth.

Lifewater International

According to William A. Ashe of Lifewater International in Arcadia, California, "Lifewater is a non-profit Christian organization dedicated to helping the rural poor of developing countries develop their own dependable, safe water supplies and systems. With the use of small, portable rotary drilling rigs, over 350 wells have been completed during the last six years. Our volunteers have been able to conduct three- and four-day well-drilling conferences, with actual on-site drilling for local leadership in over eight countries in the world, including Zambia, Tanzania, Kenya, South Africa, Philippines, Mexico and Haiti."

Since this information was provided in July 1993, Lifewater has added projects in Ethiopia, Guatemala, Burma, Romania, Nigeria, Morocco, El Salvador, Uganda, Burkina Faso, Angola, Chad, Honduras, Bangladesh and probably many other countries by the time this book goes to press. By the end of 2001, Lifewater will have installed about 2000 wells since it first began this effort in the late 1980s.

According to Lifewater, its founding purpose is "to transfer, on a non-profit basis, technology and equipment from the more affluent, technologically developed countries to benefit people of disadvantaged countries of the world. Lifewater is a Christian organization of water resource management specialists." The primary focus of these specialists is to relieve and develop mission agencies serving developing countries and to assist local churches that have no agencies to represent them. On occasion Lifewater will help with other water projects for requesting groups, based on priority as determined by Lifewater's Board of Directors. In this way, Lifewater assists other churches and organizations in water development. After a water project is completed, Lifewater offers to continue as a partner in ministry with the sponsoring church or organization on an as-needed basis.

Lifewater International does such a good job with getting the most for their money that the Motley Fool selected it and four other selected organizations as "the world's best charities." This selection came after the Motley Fool evaluated hundreds of other nonprofits that receive donations.

Hollywood and the Water Picture

Around the globe there are many people who follow the lifestyles of celebrities, especially movie stars. Without a doubt, the powerful medium of film impacts the behavior of many people. Recognizing this, a group of enlightened people got together in Hollywood in the late 1980s and created the Earth Communication Office (ECO) to use the influence of the entertainment industry to help save the global environment through education and awareness.

One of the most visible efforts of ECO is its Public Service Announcement (PSA) campaign. According to Ruben Aronin, "ECO's PSAs have been seen on tens of thousands of movie screens and have been broadcast on hundreds of television stations around the world." These PSAs are short film pieces with beautiful imagery and concise messages to help educate viewers. To date, almost all of ECO's PSAs have focused on the subject of our water environment.

In 1996 ECO produced its first national thirty-second television PSA featuring narration by Pierce Brosnan. In the same year, ECO produced and launched a national radio campaign on "health and the environment" on more than 6000 radio stations. At the end of the PSA about our oceans entitled "Neighbors," there is a toll-free telephone number for callers to receive information on ways to protect our oceans and to send an Eco Gram to the president urging him to keep our water clean.

Besides being a creative voice in helping to awaken people about Earth's water, ECO represents the cutting-edge use of communications for a positive purpose. Recently ECO has plugged into the

Information Superhighway with the launching of a celebrity-driven environmental website.

The above examples of awakening water awareness are but a handful out of thousands. We as humans, with the gifts provided to us, are the world's dominating life force at this time. To some degree, each and every one of us can do something to participate in the protection and conservation of water. It is in this way that there will truly be a water awakening. Or, to put it in the words of Lao Tzu: "The sage's transformation of the world arises from solving the problem of water."

NINETEEN

One Water Family

For all at last return to the sea—to Oceanus, the ocean river,
like the overflowing stream of time, the beginning and the end.
—RACHEL CARSON

THROUGH WATER, we are all related as brothers and sisters.

As we are connected to each other through water, so too are we connected to every other life form that exists, has existed, and will exist.

Water existed long before the coming of humankind, and water will exist long after the going of humankind. However, how we treat water during our brief passage on Earth will determine whether we and our children pass time in a dying world or a living Garden of Eden.

Simply—the choice is ours.

As prophesied in the Bible and elsewhere, humankind has finally gained dominion over every life form that walks, crawls, slithers, or swims on the face of Earth. This dominion over other life forms has come to us through our control of water.

In the future, which ecosystem survives or dies will be determined by our manipulation of water. If we decide to capture water for growing our food, quenching our thirst, watering golf courses, generating electricity, making snow for skiing, or running a water park, the downstream ecosystems will suffer deadly consequences.

Physics teaches us that for every action there is a reaction. On the face of our Earth, for every alteration by humanity or nature, there is a reaction in the environment. Place a dam across a river, and many life forms downstream wither and die, water tables change, evaporation rates are altered, and the ocean and its beaches lose nourishment. Drain a wetland, and death comes to the life forms living in the water, to life in the surrounding uplands, and to many migratory life forms. Cut down a forest and soon the water table drops, erosion sets in, and nearby streams become choked. No matter what action we take—whether building a road or a consumer good such as an automobile or some useless plastic gizmo—there is always an impact on our watery biosphere.

For every human action, for every choice, there is a reaction in the world of life—a ripple of change.

For example, the following brief story was published in the July 1997 issue of *Water Conditioning and Purification:*

> The desert, normally a dry land, has blossomed in recent years as result of the U.S. Bureau of Reclamation irrigation projects. It now appears that was a bad decision.
>
> In an effort to bring water to the West, the bureau became one of the nation's largest users of pesticides to kill the weeds, algae and pests that clog canals and irrigation trenches.
>
> What the bureau didn't do was monitor the long-term effects of such poisoning. Several communities such as Medford, Oregon, and the Tulelake National Wildlife Refuge on the Oregon-California border have experienced significant losses as a result of irresponsible poisoning. In Oregon, more than 90,000 juvenile wild steelhead were killed when a poison used to kill weeds flowed from an irrigation system into Bear Creek. And, at the Tulelake National Wildlife Refuge, the deaths of fish, birds, including bald eagles, and other animals have been attributed to the use of pesticides.

For every action there is a reaction.

If you alter the natural flow of water, you create a ripple effect that has many consequences. Bringing water to make a desert blossom sounds like a good idea. However, even though the professionals at the Bureau of Reclamation thought they knew and understood water, they still have much to learn. The unplanned heavy use of herbicides and pesticides has turned the dream of making the desert blossom into a deadly nightmare.

What the above article failed to explore was the source of the water for these irrigation projects, and what the many short-term and long-term impacts will be on that source.

The very fact that bald eagles, animals at the top of the food chain, are dying is a sign of warning to us humans. However, the death toll from this project is easily dwarfed by the number of birds killed off each year by pesticides. As reported in the September/October 2000 issue of *Organic Gardening*, "An estimated 67 million birds die of pesticide exposure each year in the United States." This staggering statistic was provided by the Pesticide Action Network. With this great number of birds dying from pesticides, I can't help but think of Rachel Carson's *Silent Spring*.

In the past, when I read stories like the above, I would get a feeling of helplessness. Sometimes I would ask, "What can I do to stop the apparent insanity of building large dams, using poisons in our environment, destroying rainforests, overfishing our oceans?"

I meditated, I prayed, I thought. I took long walks along the ocean and into the forest.

Time after time the same thoughts surfaced: "Think of water as your life-giver. Think of water as a close friend. Think of water as someone you can trust, love, and share your deepest secrets with. Think of water as your healer."

"Yes," I say to myself, "water is all these things and so much more."

Whenever I take a beach walk or sit for a while beside a lake or river, there is always a feeling of peace and wonderment. At times, while relaxing near a large body of water, I just naturally fall into a kind of daydream.

How relaxing and cleansing it is to share time with water.

Other times, I find myself meditating on the mesmerizing motions and sounds of moving water. It is fascinating to watch the "light show" as the Sun or Moon reflects off the undulating surface.

"What is this emotional connection we share with water?" I ask myself. "Is there some sort of communication happening on another level when we take a moment to think of or to share time with water?"

When rain falls on my head, or a misty cloud of fog kisses my face, I sometimes wonder why this reality was set up this way. "Why water?" I ask. "How can an entity that gives us so much be taken for granted by so many? How mysterious water is. How forgiving! No matter what we do to it, water continues to quench our thirst, clean our pollution, bring forth life."

Somewhere along the quest for answers, guidance was provided.

I feel water continually creates the reality we live in. By doing so, water provides an environment for us to come forth as a life form. The life form we inhabit will spend only a limited time on Earth, but our thoughts and actions in this reality will join with us for eternity.

As our souls pass through this watery creation, we make choices that alter the physical reality surrounding us, as well as the physical reality within us. In this way, our choices create changes in the world without and the world within.

For this reason, when we alter any part of this material world, there is a ripple of change that flows through many levels of our environment. The same happens when we alter any part of our mental or emotional world—there is a ripple of change that touches every aspect of our being.

Because we live in a material reality created by water, we have the power to change that reality with our thoughts. Our thoughts give us this power because thoughts come from the water in our brains. In this way, we as humans enjoy a touch of the creative energy that is responsible for creating and maintaining this reality.

To believe for an instant that we humans can destroy this reality is to be brainwashed of our limitations. We humans, as a collective life form, represent a mere drop in an ocean that is limitless and timeless. To think that we possess the power to destroy the water that has the power to create us, to create our Earth, to create our universe and so much more—is to be lost in the puffery of our own importance.

So, why do we share in the living experience? Why the knowledge that our time here is limited in years? Why the mystery of not knowing whence we came and where we are going?

In my lifelong search for these answers, I believe guidance has flowed.

We are creations of the entity we call water, a mysterious entity that exists in various forms at one time. Water is such that it is different from any other entity we know. But yet, water is the very thing that makes up the most of each one of us.

The water that flows through our veins is the same water that flowed through the very first life forms—no matter where they were born. It is the same water that flows in a river, fills the ocean, and makes clouds in the sky. It is the same water that circulates on our sun, throughout the galaxies, between the stars in interstellar space, throughout time—forever.

On Earth and throughout the universe, water is constantly recycling itself, constantly recreating itself.

Since water flows through all things through all time, it embodies all that ever was, is, and will be. The imprint of every unique creation ever composed by water, including you and me, lives on through all time as a part of water's infinite stream. And just as it takes a million droplets to make one raindrop, so, too, a million lives make but one drop in the ocean of timeless waters.

We flowed forth into this world from the ocean of timeless waters. By doing so, we retained much of our former selves, even down to the watery cells within our beings. Each watery cell represents a hologram of sorts of our soulful imprint. Therefore we now have the ability to clone another life form from a single cell.

As we pass through this earthly reality, we are given the opportunity, for a brief time, to alter the composition of the water defining our infinite soulful existence. We make choices in our time here that are imprinted on the timeless water of our souls. And, just as drops of water in this reality imprint all that they experience, so, too, will our souls imprint all that we have experienced and all that we have chosen.

When the time comes for us to again rejoin the infinite stream of water flowing to and from the great timeless ocean, our little droplet of soulful water will once again flow with the endless stream, and, in doing so, will carry along the memories gathered in our earthly passage.

Henceforth the rejoicing, or perhaps the torment, of once again rejoining water's infinite flowing stream. For what we chose to gather here will flow within our soul forever—for better or worse.

On an earthly scale, the way we treat water is, in a fashion, a reflection of how we see ourselves. If we love ourselves as a watery creation, certainly we will love that which has created us. If we care to have good health, then certainly we will do our utmost to care for the health of the water flowing in the world around us and through us.

Pollute the water—there is death and disease. Respect the water—there is life abundant and good health.

A few years ago, while I was visiting a friend on the West Coast, we decided to have a late lunch near Redondo Beach. It was a hot day, and the cast of characters parading along the beach and sidewalk were in full regalia. As usual, at Hennesy's Restaurant, there was a long line of people waiting. Since this was my first time at Hennesy's, I decided to go up the stairs and see what the topside deck was like. On the outside deck overlooking the ocean and beach was a cluster of tables, each having a large umbrella for shade. Wanting to take a look at the second-story view of the peopled sidewalk below, I walked by a half-filled table and peered over the edge. The view of such a wide variety of people skating, jogging, bicycling, and walking back and forth was most entertaining. A sharp contrast was presented by the crowd on the beach, which moved more slowly or not at all.

The waves of animated people flowing along the sidewalk appeared as a counterbalance to the waves of water breaking along the shore.

At a nearby table, a middle-aged man sitting with his wife commented, "Some view. We come here mostly just to sit and watch." I laughed at the idea, because it was exactly what I was doing. After a brief conversation, the couple invited me, and my friend, to join them at their table.

As the warm, breezy afternoon passed, I learned that the couple were very involved with saving the ocean through a California surf riders association. The man, named Tom, who was an American Airlines postal manager, explained how the West Coast surfers had decided to organize to protect the quality of the coastal waters they surf and swim in.

"We share an intimate knowledge of water," said Tom. "We know how the cycles of the Moon influence the tides and surf. We know how the energy of an oceanic storm influences the size and type of waves we enjoy riding. Our educated senses often tell us when the water is clean or polluted. We talk amongst ourselves and share information. Information such as what areas of the coast are most polluted after a rainstorm. We know which storm outfall pipes carry the worst pollution. We know which areas of the coast are most likely going to give us eye, ear, nose, and throat infections. That's why the surf riders decided to organize and do what we can to protect our coastal waters. Not only for ourselves, but for fishermen, bathers, and everyone else in the LA area who uses these coastal waters."

After a while, the conversation grew silent, and the four us quietly sat watching the ocean as the sun tickled its surface. Eventually, Tom's soft voice broke the silence. "You know," he said, "at times I feel a deep personal relationship with the ocean. When it is polluted, I sometimes think I feel its sadness."

Living the Future

With all I know and sense about water, I think we as humans now face one of the most profound decisions in our entire history on Earth. For the first time in our evolution, we are facing a worldwide crisis that requires us to think and act collectively for the survival of civilization and all life on Earth.

As challenging as it may seem, we have the potential to influence the course of all life on Earth for the better.

You can begin helping this change by acting immediately. Even if you are a bum on the street, you can do your part by picking up litter and putting it in a nearby garbage can.

There is little doubt that, as evolving living beings, we can change the course of human history and all the history of life on Earth.

You, as an individual, can help do this simply by awakening to water. Just say in your mind each day, "I CAN HELP DO THIS!" With these words in your mind, try and do something in the interest of water each day. It doesn't matter what you do. No matter how small or large your effort, the reward from it will ripple through the entire world.

Remember, through water, you are related to all others as one family.

Those people who try to cling to the "old way" of doing things will soon realize they are missing the boat, that humanity is evolving upward without them.

The answer to your health, to your peace, to your happiness, to your success as a life form can be found in water. You have nothing to lose by trying to live an awakened life to water. It will cost you nothing. But yet, your reward will be felt immediately.

As you lay your body down to rest, and close your eyes and go to sleep, recall the water deed you performed during your waking time. Carry that thought into your dreams. While you are asleep, your mind will process that thought and give you guidance.

As surely as thoughts flow from your mind, so too will your thoughts flow forth to alter the course of history. The meek and the humble shall inherit the Earth. It is the meek and the humble masses of people who truly have the power to alter the course of history.

When it comes to money, remember to spend it wisely. Teach your children not to spend money on consumer products that pollute our water and air. When your children bring home news of a school project that focuses on water, become involved and ask questions. Who knows what you may learn about water from your children?

Remember, WE CAN DO THIS.

When it comes to supporting or voting for political leaders, do so based on what they have done to help protect water. Do your best to understand what politicians are promising to do for water.

Remember, you can help alter the course of history just by thinking about water.

Through water, we are all members of one family.

The time has come to set aside your petty agendas of power, greed, race, and religion. You, and your offspring, as members of the human race, will either survive or die according to your relationship with water.

The time to begin your relationship with water is now.

Bibliography

Books

Alexandersson, Olof. *Living Water: Viktor Schauberger and the Secrets of Natural Energy*. Translated by Kit and Charles Zweigbergk. Bath, UK: Gateway, Bath, 1990.

Ash, David, and Hewitt, Peter. *The Vortex: Key to Future Science*. Bath, UK: Gateway, 1994.

Baker, Richard St. Barbe. *Man of the Trees: Selected Writings of Richard St. Barbe Baker*. Edited by Karen Gridley. Willets, CA: Ecology Action, 1989.

Barker, Ernest, ed. and trans. *The Politics of Aristotle*. New York: Oxford University Press, reprint 1971.

Batmanghelidj, Fereydoon, M.D. *Your Body's Many Cries for Water*. Falls Church, VA: Global Health Solutions, 1992.

Bauval, Robert. *The Orion Mystery*. New York: Crown, 1995.

Becker, R. O., and G. Selden. *The Body Electric*. New York: William Morrow, 1985.

Begich, Nick. *Towards a New Alchemy*. Anchorage, AK: Earthpulse Press, 1996.

Bird, Christopher. *The Divining Hand*. New York: E. P. Dutton, 1979.

Brabazon, James. *Albert Schweitzer: A Biography*. New York: G. P. Putnam's Sons, 1975.

Braun, Stephen. *Buzz: The Science and Lore of Alcohol and Caffeine*. New York: Oxford University Press, 1996.

Brennan, Barbara Ann. *Hands of Light*. New York: Pleiades, 1987.

Briggs, P. *Water: The Vital Essence*. New York: Harper & Row, 1967.

Brittain, R. E. *Rivers, Man, and Myths*. New York: Doubleday, 1967.

Brooks, Paul. *The House of Life: Rachel Carson at Work*. Boston: Houghton Mifflin, 1972.

Buchman, Dian Dincin. *The Complete Book of Water Therapy*. New Canaan, CT: Keats Publishing, 1994.

Burt, Bernard. *Healthy Escapes*. New York: Fodor, 1998.

Cairns-Smith, A. G. *Genetic Takeover*. Cambridge, UK: Cambridge University Press, 1980.

———. *Seven Clues to the Origin of Life*. Cambridge, UK: Cambridge University Press, 1985.

Campbell, Joseph. *Occidental Mythology: The Masks of God*. New York: Penguin, 1964.

Carson, Rachel. *Silent Spring*. Boston: Houghton Mifflin, 1962.

———. *The Sea around Us*. Introduction by Maitland A. Edey. Illustrated with photographs by Alfred Eisenstaedt. New York: Limited Editions Club, 1980.

Chambers's Encyclopedia. New York: J. B. Lippincott & Co., 1871.

Chopra, Deepak, M.D. *Quantum Healing: Exploring The Frontiers of Mind/ Body Medicine.* New York: Bantam, 1990.

Coats, Callum. *Living Energies.* Bath, UK: Gateway, 1996.

Cocannouer, Joseph A. *Water and the Cycle of Life.* New York: Devin-Adair, 1962.

Cochrane, Amanda, and Karena Callen. *Dolphins and Their Power to Heal.* Rochester, VT: Healing Arts Press, 1992.

Coffel, Steve. *But Not a Drop to Drink: The Life-Saving Guide to Good Water.* New York: Ivy Books, 1991.

Colborn, Theo, et al. *Our Stolen Future.* New York: E. P. Dutton, 1997.

Cranston, Ruth. *The Miracle of Lourdes.* Updated and expanded by Bureau Medical. New York: Image Books/Doubleday, 1988.

Creed, Virginia. *All About Austria.* New York: Duell, Sloan & Pearce, 1950.

Croutier, Alev Lytle. *Taking the Waters: Spirit, Art, Sensuality & Bathing Customs.* New York: Abbeville Press, 1992.

Davis, K. S. *Water: The Mirror of Science.* New York: Anchor Books/Doubleday, 1961.

Dean, Cornelia. *Against the Tide.* New York: Columbia University Press, 1999.

Deming, H. G. *Water, the Fountain of Opportunity.* New York: Oxford University Press, 1975.

Devereux, Paul. *Earth Memory.* St. Paul, MN: Llewellyn, 1992.

———. *Shamanism and the Mystery Lines.* St. Paul, MN: Llewellyn, 1994.

Diamond, Harvey and Marilyn. *Fit for Life.* New York: Warner, 1985.

Dictionary of Scientific Biography. American Council of Learned Societies. New York: Charles Scribner's Sons, 1976.

Douglas, Nik, and Penny Slinger. *Sexual Secrets: The Alchemy of Ecstasy.* Rochester, VT: Destiny, 1979.

Eisenberg, Arlene. *What To Expect When You're Expecting.* New York: Workman, 1996.

Eliade, Mircea. *Patterns in Comparative Religion.* Translated by Rosemary Sheed. Cleveland, OH: World, 1963.

———*Encyclopedia of Religion.* New York: Macmillan, 1987.

Flanagan, Patrick, and Gael Crystal Flanagan. *Elixir of the Ageless.* Flagstaff, AZ: Flanagan Technologies, 1986.

Forman, J., ed. *Water and Man.* Columbus, OH: Friends of the Land, 1950.

Fortune, Dion. *The Mystical Qabalah.* York Beach, ME: Samuel Weiser, 1997.

Franks, F., ed. *Water—a Comprehensive Treatise.* New York: Plenum, 1972.

Gardner, John, and John Maier, trans. *Gilgamesh.* New York: Knopf, 1970.

Gardner, Robert. *Water: The Life-Sustaining Resource.* New York: Julian Messner, 1982.

Garrison, Fielding H. *History of Medicine.* Philadelphia: W. B. Saunders, 1929.

Goldberg, Burton. *Alternative Medicine.* Tiburon, CA: Future Medicine Publishing, 1999.

Green, Maureen and Timothy. *The Good Water Guide: The World's Best Bottled Waters.* London: Rosendale, 1994.

Hanniford, Carla. *Smart Moves.* Arlington, VA: Great Ocean Publishers, 1995.

Harsha, David. *The Principles of Hydrotherapy, or the Invalid's Guide to Health and Happiness.* 1852.

Hunt, C. A., and R. M. Garrels. *Water: The Web of Life.* New York: W. W. Norton, 1972.

Illich, Ivan. *H₂O and the Waters of Forgetfulness.* Dallas, TX: Dallas Institute of Humanities and Culture, 1985.

Ingram, Colin. *The Drinking Water Book: A Complete Guide to Safe Drinking Water.* Berkeley, CA: Ten Speed Press, 1991.

Kaysing, Bill. *Great Hot Springs of the West.* Santa Barbara, CA: Capra Press, 1990.

Kersten G. H. *A Treatise of the Compendium.* Grand Rapids, MI: Inheritance Publishing Co., 1956.

King, Jonathan. *Troubled Water.* Emmaus, PA: Rodale, 1985.

King, T. *Water: Miracle of Nature.* New York: Macmillan, 1953.

Leopold, Luna B. *Water: A Primer.* San Francisco: W. H. Freeman, 1974.

Lister, Robert H., and Florence C. Lister. *Chaco Canyon.* Albuquerque, NM: University of New Mexico Press, 1981.

Littleton, C. Scott, ed. *Eastern Wisdom.* New York: Henry Holt, 1996.

Masani, Rustom P. *Folklore of Wells: Being a Study of Water-Worship in East and West.* 1918. Reprint, Norwood, PA: Norwood, 1978.

Mason, Herbert, trans. *Gilgamesh.* New York: Mentor, 1970.

Mickelsen, Olaf. *Food: Yearbook of the U.S. Department of Agriculture.* 1959.

Milne, L., and M. Milne. *Water and Life.* London: Andre Deutsch, 1965.

Mishlove, Jeffrey, *Roots of Consciousness.* New York: Marlowe & Co., 1993.

Mitchell, Stephen. *Tao Te Ching: A New English Version.* New York: Harper-Collins, 1991.

Mollison, Bill. *Permaculture One.* Melbourne, Australia: Transworld, 1978.

———. *Permaculture Two.* Stanley, Tasmania, Australia: Tagari, 1979.

Morgan, E. *The Aquatic Ape.* London: Souvenir, 1982.

New Larousse Encyclopedia of Mythology. Translated by Richard Aldington and Delano Ames. New York: Hamlyn, 1970.

Odum, Eugene P. *Ecology.* Second Edition. New York: Holt, Rinehart & Winston, 1975.

Outwater, Alice. *Water.* New York: Basic Books, 1996.

Paulus, Stephen. *Nostradamus.* St. Paul, MN: Llewellyn, 1999.

Pettyjohn, Wayne A., ed. *Water Quality in a Stressed Environment: Readings in Environmental Hydrology.* Minneapolis, MN: Burgess, 1972.

Plutarch. *Writings of Plutarch, Miscellanies, Vol. III.* Edited by William W. Goodwin. Boston: Little, Brown, 1905.

Postel, Sandra. *Dividing the Waters: Food Security, Ecosystem Health.* Worldwatch Paper 132, 1996.

———. *Last Oasis: Facing Water Scarcity.* New York: W. W. Norton, 1992.

———. *The Politics of Water.* Worldwatch Institute, July/August 1993.

Powledge, Fred. *Water: The Nature, Uses and Future of Our Most Precious and Abused Resource.* New York: Farrar, Straus & Giroux, 1983.

Quigley, Robert David. *A Nutrition Education Guide for a Lacto-Ovo-Vegetarian Health Resort.* Master's Thesis, San Diego State University, 1977.

Quillin, Patrick. *Healing Nutrients.* New York: Vintage, 1989.

———. *The Wisdom of Amish Folk Medicine.* Pennsylvania: The Leader Co, 1994.

Renou, Louis, ed. *Atharva-veda.* New York: George Braziller, 1961.

Rubin, Louis D., Sr., and Jim Duncan. *The Weather Wizard's Cloud Book.* Chapel Hill, NC: Algonquin Books of Chapel Hill, 1989.

Sanford, John A. *Mystical Christianity: A Psychological Commentary on the Gospel of John.* New York: Crossroad, 1993.

Schwartz, Steven. *The Book of Waters.* New York: A&W Publishers, 1979.

Schwenk, Theodor. *Sensitive Chaos: The Creation of Flowing Forms in Water and Air.* London: Rudolf Steiner Press, 1965.

———, and Wolfram Schwenk. *Water: The Element of Life.* Hudson, NY: Anthroposophic Press, 1989.

Seebach, Christopher. *Living Water.* Bath, UK: Gateway Books, 1976.

Shah, Idries. *The Sufis.* Garden City, NY: Anchor Books/Doubleday, 1971.

Sitchin, Zecharia. *Genesis Revisited: Is Modern Science Catching Up with Ancient Knowledge?* New York: Avon, 1990.

Smith, James R. *Springs and Wells in Greek and Roman Literature.* New York: G. P. Putnam's Sons, 1922.

Swanson, Peter. *Water: The Drop of Life.* Minnetonka, MN: NorthWord Press, 2001.

Symons, James M. *Drinking Water: Refreshing Answers to All Your Questions.* College Station, TX: Texas A&M Press, 1995.

Szekely, Edmond. *Healing Waters.* San Diego, CA: Academy Books, 1976.

Templeton, John Marks. *The Humble Approach.* New York: Continuum, 1995.

Troeller, Linda. *Healing Waters.* Paris: Marval Collection Pour Mémoire, 1997.

Tyson, Donald. *Scrying for Beginners.* St. Paul, MN: Llewellyn, 1997.

Underwood, Guy. *The Pattern of the Past.* New York: Abelard-Schuman, 1969.

Versluis, Arthur. *Sacred Earth: The Spiritual Landscape of Native America.* Rochester, VT: Inner Traditions, 1992.

Vogel, H. C. A. *The Nature Doctor.* New Canaan, CT: Keats, 1991.

Walton, W. C. *The World of Water.* New York: Taplinger, 1970.

Watson, Lyall. *Gifts of Unknown Things: A True Story of Nature, Healing, and Initiation from Indonesia's "Dancing Island."* Rochester, VT: Destiny, 1991.

———. *The Water Planet: A Celebration of the Wonder of Water.* New York: Crown, 1988.

Watts, Alan, and Al Chung-Liang Huang. *TAO: The Watercourse Way.* New York: Pantheon, 1975.

Weil, Andrew. *Spontaneous Healing.* New York: Knopf, 1995.

Weiss, Harry B., and Howard R. Kemble. *They Took to the Waters: The Forgotten Mineral Spring Resorts of New Jersey and Nearby Pennsylvania and Delaware.* Trenton, NJ: Past Times Press, 1962.

Wendt, Herbert. *The Romance of Water.* New York: Hill & Wang, 1983.

von Wiesenberger, Arthur. *H₂O: The Guide to Quality Drinking Water.* Santa Barbara, CA: Woodbridge Press, 1988.

———. *Oasis.* Santa Barbara, CA: Capra Press, 1978.

Wild, Robert A. *Water in the Cultic Worship of Isis and Sarapis.* Leiden, The Netherlands: E. J. Brill, 1981.

Wright, Lawrence. *Clean and Decent: The Fascinating History of the Bathroom and the Water Closet.* New York: Viking, 1960.

Zoeteman, Kees. *Gaiasophy: The Wisdom of the Living Earth.* Hudson, NY: Lindisfarne, 1991.

Magazines and Other Sources

Anderson, Richard Feather. "Geomancy: Living in Harmony with the Earth." *Ecology Center Newsletter,* Berkeley, CA, September 1985.

The Aquifer Journal of the Groundwater Foundation.

Bashin, Bryan Jay. "The Trickle-Through Effect." *Eating Well,* July/August 1992.

"Bottled Water: Eight Is Great." *Campaign,* International Bottled Water Association, 1994.

CBS Report, "The Silent Spring of Rachel Carson."

"Christopher Bird, 1928–1996." The American Society of Dowsers, Danville, VT.

Dold, Catherine. "Hormone Hell." *Discover,* September 1996.

Nasstrom, Stephan. "A Stream Runs Through It." *Sky,* June 1993.

Pope, Carl. "Tapwatergate." *Sierra,* August 1994.

Price, Joan. "The Earth Is Alive." *Earth Energy Network,* Number 5, March 1986.

Schindler, B. "The Development of the Chinese Conceptions of Supreme Beings." *Asia Major,* Hirth Anniversary Volume, London.

Spencer, LeAnn. "Danger in the Grass." *Good Housekeeping,* May 2001.

Turner, Jim. "Flushing Away Excess Fat." *Water Conditioning & Purification,* March 1996.

"Vagen Till en ny Mansklighet" ("The Way to a New Humanity"). A. Waerland, Halsans Forlag, Linkoping.

Washam, Cynthia. "Is the Breast Still Best?" *Food & Health,* November/December 1995.

"Water: The Beverage for Life." American Dietetics Association, 1994.

Water World. Pennwell Publications.

Wiener Medizinische Wochenschrift, Nos. 37–38, 1951, H. P. Rusch and Anto.

Williams, Michele. "Water and Health." *Water Conditioning & Purification,* May 1995.

Zeilik, Michael. "Sun Watching: Prehistoric Astronomy in New Mexico." *New Mexico Magazine,* March 1985, pp. 48–55.

Index